ETHICS, ECONOMICS, AND THE LAW

NOMOS

XXIV

NOMOS

Lieber-Atherton, Publishers

New York University Press

NOMOS XXIV

Yearbook of the American Society for Political and Legal Philosophy

ETHICS, ECONOMICS, AND THE LAW

Edited by

J. Roland Pennock, *Swarthmore College*

and

John W. Chapman, *University of Pittsburgh*

New York and London • New York University Press • 1982

Ethics, Economics, and the Law: Nomos XXIV
edited by J. Roland Pennock and John W. Chapman
Copyright © 1982 by New York University

Library of Congress Cataloging in Publication Data
Main entry under title:

Ethics, economics, and the law.

(Nomos; 24)
Includes bibliographical references and index.
1. Law—Philosophy—Addresses, essays, lectures.
2. Law and ethics—Addresses, essays, lectures.
3. Property—Addresses, essays, lectures.
4. Economics—Addresses, essays, lectures.   I. Pennock, J. Roland (James Roland), 1906–
II. Chapman, John William, 1923–   III. Series.
K486.E83   340'.11   81-16882
ISBN 0-8147-6583-1   AACR2

Printed in the United States of America

CONTENTS

CONTRIBUTORS

BRIAN BARRY
Philosophy and Political Science, University of Chicago

JULES L. COLEMAN
Philosophy, University of Wisconsin-Milwaukee

HAROLD M. DEMSETZ
Economics, University of California, Los Angeles

RICHARD A. EPSTEIN
Law, University of Chicago

RICHARD E. FLATHMAN
Political Science, Johns Hopkins University

GEORGE P. FLETCHER
Law, University of California, Los Angeles

THOMAS M. FRANCK
Law, New York University

ALAN GEWIRTH
Philosophy, University of Chicago

KENT GREENAWALT
Law, Columbia University

R. M. HARE
Philosophy, Oxford University

DAVID LYONS
Law, Cornell University

FRANK I. MICHELMAN
Law, Harvard University

KAI NIELSEN
Philosophy, University of Calgary, Canada

DAVID A. J. RICHARDS
Law, New York University

HARRY N. SCHEIBER
Law, University of California, Berkeley

PREFACE

"Ethics, economics, and the law"—a Faustian topic indeed, as it was called by the author of one of the leading essays presented at the annual meeting of the American Society for Political and Legal Philosophy, held in Phoenix, 3–4 January 1980, in conjunction with the meetings of the American Association of Law Teachers. Although the contributors to this volume deal with that topic from various points of view, they by no means exhaust the angles from which it might be approached. Perhaps no more than a beginning has been made.

We thank our contributors, and David A. J. Richards, who, as Program Chairman for the meetings that gave rise to this volume, played an important role in its creation. (Nine of the fifteen contributors were either essay readers or commentators at the Phoenix meetings.) As always, Eleanor Greitzer has been invaluable in her role as editorial assistant.

The John Dewey Foundation has recently extended a second grant to our Society for which we are deeply grateful. Without its help, and the continuing assistance of the Ritter Foundation, the Society and NOMOS could not continue to flourish as they do.

J.R.P.
J.W.C.

INTRODUCTION

The derivatation of the word "ethics" takes us, via the Greek, to custom or usage, although today we tend to associate it more with moral principles. "Law," too, when we look to its orgins, leads to the same source, custom. "Economics," on the other hand, derives from "household management." From this root it is easy to derive the concept of efficiency, now so firmly connected with "economy" and "economics." Customs not only may be efficient but, if we presume any degree of human rationality, may be initially *presumed* to be efficient—prima facie efficient. Moreover, because adjustments are inevitably costly— customary practices eliminate the necessity for much calculation and decision making—further weight is added to this initial presumption. Yet in today's dynamic society the presumption more and more wears thin. The weight of history, embedded in customs, often runs counter both to economy and to ethics understood as a set of moral principals derived from abstract thought rather than from reliance on principles grounded in practice. Law today, the product of many forces, inevitably reflects the tension between past needs and present needs, between past and present capacities, as well as the tensions between the ethical demand for justice and the economic pressure for efficiency.

But what does efficiency require? Is the presumption always in favor of a system of private property and free markets? This assumption often plays an important role in that fashionable approach to the study and analysis of law that borrows heavily from the methods and assumptions of economics. Frank Michelman has dubbed this approach PET, an acronym for "presumptive efficiency thesis." He leads off Part I of this volume with an all-out attack on this thesis. He seeks to demonstrate—perhaps wc should say he does demonstrate—in great detail and with rigorous reasoning that rationality, which he takes to be the god of economists, cannot demonstrate that a system of property rights, with the implied principles of freedom of contract and competition, will necessarily be superior to some other legal system. He shows that such a result can be obtained only by injecting into the argument one or more of a number of empirical or quasi-empirical propositions, largely about human nature. He considers these propositions and finds that none of them can be known to be true. An important part of his argument is that no one of these ethical-empirical propositions can be said even to be plausible if we consider the extent to which current human behavior and value systems are the product of the very institutions under discussion and how different they might be in a different institutional environment. His final plea is for an open mind, no presumptive validity of the case for a private property regime.

Harold Demsetz argues that Michelman is attacking a straw man. Most economists, he declares, do not argue that a system of private property is necessarily efficient or that, even if efficient, it would be supportable by a universally acceptable ethic. Rationality does not necessarily lead to complete reliance on the market and private property. But he contends that the prima facie case for private property solutions is great, because they "tend to confront persons with (a measure of) the cost (to others) of their actions, and perhaps with the only truly practical and generalizable measure (p. 45). Query: Is not this prima facie case precisely what Michelman *is* attacking?

Using antitrust law as his base of operation, Richard Epstein attacks the economic approach from a different angle from that used by Michelman. After showing certain problems that economic analysis encounters when applied to antitrust law, he applies what he calls the corrective justice approach. His model, which would integrate the law of property, contract, and torts, uses the first of this trio as its baseline. The presumption is always in favor of liberty of action, but it can be overcome by the presence of either force or fraud. Absent these elements, monopoly is acceptable, with the exception that certain countervailing circumstances may prevail, justifying forced exchanges. Public necessity operates in the same way as private necessity as a legal justification. The burden of proof is considerable but sustainable. In summary, he finds that economic theory and the corrective justice theory, as applied to antitrust law, converge at many points, but not entirely.

Finally, in this first part Jules Coleman, a philosopher, attacks the very concepts of efficiency underlying economic analysis. He discusses an analysis of the distinctions among the efficiency-related notions of Pareto optimality, Pareto superiority, and Kaldor-Hicks efficiency and uses them to attack the Coase Theorem as it is usually (mis)understood. Posner's attempt "to replicate in law the special insight of the Coase Theorem" (p. 99) is also found wanting. In short, Coleman finds that the economic analysis of law lacks an ethical foundation.

In Part II five scholars consider the problem of "utility and rights." David Lyons leads off. Arguing that utilitarianism is capable of providing a normative theory of *legal* and *institutional* rights, he contends, contrary to his previous position, that it is hostile to *moral* rights. Here is the connection between Parts I and II of the volume, for, like Coleman, he is challenging the ethical foundation of the economic analysis of law. But the argument is by no means the same as Coleman's. "Although there are often utilitarian reasons for respecting justified legal rights, these reasons are not equivalent to the moral force of such rights," he maintains, "because they do not exclude direct utilitarian arguments against exercising such rights or for interfering with them" (pp. 109–10). Moral rights provide a stiffness (he speaks of "argumentative thresholds") that utilitarian (and thus welfare) arguments lack. Both the economic analysts and Bentham fail to account for the moral force of legal rights.

Kent Greenawalt, while not denying that Lyons may have a technically sound point, argues that Lyons has greatly overstated his case. Not only are the practical results of the two theories likely to be identical, but also the act-utilitarian may be able to produce an entirely coherent account of the relation of morality to legal rights—one that comes close to our common understanding.

R. M. Hare next enters the arena. Unlike Greenawalt, he goes for the jugular. Legal rights *do* have moral force. The reason is that the utilitarian justification for a system of *moral* rights would "evaporate if in particular cases people do not have and, except in unusual cases follow, the moral intuition that the law ought in general to be obeyed" (p. 154).

Having taken up a kind of middle position, Lyons now finds himself under attack by Alan Gewirth from the opposite side, that is to say, from the side of deontology. Gewirth's argument is too complex to be adequately summarized here. Only a few highlights of his position can be indicated. He attacks Lyons for not providing a ground for rights other than welfare. Moral rights must be based on the principle of generic consistency; they derive from individual needs or requirements of agency; they are part of welfare but independent of it. They are based on a distributive principle, whereas utilitatianism is aggregative. For him duties flow from rights; for the utilitarian, the derivation is in the opposite direction.

Richard Flathman criticizes Lyons from yet another point of view. He uses the concept of authority and the opposing position of the civil disobedient for this purpose. Lyons, he says, "gives inadequate attention to the fact that legal rights are part of a system or practice of authority" (p. 195). "For a utilitarian who knows what rights and authority are, there is nothing contingent about the fact that violating a right is an *ultra vires* act" (p. 199). Authority, like rights, may be recognized in general, and yet be questioned in certain cases. "Perhaps," Flathman concludes, "a theory of civil encroachment on rights would contribute importantly to the theory of rights and at least to this aspect of the dispute between utilitarianism and its critics" (p. 207).

George Fletcher concludes Part II by arguing that Lyons has overlooked an important distinction. Rights, in particular the rights of individuals to make difficult decisions affecting their own lives, may be normatively sound for either of two reasons: (1) because in general we expect people to exercise their rights soundly, or (2) because the issues are so complex that in the long run decentralized decision making will minimize error. Lyons, he contends, does not deal with the second argument, yet it "provides a modest utilitarian defense of legal rights with normative force."

In Part III, under the heading "International Redistribution," we turn to still another aspect of our overall topic. Its relation to ethics and economics is obvious; the legal connection (apart from the fact that state policies must be implemented by law) is slightly more subtle, being the fact that it is the very absence of a strong international legal system (and the degree of commonality that must support such a system) that makes this case different from distributive justice within a state.

The lead chapter here is Brian Barry's "Humanity and Justice in Global Perspective." His argument is three-pronged: that considerations of humanity require that rich countries aid poor ones; that justice also requires such transfer; and that the obligations imposed by those considerations, though not identical, are not incompatible. Under the first heading, after answering various objections, he goes on to consider limitations to them. Although he finds no clear principle, he has no doubt that the obligation falls far short of demanding that the donors bring themselves down to the level of the donees, while it still requires a much higher level of aid than the United States is presently giving. Justice too, under one or more various possible interpretations, calls for global redistribution. But movement in this direction must be very gradual, as popular sentiment can be led to support small changes, which in turn reinforce the sentiments. Barry also considers possible systems of taxation that might be used for international redistribution. His conclusion deals with the relation between the two types of argument, neither of which, he says, can be reduced to the other. One is goal-based and aims at well-being; the other is rights-based, with autonomy as its touchstone. So important is the latter, with its stress on recipient control, that he actually maintains that the former operate only after justice has been established, for "To talk about what I ought, as a matter of humanity, to do with what is mine makes no sense until we have established what is mine in the first place" (p. 249).

The two following chapters vigorously attack Barry from sharply differing points of view. Kai Nielsen's message is brief and simple. Barry is politically naive and lacking in moral idealism. Equal satisfaction of needs should be the goal. Capitalistic government can never be persuaded to provide aid on anything like the scale that is owed, or even that Barry thinks is owed. The best way to help most poor countries would be to channel money to insurgent movements, helping them rid themselves of their exploitative ruling class.

Thomas Franck, like George Fletcher in Part II, is a skeptic about the moralizing of philosophers. Like all the other contributors to Part III, he believes we should give aid to those who need it—well, at least to some of them. We should limit it to those who share "our social goals and political values" (p. 272). In support of this limitation he argues, in part, that it can be defended—up to a point—even on grounds of fairness (p. 273), in view of the fact that the Soviet Union supports its friends and sympathizers. The argument he considers more fundamental, however, is based on national self-interest. Because his program would contribute to the global support of our values and also strengthen actual and potential trading partners, Americans can be persuaded, out of self-interest, to support it, as they could not be persuaded to support Barry's universalism.

David Richards concludes this part with his own independent contribution to the subject. He holds that Rawlsian contractarian reasoning, suitably altered or interpreted, gives powerful support to the obligation—both personal and national—to support redistribution of wealth on a global scale. Contrary conclusions—even by Rawls himself—based on the Humean circumstances of justice, lay too much emphasis on reciprocal *advantage* and too little on "the deeper idea of moral reciprocity" (p. 292)—"the ethical idea of treating persons in the way one would oneself reasonably like to be treated" (p. 278). But not everything hinges on this principle: agreeing with Barry, he holds that the natural duty of mutual aid, "triggered by extreme deprivation" (p. 293), also comes into play.

The concluding part of this volume, a historical study, is in one way very different from all that has gone before; yet in another way it both complements the other essays and at the same time brings the book as a whole full circle, or nearly that. Harry Scheiber, a legal historian, here shows ethics, economics, and the law in dynamic operation in nineteenth-century America. Private rights and public values both blend and contend in an arena of reciprocal causation. Doctrinal and pragmatic considerations, public morality and private interests, share the magnetic field of legal development. Out of this tension, Scheiber shows how "the tenets of 'possessive individualism' and those of public rights" have led to the development of "modern formulations of 'the public interest'" (p. 315).

The Editors

PART I

ETHICS, ECONOMICS, AND THE LAW

1

ETHICS, ECONOMICS, AND THE LAW OF PROPERTY

FRANK I. MICHELMAN

I. INTRODUCTION

Is it true that in economics lie answers to the ethical conundrums implicit in legal coercion?[1] This chapter considers the question with respect to the law of property. Its thesis is that not even a presumptive preference for the rudiments of private property—much less a conclusive case for any detailed configuration of rules conforming to those rudiments—is obtainable by economic reason from empirically verified premises. Now, that is not to say that private property is unjustifiable, but rather that the justifications must finally appeal to kinds of premises and arguments—call them *moral* premises and arguments—that economic reason aims at circumventing.

It is true that the norm for social ordering invoked by economic analysis—that is, the norm of efficiency—seems as neutral, as indisputable, as any such norm could be. One has only to start with a factual judgment that, far from being controversial, borders on the pragmatically irresistible; that is, that our actions as human individuals are rationally motivated, in the minimal sense of aiming at general satisfaction of consistently ordered sets of privately experienced wants or preferences. Efficiency, then, just means arranging matters so as to allow for as much such satisfaction as nature's immutable laws permit.[2] The weak premises of rationality and efficiency are, however, insufficient to determine an ideal form of property law. The efficiency of private property is a hypothesis dependent, not only on behavior rationally directed toward satisfying individual wants, but on questions about the contents of the wants and the social propensities of their bearers—some of which may be empirically determinable, while others can only be imputed through moral intuition or moral reason.

The extreme counterthesis to this essay's is what we may call the presumptive efficiency thesis (PET). It is important to see that PET, at its best, is not itself insensitive to contingencies of actual wants and proclivities. PET may well regard private property (PP), not as a unique order having detailed specifications, but as a set of orders sharing the same general form, within which the details can vary while the form remains clearly opposed to that of obviously non-PP orders such as collective ownership or an unregulated "state of nature." PET, then, would be the notion that efficiency is both a general and a peculiar virtue of the PP *form*—general in the sense that efficiency is presumptively an attribute of the PP form as such, as applied to whatever domain of valued objects you like; peculiar in the sense that given any particular domain, and any proposed regime for ordering it that is identifiably *not* PP, there is always presumed to be some PP way that is more efficient than the proposed alternative (the details of which will depend on the special facts pertaining to actual wants and proclivities). The claim here is that PET is false even in this most reasonable, highly adaptable version.

II. COMPARING FORMS OF REGIMES FOR PRESUMPTIVE EFFICIENCY

A. The Private Property Torso

To think of private property regimes (PP) as presumptively efficient is, it seems, to have at least vaguely in mind an ideal type of PP—an institutional paradigm to which actual regimes may be observed to conform or not.

Some elements of the PP form are easy to identify. Any legal order must contain both rules governing *initial acquisition* by agents in the order of use and control of valued objects, and rules governing *reassignment* from one agent to another.[3] In a "private property" order, it will be readily agreed, the rules must conform to at least the following principles:

Initial Acquisition

1. *Sole ownership:* The rules must allow that at least some objects of utility or desire can be fully owned by just one person. To be "full owner" of something is to have complete and exclusive *rights* and *privileges* over it—the "rights" meaning that others are legally required to leave the object alone save as the owner may permit, and the "privileges" meaning that the owner is legally free to do with the object as he or she wills.[4]

2. *Self-ownership:* The rules must prescribe that each individual is full owner of his or her natural body, talents, and labor power.

3. *Ownership of product:* The rules must prescribe that whoever owns all the factor inputs to any product owns the product. (Rules governing cases of production using factors owned by more than one person must be designed so as to reinforce actual social respect for property in factors.)

Reassignment

4. *Freedom of transfer:* Owners are both immune from involuntary deprivation or modification of their ownership rights and empowered to transfer their rights to others at will, in whole or in part.

B. Private Property Compared With What?

We need some reasonably clear conceptions of regimes that are decidedly *not* PP, with which PP regimes can be compared for presumptive efficiency. It will be convenient to have three of these before us:

1. *State of nature (SON).* In a state-of-nature (SON) regime there are never any exclusionary rights. All is privilege. People are legally free to do as they wish, and are able to do, with whatever objects (conceivably including persons) are in the SON.[5]

2. *Regulatory regime (REG)*. The converse of SON is a regulatory regime (REG), in which everyone always has rights respecting the objects in the regime, and no one, consequently, is ever privileged to use any of them except as particularly authorized by the others.[6] (Rules for determining when such authorization exists may vary along several axes. At one extreme, authorization would require near-simultaneous unanimous consent; tending toward the other extreme would be a rule defining authorization as expressions of consent from any two persons occurring within the same twelve-month time span. The latter rule constitutes an REG: under it, each person always has a right that each of the others shall leave the covered objects alone except insofar as authorization is obtained.)

3. *Forced sharing for needs (FSN)*. SON and REG both distinguish themselves from PP by strongly negating the PP principle of sole ownership. Forced sharing for needs (FSN) instead attacks the PP principle of ownership of one's product. An FSN regime always resembles some counterpart version of PP, departing from the PP counterpart only in the following feature: anyone who "needs" a thing and doesn't have it (or its equivalent in cash or credit) may take or requisition it from anyone else who has it and doesn't "need" it, and the state will intervene, if necessary, on the side of the needy taker. (For convenience, let us imagine rules clearly defining "need" in objective terms referring only to currently observable states of affairs. These may define "need" quite broadly—e.g., having in one's possession at this moment less than two thirds of the per capita average share of privately held national wealth—or quite narrowly—e.g., being diabetic and lacking insulin for an overdue shot.)

C. Controlling for Distribution and Rights

Calling private property presumptively efficient makes sense only as a statement that, for any given non-PP regime, there is probably some workable PP regime that, while otherwise equivalent, is more efficient. We have begun to form some rough idea of the meaning of PP and non-PP. But what does the term "otherwise equivalent" mean?

Surely one might have grounds other than comparative

efficiency for choosing among regimes. A regime might be preferred for the sake of its expected distributional outcomes, or because it conforms to extraeconomic conceptions of rights. Such concerns might immediately dictate the choice among regimes without regard to efficiency comparisons; or efficiency comparisons might be relevant but not necessarily controlling, given some "social welfare function" that specifies the form and rate of exchange[7] among efficiency and other concerns.

We need some conceptual apparatus by which to control for possible concerns about distribution and rights, and so keep our comparisons among regimes (or classes thereof) strictly focused on efficiency. We need, in particular, to make sure that preferences for PP vis-à-vis SON, REG, or FSN, even when experienced or expressed as if motivated by efficiency concerns, are not really grounded in some other dimension of morality.

The appropriate set of controls is not hard to discover. We first assume that we have an adequate definition of the PP and non-PP categories. Next, we assume a distributional criterion, D, that specifies the set of acceptable distributions, and a rights criterion, R, that specifies the form and rate of exchange (which might, of course, be that of lexical superiority) of various rights with efficiency. Finally, we assume knowledge of the natural facts and laws that determine the most efficient specification of the PP form that is compatible with both D and R. This excellent regime we call PP*.

We can use the expression P̶P̶ to stand for any class of regimes that are certainly not PP. By analogy with PP*, P̶P̶* designates any non-PP regime that satisfies both D and R. PET, then, is tantamount to the view that (i) there exists at least one instance of P̶P̶*—at least one possible non-PP regime that, given all the other supposed facts about the world, will in practice allow for due recognition of all the rights in R and yield distributions compatible with D; and (ii) for every such P̶P̶*, it is the case that (or there is reason to think it likely that) there is a possible PP* that is more efficient. It is of central importance to the aims of this chapter to understand that PET entails not only point (ii), but point (i) as well. If you think (i) is false, you are committed to PP on grounds that have nothing to do with efficiency. You are, moreover, committed to *rejecting* PET insomuch as PET is the thesis that PP regimes are presumptively more efficient than *otherwise equivalent* ~~PP~~ regimes; because whatever the term "otherwise equivalent" might mean, it seemingly cannot encompass regimes that fail, where PP succeeds, in securing distributional or noneconomic rights.

Thus, if R is such as directly to require establishment of sole ownership (thus ruling out SON and REG), or directly to condemn any needs-based redistributions of product (thus ruling out FSN), then a preference for PP* over SON, REG, or FSN is fully determined by these extraeconomic considerations, and efficiency is beside the point of the comparisons. Again, if the supposed facts are such that SON simply cannot be constrained (while still remaining a cognizable version of SON) so as to generate a D-compatible distribution, then rejection of SON in favor of PP* is fully determined by a preference for a certain range of distributional outcomes, and efficiency is beside the point.

III. THE COMPOSITION PRINCIPLE OF THE PP FORM

A. The Question of Composition

The four "torso" principles of sole ownership, self-ownership, ownership of product, and freedom of transfer,[8] are not by themselves sufficient to characterize regimes that are recognizably and distinctively PP. Also needed are rules governing the composition of allowable ownership claims—or, as it might be described, for "packaging"[9] marketable goods into legally cognizable objects of ownership. A few illustrations will confirm the need.

Take first the case of airspace overlying the earth's surface. Is that legally subdivisible at all? Is it subdivisible, but only into sole exclusive ownership domains along this or that configuration of space-time coordinates—for example, by a rule that assigns to the owner of a surface parcel sole exclusive ownership of the superadjacent space?[10] Or might the subdivision occur along different conceptual axes? For example, we distinguish "rights" (of exclusion) from "privileges" (of entry and use), and then assign to each individual "sole ownership" of a privilege over the whole spherical envelope (namely, I am the sole owner of my world-encompassing privilege in that I alone determine how and when I exercise it)—with the result, by deduction, that no one initially has any exclusionary rights. Or, conversely, we assign to each individual an all-encompassing *right*, so that it becomes true for each that no other is free to enter or act within the envelope without the permission of the former—and no one, therefore, initially has any privileges.[11]

Without at this point saying anything stronger, we can safely conclude that the PP form must require *some* restriction on decomposition of full ownership into privileges held without their congruent rights, or rights without their congruent privileges. A regime totally void of such restrictions could hardly count as PP, because a scheme of universally distributed, all-encompassing privilege is, precisely, a *commons,* a type of regime (SON) that is opposite to PP if any type is; whereas the converse scheme of universally distributed, all-encompassing rights is just an extreme of collectivization (REG) no less starkly opposed to PP than is the state of nature; and schemes that go part way to either of those extremes will be cognizable, then, not as pure PP, but as mixtures of PP and something else.[12] To be the full owner of something just is to be, at once, the one who is *both* legally free to occupy and enjoy it *and* legally authorized to say what anyone else may do with it.

Further compositional ambiguity yet lurks in the notion of "something," even if we strongly rule out of PP all regimes that countenance any degree of right/privilege decomposition. Are "objects" restricted to entities describable using spatial coordinates? using space-time coordinates? to members of some discernible typology of natural wholes? Do all such entities qualify as ownable objects? Examples of the various questions crowd to mind: May it be that I am the owner of a certain ten-acre field on odd-numbered days, while you own it the rest of the time?[13] May it be that I own, continuously and forever, one half of the field while you own the other half—but our halves are spatially configured like the red-and-black halves of a checkerboard, and the blocks are each one centimeter square?[14] May I own the whole thing, permanently, as respects beet culture, while you own all the rest?[15] May I own the toothpaste while you own the tube?[16] Note that all of these may be construed as questions both about the regime's rules for initial acquisition (e.g., may I be allowed to acquire just the beet-raising "easement" by "first occupancy"?), and its rules for reassignment (e.g., may I, fully owning the tube of toothpaste, make A the owner of the tube and B the owner of the paste?)

B. Composition Constraints on PP

It will now be apparent why the torso principles do not constitute a set of sufficient conditions to qualify regimes as PP or not-PP, for purposes of presumptive-efficiency comparisons between the two classes. A regime that reserved all industrial capital to collective ownership or defined all the land as a commons of universal privilege, which would quality as PP under the torso principles, would not so qualify in presumptive-efficiency talk. For sufficient definition of a PP category suitable to presumptive-efficiency discourse, we need some principle or principles of composition stronger than those implicit in torso 1 (*some* objects have to be fully owned by individuals at least initially) and torso 4 (owners can subdivide their holdings).

As one speculates on the matter, there seem to be at least four candidate composition principles for distinguishing presumptively efficient PP regimes, which we can call the principles of *ad hoc efficiency* (composition rules are fixed from time to time with a view to efficiency in light of current knowledge of individual wants and proclivities); *mandatory sole ownership* (no privileges unaccompanied by congruent rights, or vice versa, can be initially acquired and/or reassigned); *internalization* (holdings are configured according to rules set with a view to coordination without need for large-number transactions); and *nonintervention* (no state ownership or state dictation of composition in initial acquisition or reassignment).

The first two candidates can be rather quickly disposed of.

1. Ad Hoc Efficiency

As a composition principle for distinguishing PP orders from others for purposes of presumptive-efficiency comparison, that of periodically revising the regime's composition rules with a view to efficiency would be merely illusory. The ad hoc principle cannot distinguish between private property and, say, "market socialism." It just restates the problem that sent us looking for a "strong" principle of PP composition.

2. Mandatory Sole Ownership

The conceptually cleanest way to demarcate PP from the classes of regimes perceived as opposite to it is just to rule out of PP the kinds of entitlement configurations that seem definitional for the non-PP classes—that is, privileges without congruent rights that characterize a commons, and rights without congruent privileges that characterize a collective. (Under this principle of mandatory sole ownership, PP regimes could still exhibit a variety of composition rules. For example, a regime might have a rule allowing privileges to enter the airspace envelope to be chopped into arbitrarily tiny spatiotemporal bits, or a rule assigning the privilege respecting the entire earth's envelope to just one person, or a rule assigning the privilege in a sector of the envelope to the owner of the adjacent surface[17]—and any of those regimes would qualify as PP as long as whoever had a privilege also always had the congruent exclusionary right.)

The trouble with mandatory sole ownership as a composition principle for presumptively efficient PP regimes isn't, then, that the principle fails to distinguish among regimes, but that it fails to describe a regime that is either plausibly efficient or much like the modified common-law regime we know as "private property." As applied to initial acquisition, the sole-ownership principle would imply that our own law has been presumptively inefficient when it has assigned the high seas and navigable airspace as free transit zones over which there are no exclusive rights;[18] or has prescribed that streams and lakes were subject to rights held jointly by all the riparian owners, none of whom was privileged to deplete or pollute the water without permission from all the others;[19] or even when it has imposed less than absolute liability for harm inflicted by one upon legally cognizable interests of another, by allowing such defenses as due care, emergency, duress, and fair competition.[20] As applied to reassignment, the principle would imply that individuals have acted inefficiently when they have privately and unanimously agreed to pool their several landholdings in a recreation area open to the free use of all, or to subject their holdings to a regime of collective controls on use and development.[21] It is safe to conclude that mandatory sole ownership is too strong a composition constraint for presumptively efficient PP. We need something less inflexible, though still tougher than the ad hoc efficiency principle.

3. Internalization
a. Composition and Costs of Coordination

Before proceeding to study of the third and fourth candidate composition principles for the PP form—namely those of internalization and nonintervention—it will be in order to examine the relation between composition and efficiency.

Given a society containing a large number of individuals, a stock of available resources, and a distribution among the individuals of the society's aggregate resource wealth, there is at least one "efficient" scheme of deployment of the various resources such that no alternative deployment could make each person better off even after compensatory side payments. Let us call such an optimal allocative scheme S*.

Let us say that the society would benefit from "coordination" whenever it is the case that S* does not actually obtain (some resources being either idle or used contrary to the dictates of S*). Coordination always entails some direct ("transaction") costs, and the existence of those costs always leads to some shortfall from perfect coordination: the coordinating society always to some degree approaches S*[22] and never attains it. The value of the shortfall is the society's "deadweight loss"; and the total of the deadweight loss and direct costs of coordination is the society's economic waste. From the standpoint of a concern for efficiency, the object of composition rules is minimizing economic waste.[23]

b. Internalization

Suppose that all the available resources are owned in common by each member of the society, so that no coordination at all— much less a close approach to S*—is possible without the formal concurrence or spontaneous cooperation of everyone at once. Now suppose, alternatively, that there is at least one distributionally acceptable way of carving up the resources into individual holdings in severalty, such that under conditions of moderately imperfect information and moderately costly communication the individual holders would be motivated to transact their way stepwise toward S* *by way of a series of small-number contracts and exchanges.* It is true, of course, that under absolutely perfect information and costless communications, S* would emerge out of the ownership-in-common regime as well. But in moderately imperfect conditions, the amounts of economic waste respectively attendant upon the common-ownership and several-ownership regimes are likely to differ.

The composition principle of *internalization* reflects a policy favoring several as opposed to common ownership. The principle is that the rules for composing the taxonomy of legal ownable objects must be designed so that, given what is known or believed about people's wants and proclivities and the resultant utilities attached to various classes of objects, action in accordance with the rules will yield actual configurations of holdings such that the incidence of cases in which coordination requires simultaneous agreement among large numbers of owners will be held to a feasible minimum. Using internalization as the composition principle that qualifies a regime as PP, one would assign a regime to the PP class if its rules both conformed to the torso principles and seemed aptly designed for internalization.

The strategy of internalization is to arrange matters so that the typical owner, or most owners, will have as few "neighbors" as possible. A configuration of holdings at the opposite pole from perfect internality, that is, perfect externality, is one in which everyone is always everyone else's neighbor: each person owning an undivided fractional share interest in every thing in the world.

Of course, internality is perfect only in a world entirely owned by just one owner. That possibility, while logically conceivable, is not widely endorsed as policy.[24] Still, given any criterion (D)[25] of "widespreadness" in distribution, internality seems to posit a comprehensible goal toward which an optimizing intelligence can be coherently directed.

Consider this example.[26] A large group of people, n in number, have the opportunity, at no cost, to acquire an expanse of beach and subdivide it among themselves. We assume that, while the total area of their pending acquisition is fixed, they can take it in any shape they choose—circular, square, oblong, and so forth. They have already settled upon a scheme of equal division by lottery into n parcels to be severally and exclusively occupied by individuals. The question comes as to external shape and internal configuration. Just to keep things simple, suppose for a moment that only two alternatives are available: a row of rectangular holdings adding up to an extended oblong,

or a honeycomb of regular hexagonal holdings as shown in the accompanying drawing.

etc.

It is known, we suppose, that people use beach space for just two different purposes: napping and listening to radios (various stations). Nappers don't like radio noise, and those listening to one station don't like the noise from another. At the preferred volume levels, audible radio noise crosses over just one boundary in every direction, whichever pattern—row of squares or nest of hexagons—is used.

A property system committed to an internalizing composition chooses the row-of-squares design. Under the hexagons alternative, each holder will be faced with the problem of trying to work things out, simultaneously, with each of six neighbors, each of whom also has to deal at the same time with six neighbors, three of them different from the neighbors of the first holder, and so on. Very possibly, some kind of global settlement through a political process will be the best available solution (e.g., they will elect a legislature that will enact some temporal and territorial regulations: in the northeast sector only station A can be played; in the north central, only station B; in the southwest, no radio playing; in others, the day is carved up among different rules; and so on). Under the squares alternative, by contrast, it is quite imaginable that a chain of bilateral deals (trading places, sorting out time periods between neighbors) would lead the parties to a feasible optimum. The preference for small-numbers internality reflects an assumption that economic waste[27] is lower in these bilateral-chain dealings then in the global political process. (If the parties placed an absolute value on efficiency supposedly associated with strict bilaterality, such they they were willing to sacrifice to that end their distributional preference for equal holdings, they could achieve or approach bilaterality by allowing one of their number to become sole owner [landlord] of their entire beach site. This owner would then lease out portions in such sizes, shapes, and patterns, for such durations, and subject to such restrictions on radio playing, as seemed apt to maximize rental revenues; and so a chain of bilateral deals could, again, emerge to lead the parties up Mt. Optimus.)

There is at least some degree of plausibility in the idea that by adding to the four torso principles that of an internalizing strategy for composition rules, we capture the essence of the PP category as it occurs in presumptive-efficiency assessment. This way of completing the definition of the PP form seems to find the economic essence of private property, fittingly enough, in what we may call market structure aimed at accommodating coordination through small-number contracts and exchanges as opposed to political decision or extralegal cooperation. Moreover, the regime we commonly know as private property in fact abounds in restrictions on decomposition of titles that can be understood to reflect a policy of internalization: restrictive doctrines respecting easements in gross,[28] perpetuities,[29] covenants running with the land,[30] restraints on alienation,[31] duration of co-tenancies,[32] "novel" easements and estates,[33] to name just some of the pertinent technicalities of the land law. Scholars[34] and judges[35] have associated many of the restrictive

doctrines with efficiency goals. To be sure, there may be
plausible accounts of many of them, or perhaps all, that make
no appeal to efficiency.[36] Yet it would be folly to insist that
none is, as a matter of fact, conducive to efficiency whether
designedly or accidentally.[37]

4. Nonintervention

Now, it is an unfortunate but inescapable complication—not
to say an embarrassment—to our project of defining the essential form of supposedly efficient PP that the internalization
principle for composition rules is not only market structuring,
but also market hindering. It is market hindering insomuch as
it calls for composition *rules* at all. Internalization policy is,
precisely, the policy of frustrating private parties bent upon
excessive decomposition. And yet it seems hard to deny that
market *freedom*—the absence of economic policy control by the
state—is also of the essence of the PP category in comparative-
efficiency discourse.

We have to consider, then, the possibility of defining the PP
form as consisting of the torso principles plus a fifth to the
effect that the state simply does not mandate or restrict composition (and, by deduction, never is an owner itself).[38] In this
noninterventionist or antistatist conception of PP, all objects of
utility or desire must at all times be either in private ownership
(sole or multiple, full or divided, as the parties determine) or
be unowned because lost, abandoned, undiscovered or unoccupied. If unowned, they may be taken into private ownership
by occupation (or its analogues such as invention or creation);[39]
if owned, they may nevertheless be taken into new ownership
by prescription or adverse possession; and in either case the
occupier or prescriber becomes the owner of just what he took,
bounded by whatever spatial, temporal, and functional limits
actually describe his legally operative, possessory acts.[40] Aside
from occupation and prescription, the only way to become the
owner of anything is by voluntary exercise of some erstwhile
owner's power of alienation; and such powers may be exercised
ad libitum to decompose or recompose titles. For example: I
may, over an extended period of time, regularly but nonexclu-

sively, shoot skeet on Mondays and Fridays on blocks of your field configured like the red part of a checkerboard; and I shall thereby acquire a nonexclusive checkerboard easement (privilege) of Monday/Friday skeet-shooting.[41] Or you might confer just the same title on me by voluntary grant. Obviously, the resulting composition might be a severe impediment to future coordination.

5. Reconciling the Principles of Internalization and Nonintervention

Both internalization and nonintervention seem to be of the essence of the putatively efficient private property form for regimes. Yet, as we have just seen, the two principles have contradictory implications. The problem now is how to give each principle its due in the definition of the PP form, without destroying the coherence of the notion of "private property" as a distinct class of legal orders.

The most straightforward solution is to include both principles in the PP definition, but to give them separate domains of application. Cleanest, perhaps, would be to make internalization a principle for rules governing the composition of entitlements at the point of initial acquisition and nonintervention the composition principle for rules governing reassignment. Thus, the taxonomy of titles that could be gained by occupation, adverse possession, and so on would be composed according to rules designed to minimize the cases in which large-number transactions would be needed for coordination thenceforward,[42] whereas the rules governing reassignment would deal with such matters as formality, disclosure, and duress but leave decomposition and recomposition of titles unregulated, to be determined at will by the parties to the reassignments.

This separate-domains solution, while conceptually neat, is unsatisfactory. It plainly fails to describe the traditional "private property" legal order, which both allows decomposition by initial acquisition[43] and substantially regulates decomposition by reassignment.[44] Moreover, the separate-domains solution is far from making intuitive economic sense. If decomposition hinders coordination, it does so whether arising from initially acquisitive party activity or from the activity of reassignment.

The more satisfying if less determinate solution is best approached by dwelling for a moment on the economic rationale of the nonintervention principle for composition rules. Nonintervention is a principle tending toward efficiency in composition just insofar as it is true that the configurations of holdings arrived at via the nondirected, spontaneous acts of individuals (consisting of first occupancy, exchange, gift transfer, and the like) will always or generally lend themselves to cheaper coordination than will configurations dictated or regulated by the state. Now, the truth of that premise seems to depend on that of one or both of two subpremises—a first regarding the comparative tendencies of regimes to depart from the entitlement structures that would actually be amenable to least-cost coordination under the transient circumstances; a second regarding the comparative cost of correcting for the departures.

The first subpremise is that the self-interested acts and dealings of individuals, whether or not they "decompose" ownership, will leave the universe of holdings from time to time configured more aptly for easy coordination in the service of individual wants than will the dictates of the state. (A dramatic example might be the very sophisticated decompositions of sole ownership by which aggregations of factors are gathered under the unified control of a corporation management without directly disturbing the wide dispersion of wealth claims.[45]) This subpremise does have some intuitive appeal, insomuch as the wants and interests of individuals are seen as both generating the configuration and calling for the coordination of its elements. But there seems to be no reason to suppose that *the same* individual interests and wants are doing both things, and there's the rub. The acts and dealings that continuously reassign and redivide holdings are, to be sure, those of individuals; but, to be no less sure, those acts and dealings will often affect multiple third-party interests, either immediately (again, the concentration and redirection of resources through corporations is a striking example), or under the unknown conditions of an unfolding future. You can't very easily get eggs out of an omelet. The invisible hand is forever becoming the dead hand, as every property lawyer knows.[46] And although there is no reason to confide absolutely in either the beneficence or the omniscience of the state as regulator of property composition, there is also none for trusting more to accidental regulation by individual dealings. If the state does not always act in view of the economic interest of society as a whole, neither do individuals.

The second subpremise is that whatever the extant composition of holdings may be, and however far that composition may have strayed from the one that would accommodate least-cost coordination under the current circumstances, economic waste will tend to be less if individuals are left free to recompose entitlements as they will in private dealings than if composition is dictated or regulated by the state. Thus, both subpremises lead to just the same question about the utility of state regulation of composition.

Posed thus abstractly, the question is unanswerable; or, rather, the inevitable answer to the abstract question is, "sometimes yes, sometimes no." In that irreducibly ambivalent attitude toward state control of composition lies the answer to our search for a composition principle to complete the definition of the PP form. The PP composition principle is that of no-intervention-except-for-the-sake-of-internalization, or what we may call the principle of *market facilitation*: the state may leave composition unregulated; and insofar as the state ever does regulate composition, it does so only by rules that conform to the principle of internalization—that is, the rules are designed with a view to accommodating coordination through small-number transactions.

It is important to note how this composition principle of market facilitation, while necessarily weaker than the rejected principle of "mandatory sole ownership,"[47] is also enough stronger than that of "ad hoc efficiency" to escape the objection that it fails to distinguish between regimes that are and are not PP.[48] It is true that the principle of market facilitation, like that of ad hoc efficiency, allows the possibility of decoupled privileges and rights.[49] It allows that possibility, however, only under rules that aim at market facilitation. It does not countenance rules that aim directly at efficiency, by avoidance of markets. Unlike the ad hoc principle, the principle of market facilitation excludes the possibility that a *state-imposed* commons, or a regime of *state* command or regulation, may sometimes be preferable to a

market. This preference for markets, it seems, is one distinguishing mark of the putatively efficient PP class of regimes;
another is the nonintervention bias.

We are now, at last, in a position to set forth the complete set
of formal principles for PP regimes:

Principles Governing Initial Acquisition

1. *Self-ownership:* The rules must prescribe that each
individual is full owner of his or her natural body, talents,
and labor power.

2. *Ownership of product:* The rules must prescribe that
whoever owns all the factor inputs to any product owns the
product. Rules governing cases of production using factors
owned by more than one person must be designed so as to
reinforce actual social respect for property in factors.

3. *Market-facilitating composition:*

(a) *internalization bias:* Composition of holdings may be
regulated only by rules designed to avoid excessive dependence of coordination on large-number transactions.

(b) *nonintervention bias:* Subject only to principle 3(a),
composition of holdings by initial acquisition is as determined by party action under rules conforming to principles
1 and 2.

Principles Governing Reassignment

4. *Nonexpropriation:* Owners are immune from involuntary deprivation or modification of their ownership rights.

5. *Market-facilitating freedom of transfer:*

(a) *free alienation:* Subject to principles 5(b), (c), owners
are empowered to transfer their ownership rights to others
at will.

(b) *internalization bias:* Subdivision of holdings by reassignment may be regulated, but only by rules designed to
avoid excessive dependence of coordination on large-number transactions.

(c) *nonintervention bias:* Subject only to principle 5(b),

composition of holdings by reassignment is as determined by action of the parties to the reassignment.

IV. THE "MORAL BASIS" OF PET[50]

We are ready now to return to this chapter's central claim. Take any R and any D, and any corresponding PP* and PP*.[51] Then, from the sole factual postulate that persons are rational maximizers of individual satisfactions, one cannot deduce that the PP* is—or even is likely to be—the more efficient regime. Such a deduction must depend always on additional factual or moral premises.

It is possible to compile a short list of additional premises, the truth of at least one of which would be required to make the deduction true. My aim is to show that the additional premises are either (i) false, or (ii) quasi empirical, meaning that in the present state of knowledge they are not known empirically to be true and are better understood as moral propositions than as factual ones—as statements of a view about how things might well be, not of how things are known to be.

A. Additional Premises
The list of additional premises is as follows:

a. Per Se Preferences for Institutional Roles, States, Experiences

1. People prefer the role and experience of being unmolested producers to those of (i) being predators in a state of nature or beneficiaries of forced sharing, and (ii) repulsing predators or fulfilling legal duties of sharing.
2. With regard to some specifiable list of valued objects or experiences (e.g., your body, or having total command over what you produce), people prefer the state of being legally secure in their own possessory claims to that of being legally free to disregard the reciprocal, possessory claims of others.[52]
3. People prefer the experience of private exchange through

markets to that of public decision through politics, and
to that of informal, extralegal cooperation.

*b. Effect of Uncertainty, Predation, and Forced Sharing on
Incentive and Product*

4. Potential producers, anticipating loss of product to legally unrestrained predation, regulation, or forced sharing, will substitute for some or all of the production they
   otherwise would have undertaken some combination of
   (i) leisure, (ii) production in less predation-prone or less
   shareable form, and (iii) other defensive activity.
5. Potential producers, allowed by law to help themselves
   to the fruits of other people's work (whether as predators
   or forced sharers), will substitute leisure for some or all
   of the production they otherwise would have undertaken.

c. Coordination Behavior

6. Failure of coordination, through information failure
   and strategies of freeloading and bluffing, will be lesser
   under a market process in which large numbers eventually participate through complex chains of small-number deals than under a political process of collective
   decision or an extralegal process of voluntary cooperation.

This chapter proceeds henceforth on the assumption that
belief in PET requires belief in the truth of at least one of the
six additional premises. I see no way of proving the truth of
this assumption. I can only leave it to readers to show the
contrary, if they can, by either (i) explaining how to complete
the defense of PET with nothing but the rational-maximizers
premise to go on, or (ii) supplying some other additional premise
that can do the job.

B. The Additional Premises as Quasi Empirical

1. The Per Se Preferences

Let us take first the three premises regarding per se preferences for institutional states, roles, and experiences. Neither

observation nor introspection has established, or seems likely to, that any of them is universally held; to the contrary, either common[53] or historical[54] observation, scientific investigation,[55] or introspection casts grave doubt upon the idea that any of these preferences are species-characteristic in anything like a universal sense. And once it is granted that some people may well have converse preferences, any claim to knowledge of how the balance of value lies, when it comes to choosing which among the conflicting preferences to accommodate, will be deeply unconvincing. (Worse, one's guesses about these matters will of necessity be rooted in observation of people conditioned by the prevalence of a particular set of institutions. Worse yet, those guesses themselves—one's own reading of the contaminated evidence, such as it is—will be similarly conditioned.)

The additional premises themselves assert that products and leisure do not exhaust the wants and preferences that may be more or less satisfied in a PP or non-PP regime and therefore have to be counted in the efficiency comparison. This assertion, however, opens the door to more possibilities than the premises allow—for example, that some people have a taste for the hurly-burly of SON or the political machination of REG; or for legally noncompelled cooperation or political participation of a type possible only in SON or REG; or that some have a deep aversion to uncertainty about having their needs go unmet when others are in a position to help them. There may even be some people who would take enormous satisfaction in the knowledge of being legally at liberty to go about using other people's bodies impulsively, as the spirit moves—who like even more the prospect that the persons within the bodies may fight back—and who are, by contrast, made miserable by the knowledge of being required to bargain with other people over the use of their bodies.

One cannot just dismiss such preferences as "nonrational," if rationality is to remain a "weak" premise.[56] Of course, one *might* discount them as morally unworthy and thereby perhaps arrive at a preference for PP, in some form, over SON, REG, and FSN, on noneconomic moral grounds. One can also try admitting that there may be some people with the licentious preferences, but so few that their deviant wants are plainly outweighed by those of the host of normal security-preferrers. Thus would one enter upon quasi empiricism. Surely the crucial countings and "weighings" are not empirically known or verifiable. Surely one's sense of conviction about them arises from intellectual faculties hard to distinguish from those employed in moral intuition and moral reason. Surely their stuff is the stuff of Ought, though their form be the form of Is.

2. Uncertainty, Incentive, and Product

Let us now turn to additional premises 4–6, concerned with the untoward effects on production and satisfaction of the uncertainty (or insecurity) associated with legalized predation, forced sharing, and the threat of regulation. We take up three ways in which such uncertainty may be thought to be economically detrimental, including some further analysis of the supposed per se preference for security of possession.

a. *Uncertainty as an intrinsic bad or cost.* Let us start by granting, *arguendo,* that uncertainty is, indeed, an intrinsically bad thing to experience. Comparing PP with FSN or SON, it is obvious that the choice lies not between "more" and "less" uncertainty but between the kinds of uncertainty various people must bear.[57] Under PP, owners are certain of future control of their factors and products (per contract in the case of joint products), while those whose holdings, productive capacities, or productive motivations fall short of some critical level are uncertain of having all their needs met (i.e., by voluntary charity). Under FSN or SON, uncertainty about having your future needs met may be reduced (if you are unproductive or a gifted thief),[58] while uncertainty about keeping all your present holdings is certainly increased. Since neither sort of uncertainty is any more or less compatible with rationality than the other, neither regime can be said, prima facie, to entail "less" bad uncertainty than the other.

Moreover, experience may afford an antidote to uncertainty in SON or FNS. Farmers, for example, may come to know what fraction of a planted crop they can normally expect to reap and keep. Indeed, a fairly intelligible equilibrium may emerge, bolstered and structured by informal agreement. The total of the bounded uncertainty in a mature SON or FSN regime cannot, prima facie, be supposed either "more" or "less" than that of the (one-sided) uncertainty in PP.[59]

Finally, there is nothing in the rationality premise (at least, not in the weak or neutral sense that makes rationality almost irresistible as a working assumption) requiring that uncertainty be regarded as intrinsically bad or costly. Risk aversion is no more rational than is risk neutrality or a positive adventuring spirit. Once we drop the *arguendo* assumption of the intrinsic badness of uncertainty, it obviously becomes impossible to compare the efficiency of regimes in terms of the amounts of uncertainty they entail.

   b. Uncertainty and allocation between labor and leisure. It is sometimes incautiously suggested[60] (and, one suspects, very widely just taken for granted) that minimizing the uncertainty of return faced by (potential) producers, at the same time denying any certainty of returns of potential predators, must certainly lead to increased total product. The intuitive notion is that the farmer assured of reaping where he has sown *must* be the more disposed to sow. The notion is false. In technical language, the mistake lies in a supposition, baseless so far as rationality is concerned, that the "substitution effect" of replacing PP with SON will prevail over the "income effect"[61]—that is, that since in SON the trade-off between labor and leisure is more favorable to leisure than it is in PP, people will work less and rest more in SON.

   The truth is that the net result depends on how strongly producers value increments of product vis-à-vis increments of leisure, given this or that extant combination of the two. If those relative valuations are such that the "income effect" prevails, a farmer who anticipates losing half of his crop to human predators will plant (in the limiting case) twice as much as he otherwise would have, so as to reap no less than would have been the case absent predation—and the result will be twice as much total product for human consumption under SON than under PP.

   But wait a minute. What about the predator? Isn't it true a priori that people who in SON manage to live off others, in PP will have to work for their livings; and that *their* product, at least, will be greater in PP? Supposing for a moment that this *is* true, we still have no way of knowing a priori that the *total* product output is greater in PP, given that those who produce in PP may, for all we know, produce even more in SON. Moreover, it isn't even knowable that those who are predators in SON will be workers in PP, rather than recipients of voluntary charity. Nor is the converse knowable, namely that some people who have to work for a living in PP would, if SON were instituted instead, give up work in favor of predation; since the case might be that those who, in SON, obtain a certain standard of living through predation (say, the same as the maximum standard they can achieve as workers in PP) might find that life in SON at that standard generates additional wants more cheaply satisfiable by work, given diminishing returns to predation. Perfectly possible, these people would work harder and more productively in SON than in PP—for example, if only in SON, with the predatory income base (or supplement) there available, did it become practical for them to think of striving for a total income ample enough for cruises and oriental rugs.

c. *Lawful predation and misallocation to precaution and defense.* Here the notion is that, lacking legal guarantees against predation, producers rationally must either produce less highly valued (but also less predation-prone) outputs than they otherwise would have (e.g., gather nuts rather than raise grain), or else divert labor and resources to defensive outputs (fences, private goon squads, mayhem) that have zero or negative value as final goods, thereby reducing the real value of GNP below what it otherwise would have been. Again, the argument depends on particular assumptions of fact. As we move from PP to SON, farmers may grow less, but they also may grow more; they may build fences, but they also may (it depends on comparative cost-effectiveness) just forget the fences and plant enough for both the predators and themselves (as one does with raspberry bushes, not bothering with netting or chickenwire because it's easier just to raise enough fruit to satisfy one's own wants and give the birds a free lunch to boot); the farmers may divert energies to defensive maneuvers that they find tiresome and disagreeable, but they also may affirmatively enjoy their skirmishing with predators (and goon-squad members who otherwise would have languished their ways through boring lives may find in goon-squading their true *métiers*), or—again—the farmers may just forgo defense altogether.

Just as in the cases of the per se preferences, our counter-speculations about insecurity and its consequences depend to some extent on the possibility that people have wants or traits that may seem alien or unappealing (or worse) to "us"—too little self-reliance, too narrow a dependence on some particular form of consumption, a nasty taste for combat, or whatever. It seems no more open to us here than it was there to dismiss such inclinations as irrational. But how can we, then, pretend to *know* how the balance of preferences lies? The issues here, as there, are at least partly quasi empirical, our convictions about them just as hard to disentangle from the ingredients of moral discourse. There is, to be sure, a historical and anthropological literature offering empirical evidence on some of these questions,[62] but it is controversial and, at least for now, inconclusive—too weak a foundation for strong convictions about the rightness or goodness of private property.[63]

3. Coordination Behavior

The last additional premise is that owners of interdependent holdings, confronting one another in a changing world in which further coordination always beckons, can make better progress toward perfect coordination (S^*)[64] through numerous, stepwise, small-number dealings than through more massive, if possibly fewer, feats of large-number coordination. These more massive feats might imaginably take the form either of regulation through a political process of collective decision or of cooperation outside the legally coercive institutions of regulation, property rights, and enforceable contract. What supposed facts about the human condition lie behind the belief that such processes are generally doomed to failure, by comparison with what can be achieved through contractual relations and exchanges based on individualized proprietary holdings?

a. No Natural Harmony?

Let us recall our hypothetical case of the beach.[65] The preference we there developed for an internalizing, "bilateralist" composition depended in part on a belief about the relative costliness, in forgone gains from trade, of the strategic behaviors respectively associated with large-number and small-number dealings. But it also, and more obviously, depended on the specific facts assumed about the actual substance of individual preferences and, relatedly, the utilities of beach-based activities—that is, the assumption that everyone wants above all not to have to hear noise from anyone else's radio. The example was rigged to yield a choice for bilateralist composition.

Of course, one could as easily rig a beach case of opposite import—for example, by supposing it to be known that the only thing anyone likes to do on the beach is stretch out and listen to music over the radio, everyone has just one radio of limited power, there is only one station on the air (or there are several, always simultaneously broadcasting mutually harmonious music), and the more radios you hear playing together, the better the music is. Overhearing, in short, far from being a nuisance, is an unambiguous benefit to all participants. Knowing that to be true, rational people would prefer the configuration of hexagons to the alternatives. The law has, indeed, sometimes made such choices. There are traditional legal doctrines inclining to maximization, not minimization, of neighborhood interactions understood to be mutually beneficial—for example, those establishing common rights of transit in the seas and inland navigable waters,[66] and common rights of access to communications forums.[67]

b. No Trust?

To some extent, then, the belief that a market-structuring (neighbor-minimizing) composition of holdings yields better coordination than a neighbor-maximizing regime of common privilege may depend on belief that cases of natural interactive harmony (such as our second beach case) occur less frequently than those of conflictual neighborhood relations. It is hard to fathom the sense in which such a "fact" might be "known." We need not dwell on the question, however, because the market-structuring preference can perhaps survive confession of inability to answer it.

Suppose we don't know in advance which version of the beach story is true, because we don't know the facts about future radio program content, broadcast technology, and people's likes and dislikes. If the first (conflictual) version turns out to be true after we have opted for a nest of hexagons, the way to efficient reordering lies only through cooperation or politics; but if the second (harmonious) version turns out to be true after we are committed to a row of squares, a chain of bilateral transactions conceivably might accomplish the efficient reordering. Thus, a general preference for market structure may reflect belief that *correction* is generally likelier to occur through markets than through cooperation or politics.

There remains the question of the behavioral suppositions implicit in that belief, and a crucial one seems to be that persons in potentially conflictual social situations (beyond the confines of family and friendship) are typically incapable of acting on mutually trustful premises. No doubt there are substantial risks that cooperative or political processes will "fail" because of information gaps, communication difficulties, and destructive strategic responses to such conditions;[68] but on the other hand there are exactly analogous risks of "market failure."[69] What makes the risks seem heavier for cooperative and political processes is, I suggest, their pronounced multiparty character, which seems to escalate the likelihood that they will constitute "prisoners' dilemmas" or comparably tragic strategic fixes[70] — will be, in Mancur Olson's classification, instances of "latent" rather than "privileged" or "intermediate" groups.[71] And prisoners' dilemmas just epitomize trustlessness in social affairs.

c. Rationality, Trust, and the "Tragedy of the Commons"

The pessimistic view of human capacity for trustful cooperation has found its special metaphor in the "commons" upon which preindustrial villagers grazed their cattle. "The rational herdsman concludes that the only sensible course . . . to pursue is to add another animal to [its] herd. And another; and another. . . . But this is the conclusion reached by each and every rational herdsman sharing a commons. . . . Each man is locked into a system that compels him to increase his herd without limit—in a world that is limited. Ruin is the destination toward which all men rush, each pursuing his own best interest in a society that believes in the freedom of the commons."[72]

The "commons" stands for isomorphic predicaments observed in modern life, most typically associated with environmental degradation: "The rational man finds that his share of the cost of the wastes he discharges into the commons is less than the cost of purifying his wastes before releasing them. Since this is true for everyone, we are locked into a system of 'fouling our own nest.'"[73] A comparable case is said to be presented by "freedom to breed" in the setting of a modern welfare state commitment to social support for the needy: "To couple the concept of freedom to breed with the belief that everyone born has an equal right to the commons is to lock the world into a tragic course of action."[74]

All these can be recognized as instances of the general configuration of interests called by Schelling "multi-person prisoner's dilemma," and abstractly modeled by him as follows:

1. There are n people, each with the same binary choice and the same payoffs.[75]
2. Each has a preferred choice whatever the others do; and the same choice is preferred by everybody.
3. Whichever choice a person makes, he or she is better off, the more there are among the others who choose their unpreferred alternative.
4. There is some number, k, greater than 1, such that if individuals numbering k or more choose their unpreferred alternative and the rest do not, those who do are better off than if they had all chosen their preferred alternatives, but if they number less then k this is not true.

Is the situation thus depicted truly such that self-interested agents are rationally driven to reciprocal self-destruction? Does the way to salvation truly lie only through abolition of the freedom of the commons in favor of regulation through property rights or collective control? Cooperation based on mutual trust, if that is conceivable for rationally self-interested human agents, would avoid the catastrophe as well; so if cooperative behavior is rationally possible, then commonses are not generically tragic. But cooperative behavior *must be* possible if avoidance of commonses is practically discussable at all; for the policy of extirpating commonses in favor of property rights (or other regulation) assuredly depends on the possibility of cooperation.

What is private property, regarded from the standpoint of economic policy, but a particular form of regulation,[76] a species of those "definite social arrangements . . . that create coercion of some sort,"[77] institution of which is offered as the alternative to tragedy? But then come the questions: Instituted (fashioned, decided upon) by whom? Policed and enforced by whom? Obeyed by whom, and why? Because if (and only if!) I don't obey, the constable will catch me, the prosecutor try me, the magistrate convict me, the sheriff punish me? Who will make them? Where can the regress end, if not in uncoerced cooperation, the untragic commons of constitutional practice founded on a "rule" that there is no one to enforce but that people on the whole adhere to, though adherence is in the interest of no one who does not trust that (most) others will adhere to it, by "mutual agreement."[78] In other words: no trust, no property. In the very survival of proprietary institutions we have empirical evidence of the possibility of trust; as we have in the electorate's behavior each election day.[79]

Short of absurdity, then, the metaphor of the commons cannot speak to us more powerfully of the rational necessity of social cooperation than of its rational possibility. In this dialectic of necessity and possibility, private property emerges as a possible device or instrumentality for social cooperation—available, as such, only to agents *who have, in the first place, a capacity for cooperative action.* The initial premise has to be that of cooperative capacity; it cannot be the contradictory of that.

Since cooperation is—has to be—both possible and existent without and prior to property, the domain of property cannot be coextensive with that of the commons (all commonses). Property is a scheme of social cooperation whose utility is always a question for judgment and choice, dependent on multiple considerations varying with the circumstances, rather than impelled by some universal and inexorable grim logic of welfare. In any given commons, property may offer the best mode of cooperation, but it also may not.

4. The Additional Premises in Aggregate

I have said that the truth of at least one of the additional premises is a necessary condition of the truth of PET. It is not, however, a sufficient condition. The truth of PET entails further conditions respecting the premises in partial and total aggregates. To exhibit the full complement of further conditions would be tiresome. A single example will suffice both to illustrate their nature and to advance my argument.

Suppose premise 3 were false, the truth being that people generally and strongly prefer to work out their affairs cooperatively or politically, rather than by arm's-length dealings on markets. Suppose also that there were convincing empirical evidence for the truth of any or all of premises 4–7. PET as a whole would remain empirically unverified, because the gains in product that premises 4–7 supposedly tell us will result from shifting to PP from SON or REG may be more than offset by the loss in satisfaction from that same shift implied by the supposed falsity of premise 3. But premise 3 can be no more empirically false than empirically true: it is, inescapable, quasi empirical. As long as it remains so, so does PET. Proof of PET strictly requires empirical verification of *all* the additional premises. No doubt verification of all but one or two of them would make PET highly plausible. But verification of only one or two—which seems the most that can be claimed at present— only marginally affects plausibility.

V. WHY DOES PET MATTER?

There is an illuminating literature in economics devoted to explaining how and why property institutions are efficient when and insofar as they sometimes, indubitably, are.[80] Some of that literature seems to make rather sweeping claims on behalf of private property—to treat it, indeed, as presumptively efficient. None that I know of expressly purports to deduce the general efficiency of private property without reliance on behavioral premises additional to that of rationality, and a careful reader can always infer the additional premises that must be implicit in the literature's accounts of the efficiency virtues of private property.

The aim of this chapter, then, is not to disprove an explicit thesis elsewhere espoused, but rather to urge the importance of making additional premises explicit. Doing so will, I believe, help avoid the danger that efficiency-based accounts of private property institutions will obscure the critical vision that ought to be directed toward such institutions as they are found from time to time in actual practice.

Here is the critique of PET in a nutshell. Whoever thinks that private property is a good thing is committed to some belief in addition to (i) experience accrues to individuals, (ii) individuals are rational maximizers of satisfactions, and (iii) it is good to allow for an increase in the levels of satisfaction experienced by individuals. The necessary additional belief may be quasi empirical, such as (a) every properly formed human individual places a supremely high value on secure command over his or her body, labor, and product, or (b) to a degree that makes the exceptions practically negligible, rational conation in socially situated human individuals always takes the form of the trustless "prisoner" mentality. Or the necessary additional belief may be purely moral, such as (c) irrespective of what various individuals may subjectively want, it is right that each person should be secured in the command over his or her own person; or it may be a composite of moral and empirical belief such as (d) justice requires that the distribution among members of a society of the means to satisfaction periodically satisfy the minimal requirements of D;[81] and the only regimes that will satisfy D (or will satisfy D without excessive sacrifice of efficiency) are, as it happens, private property regimes. The critique of PET, then, is a challenge to all defenders of private property to know their additional premises.

The point is not that the serviceable additional premises are all invalid or indefensible. Far from it. Rather the point is that many—it may be all—of the appealing additional premises are potentially the grounds of significantly critical appraisal of the particular, detailed embodiment of private property we may from time to time observe in practice. Suppose, for example, you think that the efficiency of private property is rooted in a species-characteristic need or craving for privacy and security of person, or for the experience of self-command over personal labor and product. Then if you observed a society in which measurable numbers of persons were selling rights over their bodies in exchange for the means of subsistence, or could live only by submitting to the productive direction of others, you would have to see that situation as problematic. Though it might turn out that there is no way, in this vale of tears, to make

things on the whole any better, you would be committed to at
least searching for some corrective. Similarly if your commitment to private property were more generally based on a
conviction that only a property regime could hope to satisfy
distributional criterion D at a tolerable level of efficiency, then
you would be committed as well to continual scanning of the
extant regime to see whether it was in fact resulting in a D-
satisfactory distribution, and to support of corrective action
whenever such was both needed and available. And suppose,
finally, that your commitment to private property was rooted
in belief that individuals do, as a matter of fact, usually exhibit
prisoner rationality in their encounters with one another. It is
at least a possibility that you would, on further reflection, think
that a world truly void of social trust would be an extremely
dangerous place, and also that the relation between the condition of trustlessness and given institutions of private property
might be not unidirectional but reciprocal—so that not only is
private property a prudent response to a given state of trustlessness, but also particular private property arrangements
sanction and reinforce trustlessness. With that provisional view,
you might want to keep on investigating, rather than considering
the matter closed.

NOTES

1. See Posner, "The Ethical and Political Basis of the Efficiency Norm
   in Common Law Adjudication," 8 *Hofstra L. Rev.* 487 (1980);
   Posner, "Some Uses and Abuses of Economics in Law," 46 *U. Chi.
   L. Rev.* 281, 292 (1979); Michelman, "A Comment," 46 *U. Chi. L.
   Rev.* 308 (1979); Michelman, "Norms and Normativity in the
   Economic Theory of Law," 62 *Minn. L. Rev.* 1015, 1043–45 (1978).
2. There is, of course, a very controversial ambiguity as between the
   norm of *collective* maximization (utilitarianism) and that of *universal*
   "maximization" (paretianism). We can avoid that controversy here
   by way of a benign pretense that these two versions of efficiency
   come practically to the same thing, on the principle of the bigger
   the pie, the bigger the slices. See generally, Bebchuk, "The Pursuit
   of a Bigger Pie: Can Everyone Expect a Bigger Slice?" 8 *Hofstra
   L. Rev.* 671 (1980); Posner, *supra* note 1; Michelman, "Constitu-

tions, Statutes, and the Theory of Efficient Adjudication," 9 *J. Legal Stud.* 431, 435–40 (1980).

3. Rules regarding adverse possession or user that eventuates in both obliteration of an old title and inception of a new one are treated in this chapter as belonging to the "initial acquisition" category.
4. It is an open question whether the notion of full ownership must encompass entitlement to be compensated for unintended or otherwise "excusable" harm to things owned. See Kennedy and Michelman, "Are Property and Contract Efficient?" 8 *Hofstra L. Rev.* 711, 767–68 (1980) (hereafter cited as "Property and Contract").
5. Compare "Property and Contract," *supra* note 4, at 754–55.
6. Compare *id.* at 755–56.
7. The preferred form and rate of exchange may be hierarchical rather than continuously substitutive—a lexical ordering. Compare Dworkin, "Why Efficiency?" 8 *Hofstra L. Rev.* 563 (1980).
8. Text accompanying notes 3–4, *supra*.
9. See B. Ackerman, *Social Justice in the Liberal State*, 170 (1980). Ackerman is directly concerned with the composition problem as it pertains to individual versus collective ownership, but not with other dimensions of the problem we are about to discuss.
10. Such was professedly the traditional rule of the common law. See, e.g., C. Donahue, T. Kauper, and P. Martin, *Property: An Introduction to the Concept and the Institution,* 359–81 (1974).
11. For fuller discussion of the concepts of right and privilege, and of the contradictory relation between them, see "Property and Contract," *supra* note 4, at 752–56.
12. See *id.* at 755–56, 766–67.
13. The traditional common law rules allow for division of ownership along temporal lines, i.e., into "present" and "future" "estates." See, e.g., Donahue et al., *supra* note 10, at 541–60. The rules do not, however, permit unrestricted temporal subdivision *ad libitum*, but only subdivision according to some one of a finite set of recognized patterns. See *id.; Johnson* v. *Whiton*, 159 Mass. 424, 426, 34 N.E. 542 (1893) (Holmes, J.: "A man cannot create a new kind of inheritance.") The alternating-days pattern proposed in the text is not among the recognized ones.
14. Nothing in the common law rules inveighs against a checkerboard subdivision, despite its obvious tendency toward economic inconvenience. Compare *Leo Sheep Co.* v. *United States*, 440 U.S. 668 (1979).
15. Such an arrangement can perhaps be approximated under the common law rules, using recognized ownership categories of "easement in gross" and "profit-a-prendre" (see, e.g., Donahue et

al., *supra* note 10, at 1028–63), or those of "fee simple on a condition subsequent" (see, e.g., *id.* at 546–47, 581–82), or "fee simple subject to a restrictive covenant" (see, e.g., *id.* at 1102–48). There is a question, however, about the degree of permanency that is legally attainable by such arrangements. See, e.g., *id.* at 703–10, 1057–63, 1096–1101, 1170–78.

16. It seems we can make such an arrangement if we are careful about it, although some degree of hostility toward proprietary separation of the functionally inseparable is expressed in the common law doctrines of "accession" and "confusion," for which see generally R. Brown, *The Law of Personal Property*, Ch. VI (2d ed. 1955).

17. I.e., the common law rule. See note 10, *supra*.

18. See, e.g., *Illinois Central R. Co.* v. *Illinois*, 146 U.S. 387 (1892); Air Commerce Act of 1926, 44 Stat. 568, as amended, 49 U.S.C. §403.

19. Such was the traditional English ("natural flow") rule. In the eastern United States it was generally supplanted by a rule allowing each riparian to make "reasonable use" of the flow (most characteristically, for modest domestic uses) despite resulting harm to co-riparians. See, e.g., Donahue et al., *supra* note 10, at 392–99. In either version ("natural flow" or "reasonable use"), the riparian system is one of right/privilege decomposition: "natural flow" is a system of joint rights without privileges, while "reasonable use" is a combination of such a system with one of common privilege without rights.

20. See "Property and Contract," *supra* note 4, at 767–68.

21. E.g., through the common law devices of easement, covenant, and equitable servitude. See, e.g., Donahue et al., *supra* note 10, at 1102–65; B. Siegan, *Land Use without Zoning*, 33–84 (1972).

22. An inconsequential qualification is required by the theory of the second best, which tells us that short of actual attainment of S*, successive "approaches" to S* may involve local reversals in the direction of adjustment of various sectors in the total system of allocation. See, e.g., Markovits, "A Basic Structure for Microeconomic Policy Analysis in our Worse-Than-Second-Best World," *Wis. L. Rev.* 950 (1975).

23. See generally R. Ellickson, "Suburban Growth Controls: A Legal and Economic Analysis," 86 *Yale L. J.* 385, 414–15 (1977).

24. To be clear, there is wide endorsement neither of the policy of extreme concentration of wealth nor that of extreme concentration of management authority over everything in the world. See notes 45, 46, *infra*.

25. See p. 7, *supra*.

26. Adapted from Heymann, "The Problem of Coordination: Bar-

gaining and Rules," 86 *Harv. L. Rev.* 797, 800, 817, 831 et seq. (1973).

27. See text accompanying note 23, *supra*, for the definition of this term.

28. See, e.g., Donahue et al., *supra* note 10, at 1053–63.

29. See, e.g., *id.* at 686–71.

30. See, e.g., *id.* at 1114–38.

31. See, e.g., *id.* at 667–78.

32. E.g., *Clark v. Clark,* 99 Md. 356, 58 A.2d 24 (1904), refusing to enforce a stipulation, in a gift of land to seven persons as tenants-in-common, that the usual recourse of tenants-in-common to judicially supervised partition would be suspended for ten years.

33. See, e.g., Conard, "Easement Novelties," 30 *Calif. L. Rev.* 125 (1942); note 13, *supra.*

34. E.g., M. McDougal and D. Haber, *Property, Wealth, Land,* 246–51, 479–83 (1948).

35. E.g., *Northwest Real Estate Co. v. Serio,* 156 Md. 229, 144 A. 245 (1928) (Bond, C. J., dissenting); *Norcross v. James,* 140 Mass. 188, 2 N.E. 946 (1885) (Holmes, J.).

36. For example, the Rule Against Perpetuities is often explained as motivated by a concern for intergenerational equity, or for countering social stratification arising out of long-lasting concentrations of wealth within particular families. See, e.g., L. Simes and A. Smith, *Future Interests* §1117 (2d ed., 1956).

37. See "Property and Contract," *supra* note 4, at 764, 767.

38. State ownership is a form of state-mandated decomposition, insomuch as there is no individual who has coextensive rights and privileges respecting state-owned objects. Compare the case of corporations discussed in note 45, *infra.*

39. Compare Epstein, "Possession As the Root of Title," 13 *Georgia L. Rev.* 1221 (1979).

40. For the approximately similar common law doctrines of adverse possession and prescriptive easement, see, e.g., Donahue et al., *supra* note 10, at 100–140.

41. A common law court undoubtedly would require clear and strong evidence of an obviously regular pattern of implicitly assertive conduct before it would recognize such an economically vexatious prescriptive easement. See, e.g., *id.* at 108–9, 130–32.

42. E.g., one who acquires title to a parcel of land by adverse possession might take it (i) subject to the privileges of others to interfere accidentally and nonnegligently with its use and enjoyment; or (ii) subject to the liability that intentional or unreasonable interference may not be enjoinable but only compensable by a damages award.

See generally Calabresi and Melamed, "Property Rules, Liability Rules, and Inalienability: One View of the Cathedral," 85 *Harv. L. Rev.* 1089 (1972).

43. E.g., the doctrine of prescriptive easement, *supra,* note 40.
44. See text accompany notes 28–33, *supra.*
45. The corporation is, of course, well recognized as an "internaliza-tion" device. That the device works by complex decomposition rather than unification of individual ownership claims is clear, if perhaps not so widely recognized. It is of the essence of "corporate" ownership that no individual has coextensively broad rights and privileges respecting the objects "in" such ownership. Directors can act with regard to them only collectively; neither directors nor officers are privileged to use them otherwise than as authorized by the charter and by votes of the directors; shareholders, who have rights to prevent unauthorized uses of the objects, have no concomitant privileges of use; and so on.
46. When a given complex of "corporation ownership" claims has become inutile, by reason of scale diseconomies, monopolization, or whatever, readjustment is fraught with heavy transaction costs, whether in the form of legally compelled "divestiture"; voluntary "merger," "sale of assets," or "takeover"; or reassembly of sole ownership through "dissolution."
47. Text accompany notes 17–21, *supra.*
48. Pp. 10–11, *supra.*
49. See text accompany notes 10–12, *supra.*
50. Compare Becker, "The Moral Basis of Property Rights," *NOMOS XXII; Property,* 187 (J. Pennock and J. Chapman, eds., 1980).
51. See p. 7, *supra.*
52. Note that the list must, as a matter of logical necessity, exclude some of the objects and experiences that people might value. This is so because any subset of objects and experiences as to which people supposedly prefer a state of universal security necessarily implies a complementary subset as to which they supposedly prefer a state of universal exposure and license. *My* having a secure command over *your* body, labor, and product is not logically less eligible as a possible object of preference than is your contradictory claim to self-possession. Assuring secure self-possession to each person is equivalent to (i) denying to each person a secure claim to anyone else's body, labor, or product; and (ii) licensing each person to disregard or interfere at will with the claims (and, where present, the related needs) described in (i). For more elaborate discussion, see "Property and Contract," *supra* note 4, at 759–62.
53. E.g., it seems obvious that some individuals choose to live on public

assistance who could expect to attain a higher economic income if they worked.

54. Historical evidence of preferences for political decision modes can be found, e.g., in H. Arendt, *On Revolution* (1963); Historical evidence of preferences for reciprocity and mutual aid, as distinguished from market exchange, can be found, e.g., in K. Polanyi, *The Great Transformation* (1944).

55. See, e.g., E. Wilson, *On Human Nature* (1978) for one recent attempt to synthesize relevant implications of sociobiological inquiry.

56. See p. 1, *supra*.

57. See "Property and Contract," *supra* note 4, at 722–26.

58. It is not logically necessary that this uncertainty would be reduced, insomuch as the forced-sharing requirement might, imaginably, have such a severe depressant effect on total production that no one's needs could be met. See "Property and Contract," *supra* note 4, at 724–25.

59. See *id.* at 717–18.

60. E.g., R. Posner, *Economic Analysis of Law* (2d ed., 1977), §3.1, at 27–28; W. Blackstone, *Commentaries on the Laws of England* *4.

61. See, e.g., J. Henderson and R. Quandt, *Microeconomic Theory* §§ 2–6 (2d ed., 1971).

62. Collected and cited in Chapman, "Justice, Freedom, and Property," *NOMOS XXII: Property*, 289 (J. Pennock and J. Chapman eds., 1980).

63. See Becker, note 50, *supra*.

64. See pp. 12–13, *supra*.

65. Text accompanying notes 26–27, *supra*.

66. E.g., the "public trust" doctrine, see generally Sax, "The Public Trust Doctrine in Natural Resource Law: Effective Judicial Intervention," 68 *Mich. L. Rev.* 471 (1970).

67. Here the salient doctrines are constitutional free speech guaranties. E.g., *Shuttlesworth* v. *Birmingham*, 394 U.S. 147 (1969); *Lovell* v. *Griffin*, 303 U.S. 444 (1938). For a striking example of preference for the social benefits of unhindered communication over avoidance of the costs of neighborhood conflict, see *People* v. *Stover*, 12 N.Y.2d 462, 470, 191 N.E.2d 272, 277, 240 N.Y.S. 2d 734, 740 (1963) (Van Voorhis, J., dissenting).

68. See, e.g., G. Stigler, *The Citizen and the State*, ch. 8 (1975); A. Downs, *An Economic Theory of Democracy* (1957).

69. See, e.g., Bator, "The Anatomy of Market Failure," 72 *Q. J. Econ.* 351 (1958).

70. See test accompanying notes 72–75, *infra*.

71. See M. Olson, *The Logic of Collective Action* (1965).

40 FRANK I. MICHELMAN

72. Hardin, "The Tragedy of the Commons," 162 *Science* 1243 (1968), reprinted in B. Ackerman, *Economic Foundations of Property Law*, 1, 4 (1975).
73. *Id.* at 5.
74. *Id.* at 6.
75. T. Schelling, *Micromotives and Macrobehavior*, Norton (1978). The "commons" problem can be cast into this "binary choice" form by characterizing the choice facing each herdsman as that of grazing or not grazing more than c head on the commons, where c is a constant number.
76. See "Property and Contract," *supra* note 4, at 769–70.
77. Hardin, *supra* note 72, at 9.
78. *Id.* at 10.
79. It has often been observed that, according to rational calculation, the costs to an individual voter of casting a vote on election day must virtually always exceed the expected value to the voter of casting the vote. See, e.g., A. Downs, *supra* note 68.
80. E.g., Demsetz, "Toward a Theory of Property Rights," 57 *Am. Econ. Rev. Papers & Proceedings* 347 (1967); Agnello and Donnelly, "Property Rights and Efficiency in the Oyster Industry," 18 *J. Law & Econ.* 521 (1975).
81. See p. 7, *supra*.

2

PROFESSER MICHELMAN'S UNNECESSARY AND FUTILE SEARCH FOR THE PHILOSOPHER'S TOUCHSTONE

HAROLD DEMSETZ

The topic to which Professor Michelman applies his considerable talents is much too difficult to execute well with less than a lifetime's effort. The more's the pity that a successful treatment of it is hardly necessary to his objectives. Indeed, Michelman's tortured wanderings in the text of his paper detract from the straightforward statement found in his concluding comments. The conclusion, that private property arrangements are neither necessarily efficient nor, even if efficient, necessarily based on a universally acceptable ethic, is correct but hardly surprising.

Michelman begins by attempting to define a pure private property system. His complicated treatment of this topic indicates how difficult he must have found the task, as well he should. He puts forward three alternative definitions (which I believe hardly exhaust the plausible possibilities) and then argues that none of these definitions, nor the efficiency they may promote, reveals a compelling universal ethic. Hence, endorsement of private property solutions, or of efficiency, as practical solutions to legal problems should be smothered in a blanket of caution by lawyers.

While it is possible to quarrel with many of the details of Michelman's treatment of property right systems and efficiency,

I am quite prepared to accept his conclusion about absence of a universally appealing ethic. Whether or not special caution should be taken by legal scholars to protect themselves from the allures of private property solutions and the attraction of the efficiency criterion depends, of course, on the cost of special caution (back to efficiency!), where that cost includes encouragement of an already strong propensity to endorse nonprivate property solutions with vague and often mystical alternative criteria.

If Michelman subjects alternative institutional arrangements, whether they be socialism, communism, feudalism, a "state of nature," or any mix of these, including mixes with a private property right system, to a similar analysis, he will find that they too fail to supply a universally acceptable ethic or to promote efficiency. That is why Michelman's discussion is useless insofar as it seeks to guide the reflections of others. Of all possible social systems, all will fail to meet his test, but that does not entail that none is more appealing than the others. Whatever the system, there will be a few (or many) persons who are ethically frustrated or who fare less well than they would in some other system. Such a finding sheds no light on whether it would be (nonuniversally) "better" to change present institutional arrangements so as to conform more closely with another.

The "presumptive efficiency thesis" analyzed by Professor Michelman is not quite clear, at least to me. It seems to have three parts:

1. There is a habit of thought and argument, widespread and influential enough to warrant refutation . . .
2. in which private property is supposed to commend itself logically to whomever admits that persons are rational . . .
3. and that a large part of this commendation is based on the alleged universal acceptability of an efficiency ethic.

It matters little whether all three parts are necessary to Michelman's argument. A world, especially its intellectuals, still hellbent on governmental or utopian programs to resolve social and ethical problems, is hardly a world crazed by the desire for private property. In the much narrower world of economists, the postulated habit of thought is difficult to find. The presumptive efficiency thesis, to my knowledge, is nonexistent not only in the mainstream of economic thought but also in its major tributaries. I cannot testify with regard to every rivulet flowing into the rivers Charles or Chicago, but virtually every economist would agree with the following statements:

(A) A judgment that efficiency is good (or that it is bad) is not self-contained in the logic or substance of economics; when such judgments are made, they are based on a value scheme outside economics. These external values run the gamut from "efficiency be damned, what we want is equitable redistribution," to "redistribution be damned, what we want is efficiency," although economists probably tend to give greater value to efficiency than do noneconomists.

(B) A proposition that private property commends itself logically to whomever admits that persons are rational may be dismissed in the same manner. Indeed, economics has been at the forefront of analyzing criminal activity, the antithesis of activity consistent with private property, as an industry based on rational calculation of gains and losses; rational people in economics do not always respect or encourage private property.

(C) Certainly the considerable attention given in economics to externality, free-rider, and monopoly problems belies any simple extrapolation from private property to efficiency.

This is not to deny that many economists would value a broad enlargement in the role played by private property, or that others feel the reverse. But the notion that these prescriptions are self-contained, logical deductions from rationality, unaided by exogenous value systems, is not descriptive of economics nor of the thinking of most economists.

I am not knowledgeable about how well or how poorly economics and economists are used by legal scholars. But my inclination is to join Michelman in criticizing those who really hold to the presumptive efficiency thesis and to doubt that there are many who really do. Still, I criticize Michelman for writing off the usefulness of private property and of efficiency in contributing to a sensible solution of many legal questions, merely because he cannot produce an irrefutable proof of the universal desirability of (some version of) a private property system. The world does not deal in absolutes.

My criticisms of those who really subscribe to Michelman's presumptive efficiency thesis should be clear from my earlier remarks on the position of economics on this issue. Clearly, there are people who would be considered rational who prefer social arrangements involving more coercion than would be consistent with the operation of a private property right system. These include not only those who desire forced redistribution of wealth but also those who derive positive utility from coercing others; the bully and the rapist, for example, would probably not derive as much pleasure from voluntary submission as from coerced taking.

It is even possible to conjure up a scenario in which most rational persons would choose to violate private property precepts. Let there be a religious sect, *homo legalis*, the first persons to protect and nurture through great personal labor (thus satisfying even Murray Rothbard's principle of private property right entitlements) the world's only supply of trees yielding "Pure Ethicacious Tar." They worship their PET trees, never would they let them be tampered with in any way. It is discovered that PET is a sure cure for cancer, but the *homo legalis* refuse, for any compensation, to let these trees be touched. Now, I am not quite sure as to the moral course of action for *non-homo legalis*, but I am sure as to how most would act—they would simply take the PET. So much for the inviolability of private property by thinking, rational persons, and so much for my agreement with Michelman. Now back to disagreeing.

The standard set by Michelman is too high to be satisfied by any social system. He seeks an a priori connection of property with rationality and efficiency, a linkage independent of the wants and proclivities of people. The standard is, of course, impossible to satisfy, because it is always possible to imagine a cost so great associated with maintenance of the system that it seems best to violate the system. The impossibility of its satisfaction is in fact implied by an economics that envisages rational man as seeking many goals, all substitutable at the margin. On the margin, economic man is prepared to trade off some freedom for some security, some privacy for some wealth, some freedom for some paternalism, and vice versa; since no single, simple, pure social organization can deliver maximum quantities of all good things, some mixture of systems is implied. Hence, the defender of a private property right system may accept government enforcement of private rights and even government provision of that collective good called national defense. The impossibly high standard set by Michelman, however useful it may be for attacking his understanding of the presumptive efficiency thesis, is of little, if any, use in delivering practical guidance to legal decisions about social and economic organization. For example, it seems to me incredible to refuse to endorse a private property right solution because some rational people delight in coercing others. Behind the acceptability of any real solution *is* some implicit acceptable pattern of preferences. These preferences might give some scope to income redistribution, to paternalism, to externality or monopoly problems, and because of these considerations, the place of purely private property rights in social organizations may be more limited than when such preferences are not recognized as worthy.

But the prima facie case for private property solutions is strong, for these solutions more than others tend to confront persons with (a measure of) the cost (to others) of their actions, and perhaps with the only truly practical and generalizable measure. Private property allows the market to weigh and compare the beneficial and harmful effects, measured by the money that people are willing to pay, and to filter out actions that would yield a net loss in this web of calculations. The free market does not prohibit harmful effects. Great companies go under; Swift yesteryear, perhaps Chrysler next year! Indeed, a system that did, such as one based on the unanimity principle, would be so intolerably impractical (inefficient!) that it would soon give way to other arrangements.

That harmful effects arise through operation of free markets can be illustrated clearly by competitive reduction of the price of a product. However beneficial the price cut is to consumers, it hurts other producers of the product. The new price will succeed only if the harm done to rivals has a lower value attached to it by these rivals than is the gain to the price cutter and buyers. For otherwise his rivals would be willing to offset his price cut with one of their own that is large enough to keep their buyers.

It is this aspect of the private property rights system that is one of its great strengths. It is difficult to know, in the absence of individualized voluntarily given consent to a transfer of resources, whether a reallocation of resources yields a net gain since such transfers also impose costs. The net gain so measured, it is worth repeating, is an index based on willingness to pay, not on some global utility maximization. The market, or indeed any practicable social system, must tolerate activities that impose costs on *some* individuals; hence, social systems cannot be rejected because some actions intrinsic to these systems are complained about by those who would suffer. It is important to realize that scarcity implies cost, and it is impossible to reallocate resourses without some bearing, by some persons, of this cost. It is highly desirable, therefore, to have some index of whether gains exceed cost. Private property markets provide a highly workable index, but it is not the only index that may be applied to a specific situation, nor is its value always determinative. But it is always useful information—and information impossible to secure through coercive techniques. It is amazing how tolerant we are of such costs when they are embedded in a private property rights system in which willingness to pay is the index. Perhaps one of the redeeming features of such a system is its apparent ability to attenuate the intensity of group conflict that seems to infect those socialistic systems in which collective decisions on resource allocation and wealth distribution are made apparent as in Great Britain or Poland.

The use of private right practices, which, in a practical sense, precede market negotiations, introduces this useful calculation into the calculus of scarcity. Situations may arise for which the advantage of having this metric is offset by distributional considerations, or in which, as in the case of externalities, the efficacy of the metric is reduced. Well, then, perhaps some attentuation of private rights is in order. But in these issues, as lawyers well know, it is important where the burden of proof lies. The desirability of having an operable cost-benefit confrontation, especially one that is consistent with a goal that many value highly—individual freedom—argues strongly for a prima facie solution based on private property rights, even if principled doubts may arise about it.

Michelman's rejection of the claim that a private property system is logically derivable as *the* appropriate ethic of rational people in no way undermines the day-to-day practical solution it offers to many legal problems. This is especially the case when blindfolded courtroom justice must avoid looking to the income of the litigants, to their color, sex, or to other dimensions extraneous to the facts. What, then, are the facts to which the law looks? One set of facts determines the applicable precedent. But if we are starting anew, reconsidering all precedents and creating new ones, then to what facts should the court look? Surely, the private costs and benefits, measured by the implicit market values that accrue to alternative solutions, constitutute an important, definable and nonpersonal set of relevant facts.

3

PRIVATE PROPERTY AND THE PUBLIC DOMAIN: THE CASE OF ANTITRUST

RICHARD A. EPSTEIN

I

It takes no acute observer of the modern scene to note the massive impact of economic analysis upon the normative and positive studies of legal rules and institutions. While economics is but one of many social sciences, it is a social science with a difference—or more precisely, with a theory. With its postulate of rational self-interest of individual actors, it is able to convert statements about human behavior into propositions about the maximization of benefits or the minimization of costs. Its set of formalized premises allows economists to generate insights and testable hypotheses that necessarily escape those who are limited to the more intuitive tools of hunch and experience. More to the point here, the powerful and well-thought-out vocabulary of economics is so easily incorporated into legal discourse that it seems as though law and economics must perforce become natural allies. It is difficult to talk about the public interest without mention of transaction costs, public goods, holdouts, and free-rider problems; about anittrust law, without competition and monopoly; about negligence without risk preference, risk neutrality, and risk aversion; about the duties of trustees, without portfolio theory and efficient markets; about tort damages without discounting the present value. The list of examples can be expanded almost at will to show how economic concepts are embedded in the fabric of legal thought. Indeed, the real question is not whether economics has any relevance to law but, Is there any other game in town?[1]

In his contribution to this volume, Michelman gives one line of reasoning as to why economics cannot supplant the traditional forms of discourse in resolving disputes within the legal system. The general principles of rationality and neutrality cannot, even if taken together, generate a unique system of property rights unless we know something about the tastes and preferences of the individuals who are to be governed by the system.[2] In this chapter, I wish to approach the question of the limitations of economics from a somewhat different perspective, which in many ways parallels Michelman's inquiry. I hope to examine the limitations of the economic theories by placing them in contrast with what may be properly called a corrective justice approach to the insistent question, What are the general rights and duties of individuals in society?[3]

A complete theory of corrective justice requires the integration of the law of property, contract, and torts, as these are traditionally understood within legal circles. Thus, in order to correct injustices, some baseline, some initial distribution of rights, must first be established. This is generally done by the law of property, which specifies the means whereby ownership can be acquired in certain things, be it the person, land, wild animals, the electromagnetic spectrum, or inventions.[4] Thereafter the law of contracts is designed to indicate the means whereby the property rights so established (including the rights in the person) may be transferred from one individual to another. And the law of torts is designed to protect both the things reduced to ownership and the rights of transfer associated with those things from the unacceptable interference of others— generally defined in terms of the use of force or misrepresentation of one person against the person or property of another.

This private law model of corrective justice has been developed largely in relation to disputes with two particular attributes. First, the number of interested parties is small—often only two.[5] Second, none of the parties can claim the special advantages and privileges that are normally lodged in the state. The question in this essay is whether a theory of rights and wrongs so developed in this limited context has any application to decisions that must be made on so-called public law matters, that is, those in which the number of parties is necessarily large and the role of government evident, and even unavoidable. The general view today, held even by those distrustful of the new law and economics, is that such questions of general "economic" regulation are left virtually unconstrained by any theory of individual rights and corrective justice. Indeed, the salient point of the new law and economics in a sense has been to move out from its secure public policy base into novel areas, in order to demonstrate that the approach that governs the antitrust laws or zoning regulations can apply with equal force to the ordinary rules of contracts and torts. The pattern of argument here is precisely the opposite. I hope to show that it is possible to extend the arguments of corrective justice into the domain of public policy that is sometimes thought to be reserved to economic or political arguments. It is, however, one thing to show the application of corrective justice principles to large social and economic questions. It is quite another to demonstrate their complete dominance on those same questions. Indeed, in my view that claim for dominance, while it can be made, cannot in the end be secured. Instead, it is necessary, as we move from cases with few parties to those with many, to indicate how limitations on corrective justice—often based upon the strength of overt, if constrained utilitarian arguments—can be given their due. In the end, the interaction between two separate types of thought produces very uneasy edges along the margins. Indeed, no amount of analysis and evidence can eliminate honest differences of opinion about the proper ways to proceed in concrete settings. In principle, this coordination of corrective justice and utilitarian arguments is one that can take place over the length and breadth of the entire law; and it is far too broad a task to consider them all in this context. The task thus set is too vast to be accomplished for all possible areas of legal control. In order, therefore, to explore the program I have set myself, I have confined my attention to one area that has long been thought to lie within the province of economic theory: the law of antitrust.

II

The central tenet of antitrust law is that the preservation of competition between various sellers of a given good or commodity is the most desirable form of economic organization. In this connection it is necessary to beware of overstatement, and to note that monopoly, the end to be controlled, is not necessarily regarded as illegal in and of itself, wholly without regard to the circumstances of its origins. Instead, it is said that some form of illegal conduct is required, that the objection is to the process of monopolization rather than to the state of monopoly itself.[6] Yet notwithstanding this qualification, the fact remains that monopoly—a situation with an exclusive seller in a given market—is regarded as suspicious for reasons that are often put into explicit economic terms.[7] Where there are many sellers and many buyers, no seller will have any control over price, and each will be able to sell as much at the market price as he desires. Price will, moreover, be equal to marginal cost, so that it can be said that all those units of a given product that should be made and sold will be made and sold, neither more nor less. Errors of overproduction and underproduction are both monitored by the competitive process, which in turn rests upon the self-interested decisions of individuals. Whether the proposition is stated in terms of efficiency, wealth, consumer welfare, or utility, the same general message is clear.[8] Some desired collective measure of the good is maximized in the competitive equilibrium.

Monopoly stands in sharp opposition to perfect competition. Here the existence of the single profit-maximizing seller in the market insures that production will be reduced to a point where in fact price exceeds marginal cost. All units that are made should be made, but some units are not made that could be made. As gains from trade are left unexploited, the situation can no longer be regarded as optimal from a social point of view. In some accounts the social loss is said to be equal to the so-called welfare triangle, which assumes that most of the increased costs to those buyers that remain in the market is simply a transfer payment to the monopoly seller.[9] Yet in truth this position may understate the welfare loss if the monopolist has expended social resources in order to acquire the monopoly position in the first place. The argument, reduced to its simplest terms, is that the monopoly sellers will earn on average only a competitive return, because they will themselves expend resources in "rent-seeking" activities in order to acquire their monopoly position, be it in the form of efforts to influence legislation or in the form of marketing practices—be it predator pricing or in the organization of cartels.[10] Here, to be sure, there may be some opportunity to reduce the size of the asserted welfare loss by price discrimination. But this tactic is not possible in every market, especially where legal and practical means are not available to prevent resale by original purchasers, and are, in any event, very difficult to implement even in an unregulated environment without clear knowledge of the levels of demand in various segments of the seller's original market. The variation upon the basic themes should not, however, be allowed to obscure the basic point. On the economic view of the world it is quite a mistake to view competition and monopoly—or at least monopolization—with detached neutrality, as two alternative social states that ebb and flow as the tides. Monopolization is regarded as an improper social activity, one that is to be prevented chiefly by the civil and criminal sanctions of the antitrust laws. Indeed, given the available sanctions, the difficult task for legal theory is to find any reason to distinguish between antitrust violations and ordinary crimes and torts, such as theft, rape, and murder, which also carry with them civil damages and criminal penalties. Why, in other words, is not blowing up the plant of a competitor treated as an antitrust violation instead of an ordinary tort? For if conduct is known by its legal consequences, then antitrust damages must be regarded on a par with any other legal type of wrong. In fact, the treble damages feature unique to the antitrust law suggests that antitrust offenses are wrongs of exceptional severity, as might easily be concluded by the potential dollar level of the damages and the number of persons on whom they are inflicted.

Here, however, it should be noted that confidence in the judgments as to the wrongful nature of monopolistic acts is perhaps stronger than the facts of the matter warrant. In particular, this attitude toward antitrust violations is sound or reasonable in many circumstances but not necessarily in all:

many think rational self-interest is the exception, not the ordinary state of affairs, given the psychological and cognitive barriers to rational decision making.[11] Here it is possible to take a leaf from the pages of Hayek[12] and Coase.[13] They do not cast the argument for markets in terms of the perfection of outcomes because of the interplay of fully rational behavior. To the contrary, they hold that benevolence, gratitude, compassion, sympathy, not to mention fraud, greed, error, shortsightedness, and simple stupidity are the very stuff of economic and social life. On this view there can be no confident assertion that the competitive ideal will ever be realized in practice even with the most favorable institutional arrangements. Instead, the goal is to make sure that undesirable individual traits are localized (but not wholly neutralized) by a network of institutions that diffuse power in ways political scientists interested in pluralism have long stressed. The driving fear is the takeover of the instruments of government by narrow and parochial groups, not the obvious preference for one type of market structure over another. Monopoly may turn out to be bad, but only because monopolists have (if they have) increased access to the powers of the state. Yet stripped of this political dimension, monopoly simply becomes one of several forms of economic organization, and one that contains within it the seeds of its own destruction, for its high prices place an effective umbrella over those who would enter the market against it.

Doubts about the social virtues of competition do not stop here, for it is also possible to question the dominant position of competition even if the assumptions about rational self-interested behavior receive more credence than perhaps they deserve. Thus, even in economic terms there are some advantages to monopolies, especially in the way in which they tend to mitigate certain public goods problems. Firms with large market shares are apt to invest more resources in forecasting future demand and future costs because they will be able to capture a large section of the welfare gain.[14] They may also invest more in research and development because here too they can keep the gain without entering into risky transactions—for example, licensing agreements—with individuals who could misappropriate the information provided, notwithstanding any patent or trade secret protection that law might provide.[15]

Still further complications arise for the competitive model at
the institutional level because of the now familiar problems with
the "second best." Briefly stated, the proposition is that it is not
merely difficult, but impossible, to make any social judgment
about whether monopoly or competition is "better" in any given
market unless and until it is established that all other markets
are at their competitive equilibrium. Once some deviation in
market A is established, one cannot make any arguments that
a monopoly in market B will necessarily create some social loss,
regardless of the relation between markets. To take a simple
example, suppose there is a monopoly in industry A, whose
products are components of the output of B. Given that the
firms in B do not acquire their supplies at competitive prices,
of what social benefit is it for them to sell their goods at
competitive prices, which in the case at hand are apt to be too
high given the monopoly element embedded in their costs.
Here, of course, subsidy might be suggested for the second
market, but its extent will be difficult to calculate and can only
upset the operation of other markets. Nor should the fact that
one firm in the above example is a supplier to another make
any difference. Even if the firms do business in wholly unrelated
markets, any changes in the relative prices and demands for
their inputs will work back through the rest of the market (as
by influencing the price of complementary or substitute goods)
in ways that as yet are at best dimly understood. There is in
short no way to deny the truth of the "second best" simply
because its consequences for social planning seem to be generally
negative.

These complications, based upon the second best, do not of
course undercut the descriptive side of economic theory; monopolists will still tend to raise price, restrict output, discriminate
among consumers, and (perhaps) reduce quality; economic
theory can tell us how much and in what proportions. Yet the
problems of the second best are acute for any normative system
that purports to base its criterion for judgment exclusively upon
some aggregate measure of social satisfaction, whether stated in
the form of utility, welfare, or wealth. It requires some limited
article of faith to use any form of partial equilibrium analysis
to make aggregate social welfare judgments. The problem of
the second best, moreover, does not go away even if we posit

the most ideal of social orders, for some public goods—defense—will have to be provided even at the cost of some distortion in competitive markets. Our society is, of course, far from ideal as, outside the antitrust law, it excels in the very kind of special-interest legislation that is so antithetical to the basic theory of competition itself: subsidies, regulations, penalties all in bewildering size and assortment.

Economists and lawyers who believe in the edifice of antitrust will argue in response that complications of the second best must be ignored if *any* social choices are to be made. The simplifications required for antitrust analysis should therefore not be seen only as a convenience for model builders but also as an antidote to social paralysis. The economic edifice might not be perfect, but economics is the only public policy game in town, and its basic conclusions must be beaten back within its own terms and on its own premises. That on this view public goods or natural monopolies may embarrass a general preference for competition can be conceded. Yet only economic calculations can determine what mix of private monopoly and public regulation will achieve the desired social goal. Within this framework, therefore, the debate over the regulation of, for example, natural monopolies is reduced to a debate over the proper application of admitted principles;[16] it is not a debate over the fundamental soundness of those principles themselves. Hegemony of economic thought remains unimpaired even if the preference for competition contained in antitrust law is somewhat weakened.

III

So much, then, for economic analysis of antitrust law. What remains is to sketch an alternative account of the subject, one that derives from traditional common law concerns with private property, individual liberty, and corrective justice. Here the initial ethical premise of the system is that possession is the root of title, or that taking possession of an unowned thing is prima facie evidence of individual ownership, as lawyers say, in a fee. The rule is stated as a presumption that can be rebutted only by a person whose earlier possession gives rise to a higher title.

It cannot be contended, of course, that the proposed connection between possession and ownership has the status of a necessary ethical truth. The premise—possession—is a term that describes a natural state of affairs. The conclusion contains references—always implicit in the notion of ownership—itself a *social* conception—to rights and duties between the owner and the rest of the world. Nonetheless, want of demonstrative proof is not a fatal objection to the proposition. If it were, the economic alternative would also fail because it too requires bridging statements to move from assertions about facts—chiefly individual preferences and satisfactions—to conclusions about social rights and wrongs. David Hume's proposition—that propositions that contain "ought statements" cannot be derived from those that contain "is statements"—is for these purposes like poison gas: too powerful to be used in ethical combat. In any event, I do not want to make a defense of this premise here, having done so elsewhere.[17] For present purposes it is sufficient that the rule has unqualified acceptance both in common law and civil systems. Instead, my primary concern is to reveal the system of rights that evolves from its acceptance and why such *necessarily* precludes on corrective justice grounds the adoption of any antitrust law at all.

The key question is: What is embodied in the conception of ownership? At a minimum the conception should satisfy two separate formal constraints of general applicability. First, the rule should be of sufficient power so that its operation can reduce all those unowned things to ownership.[18] Second, the rights and duties that emerge will be at all times well ordered among all individuals. The first of these principles is designed to prevent *gaps* in ownership rights; the second, to prevent *overlap*. The concern with overlapping rights is clear enough: rights cannot discharge their central social function if they do not tell individuals what behavior is forbidden or permitted. The concern with gaps is perhaps a little more subtle but every bit as important. Allow gaps into the system, and one of two consequences, both unacceptable, follow. One possibility is that certain things cannot be reduced to ownership, such that there is a constraint upon all for the benefit of none. The second possibility is that some additional principle must be introduced in order to reduce those things otherwise unaccounted for to ownership. It might be said that things that are not covered by the first possession rule are owned in common by all citizens.[19] In this case, however, it must be explained how that second principle—common ownership—is reconcilable with the first possession rule, and why it does not have sufficient generality of its own to replace it.

With these two constraints in mind, the question then is: What rights ought to be included in the original ownership rights acquired by first possession? Here the traditional answer groups three sets of ownership incidents, which taken together satisfy these dual formal constraints: possession, use, and disposition.[20]

The sense of the first two terms is more or less straightforward. The third—that of disposition—needs some clarification. Here it must be stressed that the right of disposition entails only the right to *offer* property to others, not to compel them to take it. Any assertion of a broader right would necessarily create an endless instability with respect to all things, for if A can compel B to transfer what he owns to him, then surely C can—at least in a world of equal rights—compel A to transfer the thing to him, ad infinitum. Limited therefore as it must be to consensual transactions, the rights of disposition can account for the out-and-out sale of any given form of property. In addition, they permit much more complicated reassignments of original property rights, limited only by the invention of individual owners. In particular, A and B may make a partial conveyance between themselves so long as they do not by their own actions trench upon the ownership rights of C, a stranger to the transaction. If, moreover, ownership rights were consistent and exhaustive in the original position, then the rights, however divided or repackaged, remain consistent and exhaustive at all subsequent times. The legal order, therefore, that starts out without any gaps remains without gaps no matter how many proper transactions are executed in sequence. As a matter of right, parties may create life estates, restrictive covenants, easements, profits, mortgages, joint estates at their will, so long as they pool their own assets and not those of strangers.

The discussion thus far has dwelled exclusively on the question of rights. There is still the question of what types of action are forbidden to others, who are after all bound without their

consent by any valid individual claim of ownership. To put the
point another way, it is insufficient to specify the types of right
that ownership creates unless something is said about the
correlative *wrongs*.

Let us begin with the core case of a wrong against property.
By definition, it is not possible to say that A remains an owner
of property if B has the right at will to take the property from
him and use it as his own. What, then, is left to A's ownership
at all? The nature of the inquiry must therefore shift from the
question of what ownership by A forbids of B to the question
of what types of conduct of B are sufficiently like the outright
taking of the thing that they should be treated in the same
fashion. Here the first extension that is everywhere adopted is
the move from the taking of a given thing to a taking of a
part.[21] The difference between whole and part is clearly relevant
to the quantum of damages, but hardly to the question of right:
one can steal half a loaf of bread. A partial taking is not "partial"
wrong, but a full wrong, but one with of course a diminished
severity.

The next extension of the basic system moves us from the
property conception, narrowly conceived, to the domain of the
law of tort. In particular, if A cannot take B's property, it
follows that he cannot take it, break it, and return the pieces.
The duty of restoration is total, and here the restoration
tendered is but partial. What difference can it make therefore
if destruction takes place without the taking? The loss to the
owner can be the measure of the damages even where there is
no benefit to the other side. Nor, as noted above, need the harm
inflicted be total. The law of nuisance is directed, for example,
at physical invasions of property that interfere with the ordinary
use thereof, even though they leave the owner in possession
with full rights of disposition.[22] The compromise of a single
incident of ownership is like taking half a loaf of bread. It may
influence the measure of damages to be awarded, but it does
not cleanse an act that is prima facie wrongful because of its
invasive nature.

The principle of ownership also places like limits upon duress
and misrepresentation. If A cannot take B's property, then he
cannot by force make B give it to him. So too he cannot mislead
B into giving it over to him. In line with the traditional moral

conceptions of action, the voluntariness of B's act is undermined by both force and misrepresentation.[23] Both cases should therefore be treated like the simple taking by A that ownership principles necessarily prohibit. The benefit to the wrongdoer is not essential. The party who takes property cannot cleanse his wrong by a gift to a third party. So too a party that harms or misleads another cannot defend himself on the ground that he has provided in whatever form a benefit to a third party or to no one else at all. As with the taking, it is the loss to the owner, not the gain to anyone else, that stamps conduct as tortious.

Yet it is here that—taking, force, misrepresentation—catalogues of wrongful conduct must in principle end. Suppose, for example, that A tells B the truth about why he wants B's thing, and B decides to give it to him. What possible reason can be advanced to set aside the transaction in question, given that the right of disposition is inherent in the nature of original ownership? Just as persons who own things might sell them for cash, so too they may choose to give them away, or in fact allow others to take them with permission. Nor does it matter that the individual is subject to personal necessity or deprivation that induces him to enter into certain transactions. Even the extreme case—one in which a given individual offers to give away his entire fortune to a person who can rescue him from drowning at little or no cost—is not one in which the promise can be avoided in a system of pure corrective justice. The prospective rescuer has not constrained the choices otherwise available to the victim. He has expanded them beyond what they would be if he disappeared, as he might without the use of force or fraud do. Whether one likes situations in which one person "takes advantage" of another is of course a subject on which differences of opinion can arise.[24] But if one does, then there is need to develop a theory that is not dependent upon corrective justice notions to support that particular result.

In essence, therefore, force (taking or breaking) and misrepresentation are the only types of conduct that are constrained in B by a social recognition of ownership in A. This is not to say that they may never be invoked, for it still remains possible in principle to justify their use.[25] Yet justification presupposes a prima facie wrong that stands in need of justification. And what is important is that a system of liberty and private property is able to identify as well those actions that need no justification at all. The social presumption is set in favor of liberty of action, notwithstanding the ownership claims of others. Only force and fraud against person or property upset that presumption.

IV

All of this might seem to be far removed from the law of antitrust with its concern for the grand social questions of competition and monopoly, but in truth it is not. Just as the tort of nuisance is directed at interference with the use of property wholly apart from its possession and disposition, so too some torts are directed toward the disposition of property wholly apart from its possession and use. In this connection, one obvious illustration is the interference with advantageous relationships by the use of force. This is, for example, what happens when some individuals shoot persons who want to trade with their competitors[26] or, in somewhat more subtle fashion, barricade the path into their shops even if they do not trespass on their land.[27] Yet just as force is paired with misrepresentation in other contexts, so too is it paired with misrepresentation in cases involving rights of disposition. The law of defamation, far from being inconsistent with a theory of private property, is necessarily entailed by it, wholly without regard to questions of physical invasion or interference. It is in essence the wrong of misrepresentation to a third party about the plaintiff that (in ways that are not voluntary because of the misinformation) induces the third party not to do business with the plaintiff.[28] All of these wrongs involve various kinds of economic injuries that are as amenable to the traditional analysis as physical injury cases. What must be noted, however, is that neither of these wrongs against the right of disposition can be stretched or twisted to make ordinary competition between individuals in the marketplace even a prima facie wrong. Again, the question is not one of the justification of the harm inflicted. Instead, the infliction of harm to protected interest for which justification might be required, is missing altogether.

Note the conduct that competition entails. A and B each own property, which gives them the right to offer to sell or dispose of that property on whatever terms and conditions they see fit. A has offered to sell his property to C for $8; B has offered his for $10; C for whatever reason, is in a position where he wishes to accept only one of those offers. A and B are, therefore, in competition with each other. Neither A nor B violates the rights of the other by making his own offer; and C does not violate the rights of A if he chooses to accept the offer of B, or of B if he chooses to accept the offer of A. This is no economic account of competition. It is simply a statement of what may properly happen when two or more individuals exercise the rights they have in the property they own. True, as a matter of economics we can predict that if the goods offered by A and B are perfect substitutes for each other, then C will choose to accept A's offer instead of B's. But the transaction derives its legitimacy, *not* from its economic rationality, but from the fact that both A and C acted in ways that left B worse off but did not violate any of his rights. Indeed, whatever an economist might think of the situation, the legal analysis is precisely the same if C decided to accept B's offer and pay the higher price. It matters not how we characterize the transaction. It may be a blunder by B; but that is B's problem, not ours. It may be that the so-called sale by B to C was both a sale by B for $8 and a gift by C to B of $2. Yet as neither sales nor gifts violate the rights of third parties, A is not in a position to protest the sale, even if he is left worse off thereby. Note the two modes of analysis. For an economist the task is to find out what acts are efficient or rational; for a lawyer it is to ground permissible behavior on a conception of individual autonomy and ownership that specifies both individual rights and—necessarily—their correlative duties.

The examples above show that it is important to draw distinctions among the various types of harms that are alleged to follow from certain actions. Economists are prone to speak of "third-party" effects, but they do not recognize that these are not defined in economic terms alone but, to the contrary, presuppose a framework of rights of the sort developed here.[29] As the common law dimly understood from it own premises, certain economic harms are *damnum absque iniuria*; economic losses that go uncompensated because they were not preceded by any violation of right.[30] Losses inflicted through competition are—by definition—always of that sort, as they are never preceded by force or misrepresentation. They are never compensable. It is, moreover, wholly unnecessary to import any analysis of "assumption of risk" into the case, because we worry about whether the risk of harm was assumed only if defendant's conduct reveals the prima facie violation of a right, as it does when Smith breaks Jones's skull. Here, however, without the violation of right the defense simply does not come up at all. In the same manner we cannot account for competition by an appeal to the notion of ex ante compensation, whereby it is said that the losses suffered by one competitor have already been compensated in advance by virtue of his having the right to compete, as it were, in self-defense.[31] Yet normal (ex post) compensation is required only after a violation of rights is established. Ex ante compensation, the substitute for such normal compensation, likewise is required only where a violation of rights will (or even might) occur. Since competition is a type of protected activity that does not amount to a prima facie wrong against a competitor, no compensation ex ante or ex post can ever be required. With its disappearance from the case goes a whole host of issues relating to the adequacy and nature of such compensation. In a word, the original distribution of rights means that competitive behavior need not be justified and need not be purchased. It is done as of right pursuant to the set of unqualified liberties—to dispose of property—given to all persons in the original situation.

We have seen, therefore, how competition, be it between large units or small units, is simply an outgrowth of rights of ownership and liberty of action. But what about monopoly? If, to the economist, monopoly always raises special and urgent questions, to the common lawyer, wedded to principles of property and liberty, it is an event of supreme indifference—but only where the monopoly does not depend upon the protection of an exclusive franchise granted by the state.[32] The mode of analysis is exactly as before. Just as it may well turn out that competitive economic states may arise from the original and repeated exercise of rights of disposition, so too might monopoly so arise. It is settled that A can offer his property to anyone he chooses on whatever terms he sees fit. Suppose in the example above he decides to offer his property to B, another merchant in the same line of business for, $12 instead of to C, a potential customer, for $10. We may even assume that A makes this offer only because he knows that B will in turn restrict his own sales, such that he can command a price from C of $15. All of this may be true, but for a wrong to occur, rights established by the system must have been violated. Yet neither A nor B has taken anything that C has owned; nor have they lied to or cheated him in any way. On the contrary, they can explain to C in advance what they intend to do and their reasons for doing it.

Nor does the situation change if A and B make a somewhat different agreement whereby each charges $15 for the product in question. That precise result could be achieved if A first conveyed his entire stock to B, which was then reconveyed subject to the appropriate condition on resale. C, of course, is entitled to do without or to look elsewhere for his supplies, as his private search is not a violation of the rights of A or B. Yet the only prohibition created by the A-B contract is between A and B, which in a corrective justice regime should be enforced as all other agreements are. Should B try to sell to C for any price, that *itself* would be a legal wrong, even if done in an effort to thwart the cartel and to reestablish a competitive equilibrium. Damages for breach of contract, an injunction against sales to third parties, and suits for interference with contractual arrangements against third parties are therefore entirely in order as a matter of principle. The collective arrangement involved in these economic relations must be sharply distinguished from a conspiracy to rob or murder, for in the ordinary business cartel the means chosen are within the domain of rights of all. A noneconomic theory recognizes and protects noneconomic practices. The economic theories that show how and why these agreements emerge, and the welfare consequences, if any, they generate have descriptive but not normative significance. The crucial line is not between monopoly and competition but between the two together and force and misrepresentation on the other hand. A and B may agree between themselves, to reduce output, to the prejudice of C. But they cannot use force to exclude D from making offers to C, no matter how great or little the prejudice.

This common law theory of rights, therefore, is as complete

as the original ownership theory from which it derives. It
specifies those circumstances in which certain activities are, to
echo Mill, protected even against the combined desires of the
rest of mankind. Many modern rights theorists, following
Dworkin, have correctly pointed out that rights are indeed a
kind of "trump" that can prevail only to the extent that it
overrides all considerations of general social utility. What must
be stressed here is that, if we follow this route, private property
and individual autonomy are the only trumps we have, and that
the autonomy they demand in personal matters—marriage,
religion, speech—apply with equal force in general economic
matters as well.

The recent constitutional history, which has the Supreme
Court taking a cautious role in overturning legislation on
"economic matters" but an active role on "personal" and "social"
matters, likewise rests upon a misconception of a proper theory
of private rights. Protection of economic interests should extend
no further, but no less far, than protection of other personal
and private rights. Once a theory is developed that addresses
both the scope and limitations of individual rights, its consequences cannot be disregarded simply because they clash with
the dominant sentiment as to what counts as good and proper
social control. Attack on monopoly cannot be made, therefore,
within the framework of traditional normative legal theory.
When in fact the state decides to treat monopolists as felons, it
acts in a manner that completely undermines the normative
distinction between proper and improper—lawful and unlaw-
ful—behavior. Hence, the reason that most people find punishment of antitrust offenders somewhat of a puzzle is that they
accept in their ordinary affairs a theory of corrective justice
that is much like the one sketched here, however unaware they
may be of its philosophical foundations and presuppositions.
No matter what the political rhetoric, street crime or ordinary
theft are not cut from the same cloth as antitrust offenses. It
may be said of course that the arguments just made are not
apposite, because it is still possible to conceive of a set of civil
sanctions for antitrust violations that would parallel the ordinary
tort action, say, for intentional torts. There is of course good
reason to insist that the rules that govern tort be kept quite
sharp and distinct from those that govern crime, even though

the same conduct may at times be both tortious and criminal.[33] Yet it is important to note precisely where the difference between the two areas lies. Thus, in my view the proper distinction fastens upon the mental elements that must be included as part of the plaintiff's basic cause of action. With a tort action the requirement of *mens rea* (of the guilty mind) is far too strong as a minimum condition, given that the essential question is which of two parties is to be held responsible for a loss that one of them may have caused (i.e., by the use of force or misrepresentation) but that neither has willed. Given that a victory for one party necessarily entails a loss for the other party, stringent standards of conduct can be required of tort defendants, a point that is reflected in the simple fact that in tort literature the major debate over the standard of liability has always been between strict liability and negligence, judged by an objective standard of care. But the differences in the basis of liability are not what keep antitrust offenses from being torts. Indeed, most such offenses are deliberate. Instead, the crux of the matter is that protected interests of a plaintiff are the same in both tort and criminal cases. Thus, while theft may be a criminal charge, the tort conversion will be its civil analogue. For want of an invasion of protected interests, tort liability for antitrust offenses is as inappropriate as criminal liability. It matters not whether antitrust violations are conceived of as strict liability offenses; negligence offenses; or even, in conscious parallel to the criminal law, intentional wrongs.

In this connection we should note that it is the absence of force and fraud against person or property that itself defines the very domain of antitrust offenses and see in each of them the repudiation of a common law system of rights based upon conceptions of personal autonomy; private property; and their outgrowth, freedom of contract. We have already noticed price fixing and cartels. The same analysis extends to mergers; predatory pricing; and various types of contractual arrangements such as tie-ins, resale price maintenance, and the like. While in some cases economic arguments tend to reinforce the moral sentiments behind common law conceptions—for example, assumption of risk defense in ordinary accident cases— the antitrust law is not one of them. To some it might be a matter of amazement that the rise of the antitrust law depended upon the passage of statutes, such as of course the Sherman Anti-Trust Act. In truth, no other approach was possible. The ordinary notions of common law jurisprudence are not simply silent on the question of form as antitrust law might, or should, take. The theory of corrective justice specifies both what is prohibited and what is permitted. The theory that condemns trespasses allows monopoly—pure and simple.

V

Does all this mean that the antitrust law is a giant mistake? Only if the corrective justice theory and its liberal—some might say libertarian—premises of private property and individual autonomy are given complete sway as social constructs. But is there a way in which they can be respected but moderated? Here the appropriate point of departure is the proper treatment of *forced exchanges*. One necessary corollary of a theory of corrective justice is its insistence upon the *inviolate* nature of both person and property. The point is not that individuals can never be made to surrender their property or liberty without their consent. On the contrary, this is a permissible result, but only where some wrong (as defined by the system itself) is committed by the person from whom the surrender is required. This strong view of individual rights necessarily precludes, however, the possibility that any person may take from another, even—it must be stressed—if he tenders full and adequate compensation for the property taken or the liberty denied. *Forced exchanges* are simply not permitted in a system of pure corrective justice. Restoration, not damages, is the norm, so that the latter are tolerated (and required) only when the former is unattainable.

The strict and absolute quality of the legal rules has its attractive features. It promotes clarity in the delineation of rights, and it provides uncompromising vindication of individual autonomy. Yet it is one thing to be principled and predictable and quite another to be rigid and doctrinaire. The long and the short of the matter is that every legal system when pressed recognizes at least in some limited circumstances that the absolute prohibition against forced exchanges must yield. The two classical cases that illustrate much of the sensible common law approach to forced exchanges in the tort context are *Ploof* v. *Putnam*[34] and *Vincent* v. *Lake Erie*,[35] both of which involved forced exchange in conditions of private necessity—here narrowly defined as circumstances in which there was imminent danger to person or property brought about by natural events. *Ploof* v. *Putnam* established that the party in necessity was entitled to avail himself of the use of the property of another without his consent and over his opposition. *Vincent* v. *Lake Erie* stands for the proposition that, while the property may be thus taken, compensation for the damage so inflicted was nonetheless required. In essence, private necessity justified, not the taking of property alone, but only the exchange of property for monetary compensation.

Forced exchanges under conditions of necessity are dramatic, and they illustrate the uneasy exceptions to the corrective justice model of inviolate rights. They are nonetheless of limited social importance. Of far greater importance are those undertaken by the state in pursuit of public ends. Here too the independent significance of the compensation requirement is made evident in the text of the eminent domain clause: "Nor shall private property be taken for public use without just compensation." The logic of the clause parallels that of the private necessity cases in that complete respect for private rights—that is, a system that always makes restoration the preferred remedy—causes too much social inconvenience and dislocation: no one person may block completion of a needed public highway or a facility required for national defense. Instead, however, of going to the extreme that says these property rights (once vested) may be violated by the public whenever it sees fit, the clause steers the middle course accepted in *Ploof* and *Vincent* by allowing the state, without the consent of the owner, to take private property but only upon payment of compensation for the loss sustained. The distribution of the gain, a matter of extreme indifference to the economics of wealth maximization, is central as an end in itself to even this qualified theory of property rights.[36]

The partial vindication of rights in eminent domain cases is of immediate relevance to the antitrust question. Law that makes price fixing, for example, illegal, is itself a deprivation from all persons of the right to offer their property for sale on whatever terms they see fit. That right of disposition is one of the bundle of protected property rights, for as has already been demonstrated no antitrust offense can be generated solely by corrective justice theories. There is therefore no individual wrong to justify state intervention such as might be invoked to protect against robbery or pollution. To break up a private monopoly not acquired by force or misrepresentation is itself to commit a wrong, not to redress a wrong committed by the private monopolist. Some might be inclined to stop the inquiry here, and to condemn antitrust law root and branch. Yet those prepared to essay the troubled waters of forced exchanges cannot be silent on the compensation question. If the state believes therefore that the economic case against monopoly is so strong that public intervention is required, then compensation should be tendered just as it is when the state takes any other property.

Here the great question arises: Who should pay the compensation and to whom? If every person had retained only his original endowments and none had entered into any gainful arrangements, then everyone must pay everyone else not to enter into certain types of anticompetitive arrangements. The payments themselves would be a wash, like the crossing of checks in the mail. Ignore the checks and it could be said with some accuracy that the implicit-in-kind compensation received by each for not entering into a monopoly arrangement is the freedom from the monopoly prices charged by others. If in fact the social product is greater with this restriction upon liberty and property, then restrictions upon the disposition of private property are imposed upon all for the benefit of all; everyone is better off, even if not freer than before. The public condemnation of property rights to enter into certain types of contracts is paid for by the benefits gained when the same restrictions upon contractual freedom are imposed by others. As both the restrictions imposed and the benefits received are themselves property rights, the compensation demanded for the admitted taking is met, and exceeded. Regulation of monopoly has a dual aspect. It is a taking of private property and payment of adequate compensation for the property taken.

This approach will in truth permit passage of general antitrust laws without explicit compensation in many circumstances. But it is not the equivalent of a proposition that states may break up monopolies because they are wrongful in their inception, or because economic regulation and taking are wholly distinct concepts, occupying wholly distinct realms. The difference between the approach here and the alternative view becomes crucial in a society in which legitimate moves have been made from the original situation, for example, our own. Thus, suppose certain persons have invested resources to acquire a monopoly from which they are now poised to reap the benefits. The state could not *just* call the conduct a wrong and expropriate the monopoly gains. In truth, the situation here is no different from one in which the state seeks in its zoning activities to avoid payment of compensation to a landowner by declaring his current activities a nuisance that warrants extensive regulation under the police power.[37] The justification for state control must come from some type of *normative* theory that binds the state (and the citizens it represents) as much as it binds private individuals.[38] The theory of corrective justice cannot simply be brushed aside by interposing an indefensible conception of a private wrong, which is in turn treated as the sole justification for the public takings that follow. Like private necessity, public necessity may require the acceptance of forced exchanges, which themselves presuppose an accurate delineation and full respect of the initial distribution of property rights.

The consequences for regulation of private monopolies are these. With the established monopolist it must be shown that the compensation received is adequate for the loss in question. This cannot be done when the established monopolist loses far more by the *retroactive* application of the antitrust laws against him than he gains from the *prospective* application of the antitrust laws against others. The point here is not simply that the antitrust laws are suspect because private parties have acted in reliance upon the previous legal order. It is that they had a *right* to so rely given the original distribution of rights entailed by a complete theory of corrective justice. The disproportionate impact of the regulation requires that the balance among citizens be restored by explicit compensation. And if the social benefits of eliminating monopolies are as great as is claimed, then the monopolist can be paid off in full for his losses and enjoy with other members of society his pro rata share of the gains induced by government mandate in favor of competition. The law of private property requires in connection with public takings a "difference" principle of similar form but different content from that put forward by John Rawls.[39] It is not that the worse-off members of society must be left better off by any differences in wealth. It is that the owners of property must be left better off (with full compensation for the losses, plus a share in the social gains) by any taking of their property: what might be called a constrained Pareto optimality principle. The antitrust laws represent deprivation of property rights. To them the general prohibitions stated here must apply.

VI

I wish to conclude with a brief discussion of the policy implications of this perspective for the antitrust laws. Here the key question is, Which of the standard prohibitions of the law can survive in a system that strongly sets its initial presumption against any antitrust law at all? In order to answer that question, there must be some sense of the circumstances in which forced exchanges are proper in principle. In an earlier article I wrote on the law of nuisance, I set out four separate characteristics I thought should be satisfied before any deviation from the requirements of a corrective justice theory would be appropriate. These were:

1. High administrative costs for claim resolution.
2. High transaction costs for voluntary reassignment of rights.
3. Low value to the interested parties of the ownership rights whose rearrangement is mandated by public rule.
4. Presence of implicit in-kind compensation from all to all that precludes any systematic redistribution of wealth among the interested parties.[40]

If these are the relevant considerations, then it becomes clear that the case for any antitrust law is difficult both to evaluate and to establish. In particular, the first two points cut in opposite directions. The creation of liability for economic harms where none existed before necessarily entails very high administrative costs, as it is necessary to specify not only the types of conduct that are to be proscribed but also their causal relation to the plaintiff's harm and the magnitude of harm so caused. Yet on the other side the practical barriers to voluntary rearrangements of rights are virtually insuperable, given that the antitrust laws must necessarily extend to all individuals in society. Similarly, the last two elements of the formula also raise major hurdles. Thus, it is very difficult to make some ex ante estimate of the value of the rights that will be taken from individuals once particular antitrust offenses are put into place on a generalized basis. Yet, unlike the minor infractions of property rights associated with the fine points of the law of nuisance,[41] it seems clear that the economic values, both taken and provided, are apt to be substantial and—in ways that also tie into the fourth point—subject to wide variation over the individuals who are subject to their impact. Given the fact that individuals have different aptitudes for business, some will be left better off and some worse off by the shifts. Yet even here there is some comfort, because the very generalization of the rule makes it difficult for any person so disadvantaged to be identified in advance or singled out for special treatment. Nonetheless, even if such political abuse can be controlled, a general rule can guarantee only that ex ante compensation will exist, not that it will be adequate. The case of antitrust is therefore of special difficulty, for while it is possible to identify reasons for its invocation—high transactions costs and some possible enlargement of the social pie—these are necessarily subject to the qualification that the changes introduced will demand not only major administrative costs but also forced exchanges of large magnitude, and often on uneven terms. Some might argue, therefore, that the complications are so formidable that on antitrust matters we should not depart from corrective justice principles at all, even if such action might be appropriate elsewhere. I think, however, that the better way is to take a more individuated view of the various types of antitrust offense, each with its very different strengths and weaknesses.

The most obvious targets for antitrust intervention are horizontal market arrangements, such as price fixing and territorial division of markets.[42] These are generally regarded as the most obvious routes to monopolization, and if the insistent demands of the second best are put to one side, it seems possible that a limited set of prohibitions make everyone better off ex ante than they would be under some alternative regime.

Yet even if the prohibited acts are so identified, the question of remedy remains difficult and important. One possible angle is simply to declare such contracts in restraint of trade as unenforceable between the parties to them. This was essentially the nineteenth-century common law solution.[43] A second method is to allow as well direct actions for damages and injunctions by those individuals who are left worse off by the proscribed practices. The first of these alternatives—mere unenforceability—is very cheap to administer, and it will doubtless foster the instability of various cartel arrangements. Nonetheless, disintegration of the prohibited arrangement will not be instantaneous; a case could be made for a system in which a direct action for damages by aggrieved parties is allowed in addition, even though there are very substantial administrative problems. Consider the simple question of what the appropriate measure of damages is, be it to parties who have purchased from the cartel or those who have decided to do without.[44] Given my own skepticism about the dimensions of the monopoly problem, I favor the first alternative, as it constitutes the smallest deviation from the corrective justice rules. But the compromise is uneasy. The more aggressive tortlike intervention might be justified if it could produce major welfare gains.

Horizontal mergers present a somewhat different, and easier, picture. In the first place, it seems that they represent less of a threat on economic grounds than price-fixing arrangements. Mergers are much more costly to negotiate as it is no longer simply a matter of two firms deciding to restrict outputs of a single product or single-product line. In contrast, mergers are unwieldy and complicated transactions that are confined in their effect solely to the areas in which two firms wish not to compete. The transactions are always visible, and often require the approval of the shareholders of either or both corporations. They generate very complicated tax consequences that are not always favorable to the shareholders of either corporation. They require the reorganization of ways of doing business that frequently entails some disposition of those assets that are unwanted after the merger is consummated. They always hold out the possibility of displacement of members of the management team for both corporations. Likewise, mergers are not only in search of monopoly gains, as by raising price above marginal cost; they also allow reduction of the costs of production and distribution that are normally translated into increased production and reduced price.[45] Given that these efficiencies are part and parcel of the deal, it is very doubtful that the initial corrective justice presumption in favor of freedom of contract can be displaced. The real concern with mergers, therefore, lies with the increased likelihood that large corporations will control and dominate the political process; yet there is an open question as to whether these ills are brought on by concentration in market structure. If such is the case, moreover, it seems that a different set of restraints, ones that go direct to the corporate-government relations, are required.

Whatever doubts exist in horizontal cases do not carry to other areas. This twofold test—corrective justice followed by limited forced exchanges—demands a sharp contraction of antitrust laws in a whole host of other areas. Thus, the entire range of antitrust jurisprudence on vertical restrictions—be it on territories, on tie-ins, or resale price maintenance, or franchises—should be scrapped. In each and every one of these cases it might be possible to give economic arguments to support the restrictions. But equally strong (if not stronger) economic arguments cut in the opposite direction. Where, therefore, the economic issues are not clear, the burden of displacing the corrective justice rules is simply not met. Franchise agreements with exclusive purchasing clauses, for example, might be regarded as dark devices designed to eliminate the ability of a franchisee to acquire his supplies from other firms in competition with the franchisor. Yet on the other side, it might be urged that the insistence upon exclusive supply contracts will make it more difficult for the franchisor to line up franchisees in the first instance. It is also possible that the franchisor may well insist that all supplies be purchased by him because it is too difficult or costly for him to monitor the franchisee's alternative inputs, as he must in order to protect the systemwide goodwill that is associated with his quality control and brand name. This economic debate may be difficult to resolve in the abstract, but the outcome is quite clear when the noneconomic corrective justice argument has already set up a strong presumption of full enforceability.[46]

What can be said about the various forms of vertical arrangements carries over to other antitrust doctrines as well. The idea of predatory pricing as a tort is wholly inconceivable within a pure system of corrective justice: the offer of goods for sale at below marginal cost (however defined) simply does not amount to the use of force or fraud against a competitor.[47] Extensive arguments in the literature depict the possibility that a dominant firm may be able to devise a pricing strategy that will, at an immediate cost to itself, permit it to reap enough monopoly profits to make the venture worthwhile. This case against predatory pricing runs into very strong objections.[48] To clear the market the predator must expand his output in ways that guarantee substantial immediate loss; yet when he raises his prices, he has no effective way to prevent entry of new firms that might undersell him. In the end, successful predation must rest, therefore, upon its *threat,* which must *alone* be enough to keep all competitors in line, even against the best possible counterstrategies. The possibilities are remote. Yet economists continue to argue for treating predatory pricing as an antitrust offense. At this point, the clear complexity of the argument (not to mention the enormous costs of the litigation) make the ultimate judgment too clear for argument. Even if predation might be thought undesirable on some economic grounds, it cannot possibly be actionable in the face of the strong presumption in favor of liberty of action recognized by the corrective justice system.

Another antitrust peculiarity, an odd feature of the antitrust law, is that the successful plaintiff is normally entitled to treble damages. This rule would make sense only on the assumption that antitrust violations were really serious wrongs, when in fact we have already seen that they require a very complicated justification to be thought wrongful at all. In this framework, it becomes quite incomprehensible why they should be treated as especially serious legal wrongs instead of picayune ones. It may well be that some multiple of damages is justified for antitrust offenses that are *concealed* (as with price fixing); but if so, treble damages should be awarded for concealed wrongs outside the antitrust law, such as ordinary fraud.[49]

In closing, it should be noted that on many points my analysis strongly converges with some economic appraisals of antitrust law. In one sense, this convergence is both comforting and important. Congruence in result necessarily reduces the need to choose between the operational premises held by individuals with different philosophical orientations. Nevertheless, neither the extent nor the importance of the theoretical differences can be eliminated. If, for example, one takes an exclusive corrective justice stance, then there is no place for economic arguments, and none for the antitrust law. If one adopts an intermediate position, as I have, differences from the economic portrayal will still persist, and not only on linguistic matters, but also and much more importantly on the substantive areas of price fixing, merger policy, and predatory pricing, not to mention retroactive application of antitrust law. In the end, therefore, antitrust law presents difficult questions of coordination between private right and public domain—questions on which economic analysis sheds insufficient light.

NOTES

* I should like to thank Douglas Baird and Walter Blum for their helpful comments in the previous drafts of this article.

1. For Michelman's effort to counter the imperialism encountered in much of modern law and economics, see his "Norms and Normativity in the Economic Theory of Law," 62 *Minn. L. Rev.* 1015 (1978).

2. See Michelman, pp. 3–40, in the present volume. See also Duncan Kennedy and Frank Michelman, "Are Property and Contract Efficient?" 8 *Hofstra L. Rev.* 711 (1980).

3. The original conception of corrective justice dates from Aristotle's *Ethics*, book V. Aristotle's own discussion of the concept is in many ways incomplete—it deals, for example, only with the question of the proper treatment of deliberate harms. I think that there is a close view between Aristotle's view of the subject and my own, although his own conception is too obscure to permit any definite conclusion on the matter.

4. My own qualified defense of the first possession rule is found in Richard A. Epstein, "Possession as the Root of Title," 13 *Georgia L. Rev.* 1223 (1979).

5. For application of the principle in simple three-party arrangement—"A compelled B to hit C"—see Richard A. Epstein, "A Theory of Strict Liability," 2 *J. Legal Stud.* 151, 174–77 (1973).

6. See, *United States* v. *Aluminum Co. of America,* 148 F.2d 416, 429 (2d Cir. 1945).

7. For a straight economic approach to the antitrust laws, see Richard A. Posner, *Anti-Trust Law: An Economic Perspective* (1976). Learned Hand, the author of the *Alcoa* opinion, intimated that certain other elements might lie behind the adoption of these laws, in particular the organization of an industry with small firms in direct competition with each other, or the destruction of the "great aggregations of capital because of the helplessness of the individual before them." 148 F.2d 416, 428–29 (2d Cir. 1945). I have not directed by discussion toward an evaluation of these ends. Suffice it to say that neither is legitimate in a thoroughgoing corrective justice regime because of their preoccupation of the end states of the economic process rather than a concern with the nature of the actions that led to it. See *infra,* Part III.

8. The "consumer welfare" standard is adopted in Robert H. Bork, *The Anti-Trust Paradox* (1978). The term should, however, be treated as an equivalent to general welfare in order to avoid the possible implication that producers of goods are the mere instruments of consumers, without any independent entitlements of their own, whose own welfare supply does not count.

9. O. Williamson, "Economics as an Anti-Trust Defense: The Welfare Trade-Offs," 58 *Am. Econ. Rev.* 18 (1968).

10. There is one ironic twist to the discussion in the text. The modern antitrust law contains an exemption for activities to petition the government, even if they might otherwise amount to a violation of the Sherman Act. See *Eastern R.R. Presidents Conference* v. *Noerr Motor Freight, Inc.,* 365 U.S. 127 (1961); *United Mine Workers* v. *Pennington,* 381 U.S. 657 (1965). For a thoughtful discussion of the scope of the Noerr-Pennington doctrine, and its relationship to the first amendment, see Fischel, "Antitrust Liability for Attempts to Influence Government Action: The Basis and Limits of the Noerr-Pennington Doctrine," 45 *U. Chi. L. Rev.* 80 (1980).

11. See for a classical statement of the principles of cognitive biases, Amos Tverski and Daniel Kahneman, "Heuristics and Biases," 185 *Science* 1124 (1974).

12. "The antirationalistic approach, which regards man not as a highly rational and intelligent but as a very irrational and fallible being

whose individual errors are correctly only in the course of a social process, and which aims at making the best of a very imperfect material, is probably the most characteristic feature of English individualism." F. Hayek, "Individualism, True and False," in *Individualism and Economic Order*, 8, 9 (1948).

13. Ronald Coase, "Adam Smith's View of Man," 19 *J. Law & Econ.* 529 (1976).
14. Dennis Carlton, "Planning and Market Structure," to appear in *The Economies of Information and Uncertainty*, ed. J. McCall, University of Chicago Press.
15. See, Edmund Kitch, "The Nature and Function of the Patent System" 20 *J. Law & Econ.* 265 (1977); Edmund Kitch, The Law & Economics of Rights in Valuable Information, 8 J. Leg. Stud. 683 (1979). Here it should be noted that any analysis of property rights in information is itself an extraordinarily difficult task no matter what the fundamental orientation. Information cannot be reduced to exclusive possession by the acts of its owner; and it is retained as a matter of fact even when rights to its exclusive use are transferred by agreement between private parties, such that to some extent its protection must always be viewed as a matter of positive law, rather than a matter of natural rights. Whatever the difficulties in this connection, however, there is no reason why problems with the legal rights over information should influence the treatment of property rights in tangible things and natural resources, as these can be evaluated on an independent basis.
16. See, e.g., Harold Demsetz, "Why Regulate Public Utilities," 11 *J. Law & Econ.* 55 (1968).
17. See *supra* note 4, at 1238–43.
18. The concern is an old one in the law. "Its true basis [of the proposition that possession is the root of title] seems to be, not an instinctive bias towards the institution of property, but a presumption, arising out of the long continuance of that institution, that *everything ought to have an owner*." Henry Maine, *Ancient Law* (London: Dent, 1861), p. 151.
19. "In this state the title to wild animals and game is in the Commonwealth in truth for the public to be devoted to the common welfare." *Dapson v. Daly*, 257 Mass. 195, 153 N.E. 454 (1926).
20. These are the traditional incidents that are recognized. See A. M. Honore, "Ownership," in A. G. Guest, ed., *Oxford Essays on Jurisprudence* (Oxford University Press, 1961), pp. 108–47. See also *United States v. General Motors*, 323 U.S. 373, 377–78 (1945): "The critical terms [of the eminent domain clause: "nor shall private property be taken for public use without just compensation]" are "property", "taken" and "just compensation." It is conceivable that

the first was used in its vulgar and untechnical sense of the physical thing with respect to which the citizen exercises rights recognized by law. On the other hand, it may have been employed in a more accurate sense to denote the group of rights inhering in the citizen's relation to the physical thing, as the right to possess, use and dispose of it. In point of fact, the construction given the phrase has been the latter."

21. See, e.g., *United States* v. *Causby*, 328 U.S. 256 (1946).

22. With nuisance its "very name—nocumentum—suggests the damage which he [i.e., the landowner] had suffered by conduct which nevertheless fell short of an actual dispossession." C. H. S. Fifoot, *History and Sources of the Common Law*, 3 (1949). For an extended statement of my own views on nuisance, see Epstein, "Nuisance Law: Corrective Justice and its Utilitarian Constraints," 8 *J. Legal Stud.* 49 (1979).

23. The conception dates back to Aristotle, *Ethics*, book V, 1135a, and is picked up in H. L. A. Hart and A. M. Honore, *Causation in the Law*, 38 n. 1 (1959).

24. See, e.g., Anthony T. Kronman, "Contract Law and Distributive Justice," 89 *Yale L. J.* 472 (1980), where it is argued that questions of redistribution must be taken into account even by libertarian thinkers. In my view, the argument is mistaken in that it confuses the question of whether any given promise is "voluntarily" made with the related, but quite distinct and narrower, question of whether it was induced by the force or fraud of the promisee. See for my account of contractual obligations, Epstein, "Unconscionability, A Critical Reappraisal," 18 *J. Law & Econ.* 293 (1975).

25. For a development of these issues, see my "Defenses and Subsequent Pleas," 3 *J. Legal Stud.* 165 (1974), and "Intentional Harms," 4 *J. Legal Stud.* 391 (1975).

26. *Tarleton* v. *McGawley*, Peake, 205, 170 Eng. Rep. 153 (1793).

27. Other early cases are 11 Hen IV, 47 (1410); 22 Hen VI, 14 (1444); 6 East, 573, note. *Walker* v. *Cronin*, 107 Mass. 555 (1871); *Payne* v. *R.R. Co.*, 13 Tenn. 507 (1884). These cases are ably discussed in John H. Wigmore, "The Boycott and Kindred Practices As Ground for Damages," *American Law Rev.* 21, 509, 514–21 (1887), which defended a position very close to the corrective justice model developed here.

28. See Restatement of Torts, Section 559 (1976). "A communication is defamatory if it tends to harm the reputation of another as to lower him in the estimation of the community or to deter third persons from associating or dealing with him."

29. See, e.g., Posner, "The Ethical and Political Basis of the Efficiency

Norm in Common Law Adjudication," 8 *Hofstra L. Rev.* 487 (1980), where Posner instances a case in which "a company decides to close a factory in town A and open a new one in B, and that in neither location are the significant pollution, congestion or other technological externalities from the plant." Posner himself would "allow" the transaction, but on a wealth-maximization view that leads to real complications. It seems clear that the plant moves, like any major action, will leave some in the world (employees, suppliers, etc.) worse off, such that the class of harms prima facie actionable is very broad indeed. The only way that this problem can be reduced within the wealth maximization-framework is to assume that the network of voluntary transactions yields aggregate gains that exceed aggregate losses. Yet this does not deal with the possibility that the private calculations need not reflect the social gains and losses involved in (say) the plant closing. And even if there were a perfect congruence, the absolute immunity from suit need not be required under a wealth maximization-view once the possibility of negligence—itself admitted in ordinary physical injury cases—is allowed. Nor does this approach deal with the further question of whether the winners in the relocation should be required to compensate the losers.

See also Easterbrook and Fischel, "The Proper Role of Target Management in Corporate Takeovers," 94 *Harv. L. Rev.* 1101 (1981), where it is also assumed that the market will take into account all the competing economic interests of suppliers and employees of a corporation subject to takeovers. In most cases it will not, but the point is generally immaterial, because the shareholders of stock owe *no duty* to protect these persons against such shifts in economic value of their entitlements.

30. For a further discussion, see Epstein, "Intentional Harms," 4 *J. Legal Stud.* 291, 421–42 (1975).
31. See Posner, *supra* note 26, at 491–92.
32. The early English monopolies were typically exclusive franchises created by the Crown, which thereby created legal barriers to entry of the sort that are utterly inconsistent with the corrective justice theory outlined here. See B. Malement, "The 'Economic Liberation' of Sir Edward Coke" 76, *Yale L. J.* 1321, esp. 1345–51 (1967), for explanation of the sharp divisions between Coke's antiroyalist sentiment and the economic theories of laissez-faire.
33. For a more systematic elaboration of the distinction between tort and crime that is advanced here, see Epstein, "Tort and Crime: Old Wine in Old Bottles," in Randy E. Barnett and John Hagel, III, eds., *Assessing the Criminal: Restitution, Retribution, and the Legal*

process, 231 (1977). See, for earlier developments of the same general approach, Jerome Hall, "Interrelationships of Criminal Law and Torts," 43 *Colum. L. Rev.* 760 (1943); and Henry Hart, Jr., "The Aims of the Criminal Law," 23 *Law & Contemp. Probs.* 401 (1958).

34. 81 Vt. 471, 71 A. 188 (1908).
35. 109 Minn. 456, 124 N.W. 221 (1910).
36. For a further account, see Epstein, "The Next Generation of Legal Scholarship?" 30 *Stan. L. Rev.* 635 (1978). [Review of Bruce Ackerman, *Private Property and the Constitution* (1977).]
37. See, e.g., *Mugler* v. *Kansas*, 123 U.S. 623 (1887), for an early instance in which the legislative declaration of a private brewery as a public nuisance was permitted to allow the use of this technique.
38. See *Pruneyard Shopping Center* v. *Rohls*, 447 U.S. 74 (1980), concurrence of Justice Marshall, where the analytical point is made only to be misapplied. There it was held that a state could require the owners of a large shopping center to permit the distribution of leaflets advocating causes that the owners opposed without their consent. The decision in effect allows expropriation by private use, given that the conduct in question is clearly (as a matter of private law) an actionable trespassing not withstanding the leafleter's desires and needs to use the owners' property.
39. John Rawls, *A Theory of Justice* §13 (1971).
40. Epstein, "Nuisance Law: Corrective Justice and Its Utilitarian Constraints," 8 *J. Legal Stud.* 49, 79 (1979).
41. Thus the appropriate comparison is with the so-called live-and-let-live cases, in which minor disturbances that are technical invasions of property are tolerated by all for the benefit of all. There the high frequency of the harms, and their small extent lends a certain amount of credibility that everyone will be left better off with a relaxation of the ordinary rules. *Id.* at 82–87. The antitrust law presents the same pattern of generalized forced exchanges in the economic area but with much lower likelihood that the fortunate pattern will manifest itself.
42. See the discussion in Robert Bork, *The Anti-Trust Paradox* ch. 13 (1978), where the distinction is taken between those price-fixing or horizontal restraints that are "naked" and those which are "ancillary" to some productive activities. As regards the former, he concludes on standard economic grounds that they should be per se illegal. *Id.* at 279.
43. See, e.g., *Gibbs* v. *Baltimore Gas Co.*, 130 U.S. 396 (1889) (contract of services incident to price-fixing arrangements); *Chicago Gas Light*

Co. v. *People's Gas Light Co.,* 121 Ill. 530 (1887) (territorial limitation); *Chaplin* v. *Brown Bros.,* 83 Iowa 157 (1891) (same).
44. See, William H. Page, "Antitrust Damages and Economic Efficiency: An Approach to Economic Inquiry," 47 *U. Chi. L. Rev.* 467 (1980).
45. See, on the trade-offs between restraint and efficiency, Oliver Williamson, "Economies as an Antitrust Defense: The Welfare Tradeoffs," 58 *Am. Econ. Rev.* 18 (1968); Deprano and Nugent, "Economies as an Antitrust Defense: Comment," 59 *Am. Econ. Rev.* 947 (1969). The very uncertainty of the debate over the relative size of the asserted welfare gains and losses is yet an additional reason to prefer the corrective justice approach which puts these all to one side. Needless to say, the case law on horizontal mergers is far too restrictive on any point of view. The most influential decision in the undistinguished Supreme Court literature is *Brown Shoe Co.* v. *United States,* 370 U.S. 294 (1962); for criticism, see Bork, *The Antitrust Paradox,* ch. 9 (1978).
46. See, for similar conclusions, Robert Bork, *The Antitrust Paradox,* ch. 15 (1978).
47. For a more extended statement of my views, see Epstein, "Intentional Harms," 4 *J. Legal Stud.* 391, 420–41 (1975); Epstein, "Causation and Corrective Justice: A Reply to Two Critics," 8 *J. Legal Stud.* 477, 494–96 (1979).
48. For powerful critiques of the economic arguments that support antitrust recognition of the offense of predatory pricing, see John S. McGee "Predatory Pricing Revisited," 23 *J. Law & Econ.* 289 (1980); Frank H. Easterbrook, "Predatory Strategies and Counterstrategies." 48 *U. Chi. L. Rev.* 263 (1981).

For various efforts to define some offense of predatory pricing, see Philip Agreeda and Donald F. Turner, "Predatory Pricing and Related Practices Under Section 2 of the Sherman," 88 *Harv. L. Rev.* 679 (1975); Richard A. Posner, *Anti-Trust Law: An Economic Perspective,* 184 et seq. (1976); F. M. Scherer, "Predatory Pricing and the Sherman Act: A Comment," 89 *Harv. L. Rev.* 869 (1976); Oliver Williamson, "Predatory Pricing: A Strategic and Welfare Analysis," 87 *Yale L. J.* 284 (1977); Paul L. Joskow and Alvin K. Klevorick, "A Framework for Analyzing Predatory Pricing Policy," 89 *Yale L. J.* 213 (1979); Baumol, "Quasi-Permanence of Price Reductions: A Policy for the Prevention of Predatory Pricing," 89 *Yale L. J.* 1 (1979). The extent to which these economists disagree among themselves provides still further proof that no antitrust offense for predatory pricing should be recognized or created.
49. The point about treble damages in antitrust actions has been made

to me forcefully in conversation by William Landes. The fact that the common law did not give some multiple actions in ordinary fraud cases is some indication that it did not discount the probability of nonapprehension in setting the appropriate level of damages awards.

4

THE ECONOMIC ANALYSIS OF LAW

JULES L. COLEMAN*

Proponents of the economic approach to law find in welfare economics a framework for both understanding large bodies of the common law and developing new law—through the legislative, judical, and administrative processes. The unifying principle of both analytic and normative law and economics is the principle of efficiency. The economic approach to law involves three efficiency related notions: Pareto optimality, Pareto superiority, and Kaldor-Hicks efficiency. I propose to analyze these notions and to develop the analytic relations among them. In addition, I shall explore aspects of their alleged connection to utilitarian moral theory and discuss critically their respective roles in the prevailing normative economic theories of law.

I. PARETO AND KALDOR-HICKS

When a proponent of economic analysis maintains that a change in legal rules or in the market is warranted or required because it is efficient, his claim is ambiguous. He or she may be understood to mean either that the proposed rule is Pareto optimal, whereas the existing order of affairs is not; or that his proposal constitutes a Pareto improvement, that is, is Pareto superior to the existing state of affairs; or that the envisaged change constitutes a Kaldor-Hicks improvement over the existing distribution of resources.[1]

Resources are allocated in a Pareto optimal fashion if and only if any further reallocation can make one person better off only at the expense of another. An allocation of resources, S^1, is Pareto superior to an alternative allocation, S, provided no one is made worse off in going from S to S^1, and the welfare of at least one person is enhanced. A Pareto optimal distribution has no distributions Pareto superior to it. In addition, Pareto optimal distributions are Pareto noncomparable, that is, the Pareto superior standard cannot be employed to choose among them. Another way of putting this last point is to say that the choice among Pareto optimal distributions must be made on grounds other than efficiency.

One distribution of resources, S^1, is Kaldor-Hicks efficient to another distribution, S, if and only if in going from S to S^1 the winners could compensate the losers with a net gain in welfare. Because Kaldor-Hicks requires that winners *could* compensate losers, not that they must, a Kaldor-Hicks improvement, unlike a Pareto improvement, produces losers as well as winners. Were compensation costless and actually paid, a Kaldor-Hicks improvement would become a Pareto improvement. Because the Kaldor-Hicks standard does not require compensation, it is often referred to as "the hypothetical compensation principle," or simply, "the compensation principle." Furthermore, because under the conditions of costless compensation, a Kaldor-Hicks improvement could be transformed into a Pareto improvement, it is sometimes referred to as the "Potential Pareto test."[2]

This last way of characterizing Kaldor-Hicks is misleading, however. It suggests that a Kaldor-Hicks improvement is just a Pareto improvement waiting for compensation to be paid. That would be a mistake. Not every Kaldor-Hicks improvement corresponds to a Pareto one. Whenever the transaction costs of rendering compensation exceed the difference between the amount of compensation losers demand and the gain to the winners, requiring gainers to compensate losers will make the gainers worse off than they were under the original distribution. This just emphasizes the importance of the distinction between the *hypothetical* compensation required by the Kaldor-Hicks test and the *actual* compensation required by the Pareto superior test.

II. EFFICIENCY AND UTILITY[3]

The claim that a change in the market or in the legal order is desirable or warranted because it would be efficient is a normative one that requires the proponent of economic analysis to relate the conceptions of efficiency to standards of value and right conduct, which in turn impart moral significance to the notions of efficiency. To this end, proponents of economic analysis have relied on an alleged connection between at least the Pareto standards and classical utilitarian moral theory.

According to classical utilitarianism, an individual is obligated to perform that action among the set of possible actions open to him at a given time that is most likely to produce the greatest net balance of utility over disutility. This formulation of the principle of utility calls for interpersonal comparison of utilities, a requirement that, according to the prevailing wisdom, cannot adequately be met. Since a Pareto superior redistribution of resources improves the welfare of at least one person without adversely affecting the welfare of another, the standard of Pareto superiority may be used to bypass the interpersonal comparability problem of classical utilitarianism. In other words, because a Pareto improvement produces winners but no losers, no need exists to compare the relative gains and losses of respective winners and losers to determine if a course of conduct increases total utility. If a course of conduct is Pareto superior, total utility increases, though there may be increases in total utility that are not the result of Pareto improvements.[4]

Not every net gain in utility constitutes a Pareto improvement; and the use of the Pareto superior standard will not enable us to determine by how much net utility has increased.[5] For these reasons, the Pareto standard resolves the interpersonal utility problem in a limited way. Still, the fact that the Pareto standard enables one to determine in a reliable way whether a policy increases total utility makes it easy to see why one might be led to consider utilitarianism to be the normative basis of at least the Pareto superior criterion.

The argument that Pareto optimality is connected to utilitarianism is more difficult. Since not every move to a Pareto optimal distribution of resources involves a Pareto improvement, one can *not* infer from the fact that an existing state of affairs is Pareto optimal that the move to it increases total utility. Moreover, because the set of Pareto optimal states of affairs is Pareto noncomparable, no judgments concerning the relative total utility contained in them are warranted.[6]

On the other hand, from the fact that a state of affairs is Pareto optimal, one can infer that it contains more total utility than the set of distributions that may be represented by points to the southwest of it within the utility / possibility frontier. That is because every distribution represented by a point on the utility / possibility frontier, that is, a Pareto optimal distribution, is *Pareto superior* to those distributions represented by points within the frontier to its southwest. Moreover, the net utility contained in any Pareto optimal distribution *cannot* be increased by a Pareto improvement. This feature of Pareto optimality follows from its conceptual connection to Pareto superiority; namely, a Pareto optimal distribution has no distributions Pareto superior to it.

Every utility judgment warranted by the Pareto optimality standard is a logical consequence of its analytic relation to Pareto superiority. No independent argument for the claim that Pareto optimality is rooted in utilitarian moral theory is possible. Whether Pareto optimality can be defended on utilitarian grounds will depend on whether Pareto superiority can be. Moreover, even if Pareto superiority can be defended on utilitarian grounds, it will not follow that Pareto optimality can, since not every Pareto optimal state of affairs need be the result of a Pareto improvement.

The problem of constructing a utilitarian account of Kaldor-Hicks efficiency runs even deeper. Under the Kaldor-Hicks test, winners are not required to compensate losers; all that is required is the *capacity* to render full compensation. Consequently, in order to infer a net increase in utility from the fact that the Kaldor-Hicks requirement has been satisfied, we have to know that winners have won more in utility than losers have lost in utility. Such a judgment requires interpersonal cardinal comparability, which the Pareto superior criterion was originally introduced to avoid. Satisfaction of the Kaldor-Hicks test does *not* require comparability; using the Kaldor-Hicks test as an index of utility *does*.

Second, the Kaldor-Hicks test is subject to the Scitovsky Paradox. The Scitovsky Paradox is the result that two states of affairs, S and S^1, can be Kaldor-Hicks efficient to one another. The proof is simple enough. Assume a two-person (X, Y), two-commodity (a, b) universe and the preference orderings for the distributions of a and b between X and Y shown in the accompanying illustration. Consider the states of affairs S and S^1. The distribution of a and b between X and Y in S and S^1 is given by the accompanying matrix.

PoX	*PoY*
a b	*a b*
1,1	*1,1*
2,0	*0,2*
1,0	*0,1*

		a	*b*
S	X	2	0
	Y	0	1

		a	*b*
S^1	X	1	0
	Y	0	2

Here, S^1 is Kaldor-Hicks efficient to S since Y (the winner) could compensate X (the loser) one unit of b. Having done so, X would be in his most preferred state; Y would then be no worse off than in S.

Also, S is Kaldor-Hicks efficient to S^1, since X (the winner) could compensate Y (the loser) one unit of a. Having done so, Y would be in his most preferred state; X would be no worse off than in S^1.

In short, satisfaction of the Kaldor-Hicks criterion cannot entail a net gain in utility because, without appealing to any particular standard of interpersonal comparison, one can determine if Kaldor-Hicks has been satisfied; but one cannot determine if utility has been increased by a Kaldor-Hicks improvement in which there are both winners and losers without appealing to such a standard; and S^1 can be Kaldor-Hicks efficient to S and S Kaldor-Hicks efficient to S^1, though S^1 cannot have more total utility than S while S has more total utility than S^1. Because satisfaction of the Kaldor-Hicks test does not entail an increase in utility, the justification, if there is one, for pursuing Kaldor-Hicks improvements cannot be utilitarian.[7]

On the other hand, even though satisfaction of the Pareto superior standard *does* entail an increase in utility, it will not follow that the justification for *its* use is utilitarian. There is an important distinction between the claim that Pareto superiority *warrants* a utility judgment and the claim that it is this connection to utilitarianism that justifies pursuing Pareto improvements. I have elsewhere discussed at length alternatives to the utilitarian justification for Pareto superiority, so I will only summarily discuss one of them here.

The empirical content of Pareto superiority judgments is given in terms of their relation to individual preference theories, not to total utility theories. Pareto superiority is defined in terms of preference orderings: S^1 is Pareto superior to S if and only if at least one individual in S^1 is further along his preference ranking than he is in S, and no individual is any worse off with respect to hers in S^1 than she is in S. Suppose that judgments made in terms of individual preference orderings could not be made into judgments regarding total utility. In such a case, the notion of total utility would be meaningless, and the standard of Pareto superiority could not serve as an index of total utility. Nevertheless, the concept of Pareto superiority would be meaningful; and a claim that S^1 is Pareto superior to S would have empirical content. Under such circumstances, one could not *ex hypothesi* purport to justify a Pareto improvement on the ground that it increases total utility. (Remember, we are assuming that the notion of total utility is meaningless.) It would not follow, however, that a Pareto improvement or policies in pursuit thereof could not be justified. One possible justification is this: because a Pareto improvement makes at least one individual better off and no one worse off, no rational person would object to it. That is, rational individuals would choose to pursue Pareto superior policies, not because they increase utility, but because they improve the well-being of some without adversely affecting the well-being of others. This is an argument from consent, not utility.

In short, the argument for identifying the Pareto criteria with utilitarian moral theory is problematic in two ways. First, only Pareto superiority judgments entail judgments cast in terms of total or net utility. Second, the fact that a Pareto judgment of any sort warrants a utility judgment is inadequate to establish the proposition that the justification for pursuing Pareto improvements is utilitarian.

III. THE COASE THEOREM

The most influential discussion of the relation of economic efficiency to law is Ronald Coase's "The Problem of Social Cost."[8] Whenever reference is made to this article, visions of the Coase Theorem spring to mind. Often overlooked is the fact that Coase's purpose was *not* to develop a theorem about the relation of law to efficiency; his intention was to criticize and provide an alternative to the Pigouvian approach to externalities.[9]

The Pigouvian approach to externalities involves three steps. First, an appropriate civil authority identifies an activity as the source or cause of the externality. Next, the authority determines how much of the external by-product of the "offending" party is optimal or efficient. Then the requisite body imposes on the offending party a per unit tax equal to the marginal damage caused by each "unit" of the offending activity beyond the optimal level. The Pigouvian approach requires first a judgment of causal responsibility for damage, then a determination of efficient resource use, and finally the imposition of a tax in order to reduce the output of the offending party to the efficient level. The per unit tax reduces output by requiring the offending party to pay not only the *private* but the *social costs* of its activity.

An example may be helpful. Suppose no fence separates adjacent plots of land owned by a rancher and a farmer, respectively. Because cows wander, each cow the rancher raises results in damage to the farm crop. If the rancher's decision about how many cows to raise does not require him to take into account the costs of ranching on farming, he will raise cows as if no corn were being farmed. He will cease raising additional cows only when his marginal profit in doing so is equaled by his marginal *private* costs.

In the Pigouvian approach to externalities, the appropriate authority determines first that the rancher's cattle adversely affect the level of corn and beef production, so that the price of beef is too low and the price of corn too high. When the rancher's activity does not reflect its effect on corn, too much beef and too little corn are produced.

The next step in the Pigouvian analysis requires determining how much of each activity is optimal or efficient. One way of doing this is to imagine that both activites and plots of land are owned by the same person, Mr. R. F. (rancher/farmer). The question R. F. would pose to himself is this: "Given this land and the fact that it can be used for raising both cows and corn, how much of my resources should be devoted to each?" His answer, of course, will depend on what he wants to do with the land. Let's simplify matters by assuming that R. F. desires to use his resources at their optimal productive level; he wants, in other words, to maximize his revenue from the land. In order to maximize revenue from his enterprises, R. F. must consider, not only the private costs of ranching and farming, but the costs of ranching *on* farming and that of farming *on* ranching as well. His strategy will be to choose that level of each activity such that any further increase in either will mean forgoing a greater benefit that could be secured by devoting those resources to the other activity. So if the next cow is worth X, whereas the damage to the corn crop it will cause exceeds X, then R. F. will forgo *that* cow in favor of the corn crop. In general, R. F. will decide on that level of ranching and farming such that any further ranching is more costly than farming (in terms of forgone farming opportunities) and any further farming is more costly than ranching (in terms of forgone ranching opportunities). No more ranching or farming can be undertaken without imposing a marginal loss. The levels of ranching and farming R. F. decides upon are in this sense efficient.

Once the efficient levels of ranching and farming are determined, the requisite authority imposes a per unit tax on the rancher equal to the marginal damage to corn crops of each additional cow.[10] As a result of the tax, the rancher gains nothing by raising any cow beyond the number represented by R. F.'s decision. The Pigouvian tax forces the rancher to internalize into his decisions the effects of his ranching on the farmer's farming. Because the true costs of ranching are now reflected in the sum of private and social costs, the prices of beef and corn are accurate, and consumers' decisions concerning how much corn and beef they want are based on accurate relative prices.

"The Problem of Social Cost" presents an alternative to the Pigouvian approach to internalizing externalities. The Coasian method relies on private exchange rather than on public taxation. The argument that externalities can be internalized by private exchange assumes that the relevant parties have substantial knowledge of their preferences, are rational, and that transactions between (or among) them are costless (i.e., that they exhibit cooperative behavior), or that these costs are trivial. Under these conditions, Coase argues, the relevant parties will negotiate to the efficient level of the respective activities.

Suppose the rancher is not required to take into account the costs of raising cows on corn. He will raise cows as if no corn was being grown on the adjacent land. Suppose the rancher will raise one hundred cows, where R. F. would have raised only fifty. To say that R. F. would have raised only fifty cows is just to say that each cow beyond the fiftieth causes more damage to the corn crop than it produces in ranching profits. Whatever the value of each cow between the fifty-first and the one hundreth is to the rancher, the value to the farmer of the associated corn crop damage exceeds it. The farmer therefore has an incentive to pursue an accord with the rancher that will prohibit the rancher from raising any more than fifty cows in return for which the farmer will pay the rancher an amount equal to or greater than the value of each additional cow but less than the crop damage associated with each cow. The rancher will accept some such offer, since he gains at least as much from the farmer's offer as he would from actually raising the cow. The rancher and farmer will continue to negotiate until the efficient level of ranching and farming—that is, that level R. F. would have chosen—is reached.

The same outcome is secured if we begin by assuming that

the farmer would grow corn as if no raising of cattle took place
on the adjacent land. This scenario requires that we assume
that the rancher begins by raising no cows; otherwise it is
impossible even to conceive of the farmer growing corn as if no
cows were within trampling distance. Suppose, then, that the
rancher begins by raising no cows at all. By hypothesis, the
marginal value of each of the first fifty cows to the rancher is
greater than the marginal value of the associated corn crop to
the farmer. Consequently, the rancher has an incentive to
purchase from the farmer the right to raise each cow up to the
fiftieth one. The farmer will accept any offer that exceeds the
marginal benefit to him of each unit of corn the rancher's cows
require him to forgo. The rancher is prepared to make such an
offer; again the two will negotiate to the efficient level of
ranching and farming.

Whether negotiations begin with too much or too little
ranching, that is, with ranching imposing inefficient external
costs on farming or with farming imposing inefficient external
costs on ranching, the result of negotiations will be the same.
The rancher and farmer will negotiate to that level of ranching
and farming represented by R. F.'s decision about how to
allocate his ranching and farming resources. In the absence of
transaction costs the externalities of ranching on farming will
be internalized by private exchange.

Not only is the Pigouvian tax just one way of controlling
externalities, as long as the parties remain free to negotiate
after the tax is imposed, imposing the tax may lead to inefficient
levels of production. Moreover, unlike the Pigouvian approach
that requires identifying one activity as the source of an externality, the Coasian approach reveals an underlying *reciprocity*
between activities:[11] too much farming means too little ranching
even if corn doesn't harm cows in the way in which meandering
cows harm corn.

Commentators have seen in Coase's argument the basis of a
formal or analytic claim about the relation between the goal of
economic efficiency and the assignment of legal rights as an
instrument in its pursuit. This is the Coase Theorem. There
are as many ways of stating the theorem as there are illustrations
of it and controversies arising from it. I prefer to state it as
follows: if we assume that the relevant parties to negotiations

are rational, that they have substantial knowledge of their own and one another's preferences, that transactions between them are costless, that the state will enforce contracts between them, that their negotiations are not affected by their relative wealth (no income effects), that the prices on the basis of which they bid against one another are given to them rather than established by their negotiations (the partial equilibrium model), the assignment of property rights by the state to either party will be irrelevant to the goal of efficiency, provided of course that the rights are divisible and negotiable.

I state the theorem with all these qualifications, partly for effect, and partly because so much confusion arises in its application simply because commentators either ignore or are unfamiliar with all the initial conditions that must be satisfied. The basic idea is really quite simple, however. As long as two people, A and B, can negotiate with one another, it won't matter from the point of view of efficiency whether the state gives B the right to prevent A from acting in a way that adversely affects B, or A the right to act in a way that harms B. As long as transactions are costless, A and B will negotiate to an efficient level of their respective activities through the process of mutual gain *via* trade, though there is no guarantee that they will negotiate to the *same* efficient distribution.[12]

In efficiency terms, the argument is this. The initial assignment of entitlements will either be efficient, that is, Pareto optimal, or not. If it *is* efficient, no negotiations will occur. Rational parties will not negotiate away from an efficient distribution, since doing so must make one of them worse off; that is just another way of saying that there are no Pareto superior moves from Pareto optimal states of affairs. On the other hand, if the initial assignment is inefficient, a Pareto superior redistribution exists; and rational parties will reach an agreement that is Pareto superior to their current relative positions. This process of mutual gain through trade, that is, Pareto improvements through exchange, continues until further trade is unrewarding for either or both parties.

Immediately upon stating the Coase Theorem—that the assignment of entitlements is irrelevant to the goal of efficiency—analysts go on to point out that the assignment of rights does make a difference from the point of view of the distribution of wealth between the relevant parties. That is, the party who is not assigned the entitlement must purchase it from the party who is assigned it. This effects a wealth transfer between them. So if the farmer is entitled to prohibit all cows, there will be fifty cows in the end, but the rancher will have had to pay the farmer for the privilege of ranching fifty cows; whereas if the rancher was entitled to ranch one hundred cows, there will be fifty in the end, but the rancher will be compensated by the farmer for each cow he forgoes.

I have become persuaded that this way of characterizing the wealth redistributive effects of the assignment of entitlements is mistaken. For it seems to me that what the farmer would be willing to pay for the farmland in the first place would depend on his future liabilities and, in particular, on whether he will have to *bribe* the rancher to reduce the level of ranching. Certainly, he would pay less for the right to farm the land if he is not assigned as well the right to prohibit cows on the adjacent property. Concern for his liability to the farmer would also effect what the rancher is willing to pay for the right to ranch. The financial gains and losses in relative wealth between rancher and farmer associated with the right either to raise or prohibit cows appears to be discounted in the purchase price of the *prior* rights.[13] Generally, the standard understanding of the redistributive effect of the assignment of entitlements looks at individual right assignments in isolation, piecemeal. The piecemeal approach misses the crucial point that the value of any right to a person depends on associative rights, on clusters or bundles of rights. When the respective bundles of rights and liabilities of the rancher and farmer are taken into account, it may well be that the relative wealth of the parties is not affected by any *particular* assignment.

IV. AUCTIONING ENTITLEMENTS

Having expressed my skepticism concerning the universally accepted understanding of the redistributive aspects of the Coase Theorem, I want to move on to the application of the theorem to law when the conditions necessary for its satisfaction are not met; in particular, when transaction costs are not insignificant. In many cases the existence of transaction costs may make it impossible for the relevant parties to reach an accord that will improve their well-being. For example, if the cost of the transaction exceeds the difference between what the rancher values adding another cow at and what the farmer values the corn he will lose at, the rancher will not purchase from the farmer the right to that cow (assuming the farmer is initially assigned the right to prohibit it). Because no transaction occurs, the farmer maintains the entitlement, though his doing so is inefficient; that is, Pareto superior redistributions exists. Failures of this sort are called market failures.

Where transaction costs create market failures, the initial assignment of entitlements makes a difference from the point of view of efficiency. Consequently, the essential question for economists concerns how externalities are to be internalized (or controlled) when transaction costs threaten the capacity of the market to promote efficiency through private exchange.

In the economic theory of law, the failure of private exchange to promote efficiency calls for some sort of public intervention. One form of intervention, which was briefly discussed earlier, would involve taxing the inefficient activity—for example, ranching—thus requiring the adverse effects of ranching on farming, to be reflected in its total costs. Another form of intervention, subsidy, would involve subsidizing the inefficient activity for each reduction in inefficient levels of its activity undertaken.

Neither the tax nor the subsidy policy involves a claim concerning the legal rights of the respective parties. Presumably the farmer would be entitled to farm as much as he would like to, and the rancher would be free to raise cows as he pleases. The tax or subsidy is intended simply to make it economically more feasible for the farmer and rancher to engage in their activities at the efficient levels.

In contrast, externalities or inefficiences may be controlled through the legal process by the imposition of either a *liability* or a *property* rule.[14] Both the liability and property rule techniques involve two steps. The first is assignment of a legal right to one or the other activity to act in a particular way; the second step involves a means for protecting the right once assigned. The alternatives differ with respect to the vehicles for protecting legal rights. A property rule protects an entitlement by enjoining others from interfering with the right bearer's exercise of the right except insofar as the right bearer may choose to forgo his liberty at an acceptable "price." A liability rule affords protection by entitling the right bearer to compensation should the liberty secured by the entitlement be abridged by others. In other words, the nonentitled party may reduce the value of the entitlement without securing the consent of the entitled party, provided he pays damages. Under liability rules, damages are set by a court and need not reflect the price the originally entitled party would have been willing to accept for the reduction in the value of his entitlement. While liability rules in effect permit nonentitled parties to bring about nonconsented to transfers of entitlements at prices set by third parties, property rules prohibit such transfers in the absence of mutual agreement.[15] If my right to my house is protected by a property rule, you may not do anything to it except as I permit you to. If, however, my right to my house is protected by a liability rule, you may do as you wish with it, provided you adequately compensate me for the infringements. We can further distinguish among liability rules. Some require compensation only if the infringement involves some kind of *fault*; others require compensation without regard to the injurer's fault.

Both the liability and the property rule assume that entitlements to efficient resource use have been assigned. They differ with respect to the vehicles employed for maintaining an efficient distribution of rights to resource uses under the dynamics of human interaction. Considerations of efficiency enter into the analysis of legal rights at two levels: first with respect to the efficient allocation of legal rights; then with respect to efficiency in the enforcement or protection of these rights. I want to confine the discussion to the common element in economic analysis of legal rights: the question of efficiency in allocating entitlements.

Richard Posner has advanced the following rule to guide the law in promoting efficient resource use in the absence of efficient private exchanges:

> Assign the relevant entitlements to that party who would have purchased it in an exchange market in which the conditions of the Coase Theorem were satisfied.

The idea is simple enough. Economic analysis relies on competitive market models of efficiency. Where efficient outcomes cannot be obtained and the law must intervene, entitlements are to be conferred to produce the result an efficient market would have. In an efficienct market, the relevant right would eventually have worked its way to the party who would have paid the most for it. The general principle, then, is to assign entitlements by simulating or mimicking the market.

The rationale for the principle is straightforward. The Coase Theorem demonstrates that, in the absence of transaction costs, any assignment of rights will be efficient. Resources will be traded to their highest value; that is, ultimately the person willing to pay the most for a resource will get it. Such a result would be efficient in the sense that no mutually advantageous trades could then be made, since an individual willing to pay any less for the entitlement would be incapable of rendering compensation sufficient to induce the high bidder to agree to part with the entitlement. When the market is incapable of securing the efficient outcome through exchanges, Posner's principle tells authorities to secure the efficient outcome *directly* by conferring the relevant legal right on the "high bidder," that is, that individual who would have purchased the entitlement in the market.

Posner's intention is to translate into the law so far as possible the implications of the Coase Theorem. But Posner's principle for assigning entitlements, what I have called the "auction principle,"[16] fails to duplicate crucial features of Coase's analysis. Most important, whereas the Coase argument relies on the model of exchange, on freely consented to Pareto superior moves to efficient or Pareto optimal outcomes, Posner's principle abandons Pareto superiority in favor of the Kaldor-Hicks standard. Assigning an entitlement to the person who ultimately would have purchased it in an exchange market is to assign it to a party who *could* have compensated the other party; that is, if he could purchase the entitlement at price, P, then he could compensate someone willing to pay less than P. For example, under Posner's rule, instead of the rancher purchasing the right to the fiftieth cow from the farmer and thereby compensating the farmer for the crop damage, the state entitles the rancher to the fiftieth cow, and the farmer goes uncompensated. The rancher *could* have compensated the farmer because he would have been able to purchase the right from the farmer—had the farmer initially been entitled to prohibit the cow. Consequently, the Kaldor-Hicks test is satisfied. Because the rancher does not compensate the farmer, and because wandering cows damage crops, assigning the right to the rancher makes him better off and the farmer worse off. Consequently, the Pareto superiority standard is *not* satisfied. To the extent the Posner principle replaces the Pareto test by the Kaldor-Hicks standard, it deviates from that aspect of the Coase argument.

Moreover, because of information problems, it is doubtful whether following Posner's rule can guarantee that the assignment of entitlements will be Pareto optimal; that is, it is doubtful that Posner's rule will duplicate the efficient outcome aspect of costless voluntary exchange. Suppose two individuals are vying for a right to use a plot of land in different, indeed incompatible ways. Following Posner's rule we are supposed to assign the use to the high bidder—as the market eventually would have done. In following Posner we abandon the market in an effort to mimic its outcome. Once we abandon the market, however, how are we to gather the pertinent information regarding the respective parties' willingness to pay? On the other hand, if a market exists, or can be established to determine relative willingness to pay, Posner's rule becomes otiose, since all the relevant ingredients of an exchange market are present. Posner's rule may be either otiose or unworkable.

Information problems also arise in determining the efficient level of activities. The efficient level of activities depends on the preferences of individuals who engage in them. For example, if we assume that R. F. desires to maximize revenue from ranching and farming, then, given the relevant prices, we can determine that he will raise fifty cows. If he had as well an aesthetic preference of cows to corn, then he would raise more than fifty cows. How many more would depend on a variety of factors. The traditional way of determining how many cows he would raise would be for him to reveal his preferences through market behavior. In following Posner we abandon the market in an effort to simulate its outcomes. But in this sort of case, where preferences are complex, we need the market to reveal the relevant preferences and to enable us to determine the efficient level of the relevant activities. This problem is further exacerbated by income effects.[17]

In short, if we follow Posner in assigning rights, we cannot be certain that we have duplicated the market in producing efficient levels of resource use; and, if we are fortunate enough to have done so, we would have achieved the Pareto optimal outcome by a Kaldor-Hicks rather than by a Pareto superior move. To that extent Posner's rule fails to replicate in law the special insight of the Coase Theorem.

In *theory* an efficiency-related intervention in the market might be justified because it constitutes either a Pareto improvement or a Kaldor-Hicks improvement, or because the effect of the redistribution of resources is Pareto optimal. In fact, however, almost no interventions involve actual Pareto improvements. Certainly interventions that follow Posner's rule do not. They involve the Kaldor-Hicks criterion.

The Kaldor-Hicks criterion is subject to the Scitovsky reversal problem. Consequently, the Kaldor-Hicks criterion does not provide an adequate linear ordering of states of affairs. It will not follow, therefore, that satisfaction of the Kaldor-Hicks criterion is adequate to justify preferring one state of affairs to another. Moreover, Kaldor-Hicks is not an index of utility. So an intervention in the market following Posner's rule would not be justifiable on utilitarian grounds. The fact that Posner's rule satisfies the Kaldor-Hicks test would therefore be inadequate to justify it.

Suppose we shift gears. Instead of arguing that the assignment of legal rights on the model of mimicking markets is justified because doing so constitutes Kaldor-Hicks improvements, a proponent of economic analysis would argue that the effect of such interventions is to produce Pareto optimal outcomes; and that interventions that follow the principle of mimicking markets are justified for that reason. This justification of assigning entitlements by mimicking markets relies, not on the efficiency of the *process,* but on efficiency of the outcome instead.

There are of course enormous information cost problems that suggest that in fact applying Posner's rule rarely results in Pareto optimal states of affairs. The problems with this defense of the auction rule go much deeper, however. We can understand the claim that the auction rule is justified because it produces Pareto optimal outcomes in two ways, depending upon the justification for pursuing Pareto optimal outcomes. If we understand the claim to be that the Pareto optimal outcome is justified on utilitarian grounds, that is, as the assertion that the optimal outcome maximizes utility, then the claim must be mistaken, since not every Pareto optimal outcome is utility maximizing. (This follows from the fact discussed above that one can achieve Pareto optimal results in a number of ways.[18])

If, however, we understand the claim to be that the intervention is justified because it is efficient, whereas the existing state of affairs is not, the argument turns on the proposition that every Pareto optimal state of affairs is, on efficiency grounds, preferable to every non-Pareto optimal one. That claim, however, is false.

Posner's rule comes into play when the market *cannot* reach a Pareto optimal outcome via exchange. At that point, the distribution is a non-Pareto optimal one. If we set aside information problems involved in applying Posner's rule, then when resources are redistributed in virtue of the assignment of rights, they are done so efficiently.[19] From an efficiency standpoint the optimal distribution is *necessarily* preferable to the nonoptimal one *only if* every Pareto optimal distribution is preferable to every non-Pareto optimal one. But as every welfare economist knows, only the set of points on the frontier that are to the northeast of points within the frontier constitute distributions preferable on efficiency grounds. So unless Posner's rule assigns entitlements that produce distributions to the northeast of the inefficient market situation, there is no efficiency-related reason for preferring the efficient outcome of the Posner rule to the inefficient market. And since Posner's principle satisfies the Kaldor-Hicks but not necessarily the Pareto superiority test, we have no way of knowing a priori that Posner's rule guarantees such assignments.

Current thinking about normative law and economics seems to me to face the following problem. On the one hand it tells us to design policy to promote efficiency. When asked why, the answer is that efficiency is ethically rooted in utilitarianism: that efficiency analysis is utility analysis without the problems of interpersonal comparability. As it turns out, however, of the various efficiency notions bandied about in economic analysis, only one, Pareto superiority, is connected to utility in a way that *might* be justificatory in nature. Unfortunately, the prevailing normative economic approach to law does not rely on the Pareto superiority standard—as indeed it cannot, since that standard, as is well known, is unworkable.[20] Instead, it relies on the one efficiency standard that logically *cannot* be an index of utility, namely Kaldor-Hicks. Moreover, to the extent that economic analysis relies on neither Pareto superiority nor Kaldor-Hicks, but on Pareto optimality instead, it afford us no utilitarian defense, since whatever claims about total utility one can make from Pareto optimality follow from its analytic connection to Pareto superiority. What is worse, any alleged justification of market interventionism that relies entirely on the optimality of the outcome is committed to the mistaken proposition that every Pareto optimal distribution is preferable (on economic grounds only) to every non-Pareto optimal one.[21]

NOTES

* Research for this paper was undertaken during a leave of absence financed by an N.E.H. research fellowship. I am grateful to participants in the law and economics workshop at Stanford University and at the University of Southern California for their helpful comments on earlier drafts of this paper.

1. For a more complete analysis of efficiency notions, see Coleman, "Efficiency, Exchange and Auction: Philosophic Aspects of the Economic Approach to Law," 68 *Calif. L. Rev.* 2, (hereafter cited as "Philosophic Aspects").

2. Here I am following Guido Calabresi and Phillip Bobbitt's means of characterizing the Kaldor-Hicks criterion in *Tragic Choices* (New York: Norton, 1977).

3. For a more complete discussion of the relationship of efficiency to moral theory, see Coleman, "Efficiency, Utility and Wealth Maximization" 8 *Hofstra L. Rev.,* 509 (1980).

4. There may be ways of increasing overall utility by making some people worse off. Determining which redistributions increase overall utility by making some people worse off and others better off, unlike the Pareto test, requires interpersonal comparability.

5. Still, the Pareto test enables us to linear-order states of affairs in terms of their utility. In other words, while we could not determine by how much total utility increases in going from S to either S^1 or S^2, and therefore determine on those grounds which is most preferable to S, provided that S^1 and S^2 are Pareto comparable,

we could linear-order by use of the Pareto standard S^1 and S^2 and determine on that basis which is most preferable to S.

6.   Provided, of course, that we rule out interpersonal comparability.
7.   The following utility/possibility graph illustrates the relationship among various efficiency distributions of resources:

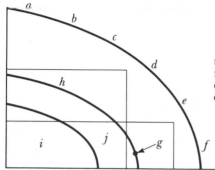

the utility/possibility frontier representing the set of all Pareto optimal distributions — e.g., distributions — a, b, c, d, e, and f.

   (i)   because c and e represents P.O. distributions they are Pareto noncomparable.
   (ii) c is P.S. to all points to its southwest, including h and i, but not g, with which it is Pareto noncomparable.
   (iii) e is P.S. to g and i, but not h. It is Pareto noncomparable.
   (iv) h and g are Pareto noncomparable; both are Pareto superior to i, but not to j, with which they are both Pareto noncomparable.

8.   Ronald Coase, "The Problem of Social Cost," 3 *J. Law & Econ* 1 (1960).
9.   Externalities are by-products of engaging in an activity that adversely affect the levels of production of other activities or the well-being of other individuals.
10.   This argument relies on the assumption that there are currently too many cows being raised.
11.   Proponents of economic analysis tend to make too much of this underlying reciprocity; critics of economic analysis make too little of it. See Coleman, "Philosophic Aspects," esp. sec. II.
12.   That is, there are instances in which assigning the relevant entitlement to either A or B will preclude further negotiations, since neither will part with entitlement at any price the other is willing to pay. This happens most often with tragically scarce resources, e.g., a bucket of water in the desert. Either distribution will be efficient in such cases.
13.   The idea is simple enough. Suppose I am interested in purchasing and then farming a plot of land you own. When we discuss purchase price, one question I ask you is who lives next door—Is

he a rancher or a farmer? If you answer "rancher," then I want to know whether his cows roam on the property. If you again answer in the affirmative, I want next to know whether he or I is liable for the losses to crops his cows cause. If you say he is, I offer you $X for the land; but if the loss lies where it falls, I offer you $(X − Y), where Y represents the costs of anticipated crop damage. If I want to increase my crop to the level it would have been had he, not I, been liable for the damages, I must bribe him to reduce his ranching accordingly. That will cost me $Y, so I am no worse off than before. And he no doubt had to pay an equivalently greater price for his ranch in the first place, because it came with the right to let his cows graze neighboring land.

14. These terms were originally introduced in the seminal piece by G. Calabresi and Malamed, "Liability Rules, Property Rules and Inalienability: One View of the Cathedral," 85 *Harv. L. Rev.* 1089 (1972).
15. The claim that the level of protection afforded by a liability rule cannot be reduced except by agreement depends on the rights being otherwise protected, for example, by criminal sanction.
16. Coleman "Philosophic Aspects," esp. sec. III.
17. "Income effects" describe the impact of one's relative wealth on one's willingness to pay to satisfy a particular preference.
18. See the discussion on pp. 85 and 86 above.
19. But it is unlikely that employing Posner's rule to assign entitlements produces a Pareto optimal outcome, since that supposes that once rights and duties are in place no gains can be obtained by further negotiations. Posner himself would argue that one purpose of his principle is to assign entitlements so as to facilitate *further* exchange.
20. This point has been made by Calabresi and Bobbitt in *Tragic Choices,* note 2, *supra,* and by Posner himself in "The Ethical and Political Basis of the Efficiency Norm in Common Law Adjudication," 8 *Hofstra L. Rev.* 487 (1980). See note 3, *supra.*
21. Whether it is time for lawyers enamored of the normative economic approach to law to abandon ship depends in part on whether these objections can be met. I consider this matter in "Strategies in Defence of Normative Economic Analysis of Law: Why They Fail," (unpublished manuscript).

PART II
UTILITY AND RIGHTS

5

UTILITY AND RIGHTS*

DAVID LYONS

Two notions concerning the relation of rights to utilitarianism seem widely accepted, by both utilitarians and their critics. The first is that utilitarianism is hostile to the idea of moral rights. The second is that utilitarianism is capable of providing a normative theory about legal and other institutional rights. This chapter chiefly concerns the second thesis, and argues against it. But it also says something about the first. In previous writings I have challenged the first thesis,[1] but here I shall suggest that it is sound. The upshot is that utilitarianism has a great deal of trouble accommodating rights.

SCOPE AND PLAN OF THE ARGUMENT

By "utilitarianism" I mean the theory that the only sound, fundamental basis for normative (or moral) appraisal is the promotion of human welfare. But my argument has implications beyond utilitarianism in this limited sense. It extends in the first place to a number of normative views that are closely associated with utilitarianism but not equivalent to it, such as normative "economic analysis" in the law. Second, it extends to many other "goal-based" theories and perhaps to other normative theories as well. All of these theories have trouble with legal as well as with moral rights.

Outside ethical theory—in economics and fields that economics has influenced strongly[2]—traditional utilitarian terminology and doctrines have sometimes been displaced by new ones. To a great extent, this change represents an attempt to secure behavioristic foundations for normative doctrines. Sometimes, utilitarian terms have been given a self-consciously behavioristic interpretation, as when references to "pleasure" and "pain" are replaced by a concern for individuals' "preferences" or one's "willingness to pay." In other cases, normative doctrines have departed from traditional utilitarianism, largely because of worries about "interpersonal comparisons of utility." For example, the utilitarian requirement that the overall net balance of pleasure over pain be maximized has been replaced, in some quarters, by notions of "economic efficiency," some versions of which do not require us (even in principle) to compare the benefits conferred and burdens imposed on one individual with those conferred and imposed on others. The result is a doctrine that is by no means equivalent to traditional utilitarianism. I believe, nevertheless, that my argument applies to these modifications and descendants of utilitarianism. Economists and theorists working in other fields frequently take normative positions that are, for present purposes, similar to those found within the utilitarian tradition. The problems that I discuss in this chapter are, so far as I can see, problems for their theories as much as they are for utilitarianism.

Later on I shall suggest how these problems beset a much wider class of theories, including some that are opposed to utilitarianism. These problems concern rights. My argument requires, however, that we distinguish two broad categories of rights, which I shall call "moral rights" and "legal rights."

Some rights are thought to exist independently of social recognition and enforcement. This is what I think we usually mean by "moral rights." These include the rights that are sometimes called "natural" or "human," but are not limited to them. Natural or human rights are rights we are all said to have (by those who believe we have them) just by virtue of our status as human beings. They are independent of particular circumstances and do not depend on any special conditions. The class of moral rights is broader, since it includes rights that depend on particular circumstances or special conditions, such as promises. Moral rights, in general, do not depend on social recognition or enforcement, as is shown by the fact that they are appealed to even when it is not believed that they are enforced or recognized by law or by prevailing opinion.

Utilitarians are seen as hostile to moral rights; I shall call this *The Moral Rights Exclusion Thesis* (*Exclusion Thesis* for short). Economic theorists who embrace doctrines similar to utilitarianism tend to ignore (rather than reject) the idea of moral rights. Moral rights have little, if anything, to do with normative doctrines of this kind.[3]

Other rights presuppose some sort of social recognition or enforcement, the clearest case being rights conferred by law, including constitutional rights. I restrict my attention here to legal rights within this general class.

It is generally assumed that utilitarians have no difficulty accommodating legal rights and providing a normative theory about them; I shall call this *The Legal Rights Inclusion Thesis* (*Inclusion Thesis* for short). Normative theorists working within economics and policy studies are concerned with telling us which legal rights should be conferred, and take for granted that their theories are capable of accommodating such rights. I shall argue that they are mistaken.[4]

The main part of my argument may be summarized as follows. The Exclusion Thesis assumes that moral rights make a difference to evaluation of conduct by excluding a range of direct utilitarian arguments that might militate against conduct (but not when it involves the exercise of rights) or that might justify conduct (but not when it would interfere with the exercise of rights). I call this the normative force of moral rights. The Inclusion Thesis assumes, by contrast, that legal rights are morally neutral and lack such force. But, when legal rights are regarded as justifiable or morally defensible, they are regarded as having moral force. In other words, the idea that legal rights are morally defensible entails the idea of a moral presumption in favor of respecting them, even though it may not be useful to exercise them or may be useful to interfere with them in particular cases. The problem for utilitarianism, then, is whether it can somehow accommodate the moral force of justified legal rights. I argue that it cannot do so satisfactorily. Although there are often utilitarian reasons for respecting justified legal rights, these reasons are not equivalent to the moral force of such rights, because they do not exclude direct utilitarian arguments against exercising such rights or for interfering with them. Specifically, utilitarian arguments for institutional design (the arguments that utilitarians might use in favor of establishing or maintaining certain legal rights) do not logically or morally exclude direct utilitarian arguments concerning the exercise of, or interference with, such rights. As a consequence, evaluation of conduct from a utilitarian standpoint is dominated by direct utilitarian arguments and therefore ignores the moral force of justified legal rights. The utilitarian is committed to ignoring the moral force of those very rights that he is committed to regarding as having moral force by virtue of the fact that he regards them as morally justifiable.

BENTHAM'S APPROACH

Of the classical utilitarians, Bentham is the one whose approach is most directly analogous to that of contemporary economic theorists as well as that of utilitarians who wish to provide a normative theory of legal rights. He accepted The Exclusion and Inclusion Theses. And so it is useful to begin with his ideas.

We are often reminded that Bentham dismissed the very idea of natural rights as "nonsense." One reason, of course, was his rejection of certain doctrines associated with natural rights, such as the notion that they are conferred by nature or discovered by the pure light of natural reason. But Bentham in effect rejected moral rights generally, that is, rights that do not presuppose social recognition or enforcement.[5]

Bentham's most direct, official reason for rejecting moral rights derives from his analysis of statements about rights and obligations. He held that meaningful statements about rights must be understood as statements about beneficial obligations, and he held that statements about obligations concern the requirements of coercive legal rules. He held that one has a right if and only if one is supposed to benefit from another person's compliance with a coercive legal rule. It follows that he could not recognize rights that are independent of social recognition or enforcement, that is, moral rights.

These analytical doctrines have no straightforward relation

to Bentham's utilitarianism. His analysis of rights neither follows from a principle of utility nor entails it. Nevertheless, it is arguable that, given his utilitarianism, Bentham could not have accepted the idea that we have any moral rights. It would seem that his utilitarianism commited him to The Exclusion Thesis.

One might argue for the incompatibility of utilitarianism and moral rights as follows. Moral rights are not merely *independent of* social recognition and enforcement but also provide *grounds for appraising* law and other social institutions. If social arrangements violate moral rights, they can be criticized accordingly. Moral rights imply the establishment of institutions that respect them. But Bentham held that institutions are to be evaluated *solely* in terms of human welfare. Unless we assume that arguments based on moral rights converge perfectly with those based on welfare, it would seem that a utilitarian like Bentham would be obliged to reject moral rights.

This reasoning appears, however, to assume rather than prove The Exclusion Thesis. Why should we suppose that arguments based on moral rights diverge from welfare considerations? The answer has to do with the normative character of rights. If I have a right to do something, this provides *an argumentative threshold* against objections to my doing it, as well as a presumption against others' interference. Considerations that might otherwise be sufficient against my so acting, in the absence of my having the right, or that might justify others' interference, are ineffective in its presence.

Consider, for example, the idea that I have a right to life. This entails that I may act so as to save it and that others may not interfere, even if these acts or the results would otherwise be subject to sound criticism. I need not show that my life is valuable or useful, and the fact that my defending it would have bad overall consequences or is otherwise objectionable does not show that my defending it is wrong, or that others' interference is not wrong. My right provides a measure of justification for certain actions of my own, as well as limits to interference. I call this argumentative threshold character the *normative force* of moral rights.

This point is sometimes distorted by exaggeration. Note, however, that my right to life does not automatically justify any course of action whatsoever that may be needed to save it; nor does it absolutely block justification for other's taking my life. Rights are not necessarily "absolute." That is why I speak of thresholds that need to be surmounted.[6]

Let us apply this to utilitarianism. From the standpoint of this theory we are entitled to assume that considerations of welfare are morally relevant, so that the promotion of welfare to a minimal degree provides justification for a course of action. Considerations like these are incremental. However, minimal increments of utility are incapable of surmounting the argumentative threshold of my rights. I may defend my life even at *some* cost to overall welfare, and others may not interfere *just* because it would promote overall welfare to *some* degree if they did. In this way, the arguments that flow from moral rights appear to diverge from those predicated on the service of welfare. If one accepts moral rights, one cannot accept absolute guidance by welfare arguments. And so we have The Moral Rights Exclusion Thesis.

Similar considerations apply to normative doctrines in economics and other fields that are developed in terms like "economic efficiency." If one believes that institutions are to be evaluated solely in terms of their promotion of such values, and not in terms of independent rights, one cannot accept the idea that we have any moral rights.

Bentham's attitude toward legal rights was of course different. His analysis of rights in terms of the beneficial requirements of coercive legal rules allows for the possibility of legal rights. And the general idea that utilitarianism is compatible with legal rights is hardly controversial, being widely assumed in law, economics, and political theory. Much the same idea is presupposed by what is called "the economic analysis of law" (though only the normative versions of "economic analysis" interest us here).

The Legal Rights Inclusion Thesis assumes that institutions serving the general welfare or economic efficiency are capable of conferring rights. Critics of utilitarianism as well as critics of normative economic analysis (including those who believe we have moral rights) do not challenge this assumption. They may claim that utilitarian or economically efficient institutions would establish some rights that ought not to be established (such as certain property rights) or would violate some rights that ought to be respected (such as rights to privacy or to personal autonomy), but they do not claim that such institutions are incapable of conferring any rights at all.

This is a plausible assumption, at least when it is coupled with a morally neutral conception of legal rights, by which I mean a conception that generates no moral presumption that those rights should be respected. Furthermore, the idea that utilitarian and efficient institutions confer rights leaves plenty of room for opponents of utilitarianism and of normative economic analysis to criticize those institutions, on the basis of moral rights or other values.

I am sympathetic to the morally neutral conception of legal rights, for reasons such as the following. The law of a society may be understood as implying that people have certain rights. But the law may be outrageously unjust and hence the rights it confers morally indefensible. There is absolutely no moral presumption favoring respect for those legal rights conferred by chattel slavery. Circumstances may of course provide some reasons for respecting morally objectionable entitlements. Those on whom such rights may be conferred are, after all, human beings who can claim some measure of respect and consideration from others too. But, while these considerations may affect what we ought to do in the context of morally outrageous institutions, they do not show anything about the moral force of legal rights themselves. So I am prepared to say that, from the fact that I have a right conferred on me by law, *nothing follows* concerning what I or others may do. We might put this point by saying that *merely* legal rights have *no moral force*.

Some writers do not share my view of legal rights, though their reasons are unclear.[7] In any case, if I am wrong about legal rights in this respect, then all have moral force. If we could assume that, my argument would be simpler. Since I deny it, I must limit my attention to those legal rights with moral force. These are legal rights that are taken to be morally defensible, the rights conferred by laws that are supposed to be justified. Let us see what this amounts to.

LEGAL RIGHTS WITH MORAL FORCE

Suppose that Mary rents a house that comes with a garage for her car. Access to the garage is provided by a private driveway, which she alone is authorized to use. Sometimes, however, she finds someone else's car parked in the driveway, which prevents her from parking or leaving with her own car. This may be inconvenient or it may not. Whenever it happens, however, Mary's rights are not being respected by other individuals.

Mary's rights depend on social arrangements, and they are enforceable by legal means. They thus qualify as legal rights. I shall assume, however, that these rights are *not merely* legal. I am supposing, in other words, that the social arrangements presupposed by Mary's rights and their enforceability are justifiable; those institutions or their relevant parts are morally defensible. This does not seem an implausible assumption to adopt. From the fact that Mary's rights are not shared by others, for example, we cannot infer that they are morally objectionable. I would suppose that ordinary rights like Mary's can arise and be justified in otherwise unjust as well as just societies, though this is not required for the argument. Within a society in which people have fair shares of the resources and considerable freedom to decide how to use their respective shares, for example, some individuals, with needs that are different from Mary's, may reasonably decide to make arrangements that are different from hers. And in such a society there may be good reason to have rights like Mary's made enforceable by law. Of course, Mary's rights are meant only as an example. If one has objections to private parking arrangements, it should be possible to substitute another example for the purpose. It is useful, however, to choose *very ordinary* rights, which clearly depend on institutional arrangements and legal recognition or enforcement. What I think we can agree about Mary's rights applies to many other routine legal rights, that is, to those we think of as morally defensible.

Given the arrangements that Mary has made, she may use the garage and driveway as she wishes. She may permit others to use them or refuse to do so. Others may not use them without her permission. In other words, Mary's rights make a difference to what she and others may justifiably do.

The principal assumption I shall make is this. When we regard Mary's rights as morally defensible, on any basis whatsoever, we also regard them as having moral force. The differences that her rights make to evaluation of conduct obtain, not just in the eyes of the law, but also from a moral point of view. We may disagree about the conditions that must be satisfied if legal rights are to be morally defensible. But if we hold that Mary's rights are morally defensible, then we are committed to agreeing that they have such force. Utilitarians and nonutilitarians will disagree about the conditions that justify legal rights. This is compatible, however, with their agreeing that certain legal rights are morally defensible. And the latter entails, as I shall assume, that such rights have moral force. To deny that Mary's legal rights have such force is to deny that they are morally defensible.

Mary's rights make a difference even when they are infringed. If others encroach upon her rights thoughtlessly or for their own private convenience, for example, it is incumbent on them to apologize or even, perhaps, to compensate her for any inconvenience she has suffered as a consequence. If they fail to do so, then they act wrongly. If compensation should be offered, then Mary is free to accept it or refuse it, as she prefers.

Of course, Mary's rights are limited. The driver of an emergency vehicle on an urgent errand might justifiably block Mary's driveway without first obtaining Mary's permission—even, perhaps, in the face of her refusal to give permission. This holds from both a legal as well as a moral standpoint. And, to simplify matters here, I shall assume that the legal limits of Mary's rights correspond perfectly to what we should regard on reflection as their proper limits from a moral point of view. Limits like these on Mary's rights are compatible with the idea that her rights make a difference to moral arguments. We need not assume that Mary's rights are "absolute" and overwhelm all conflicting considerations. My point is simply that Mary's rights entail an argumentative or justificatory threshold. Certain considerations are capable of justifying encroachments on Mary's rights, but not all are. Let us look at this more closely.

If one regards Mary's moral position from a utilitarian standpoint, then one might be presumed to reason as follows. Mary is fully justified in exercising her legal rights only when and in a manner in which she can promote human welfare to the maximum degree possible, and others are fully justified in encroaching on Mary's rights in the same sort of circumstances and for the same sort of reason.

This reasoning may be framed in probabilistic terms. What

may be thought required, then, is not that human welfare actually be promoted to the maximum degree possible, but that Mary's acts, when she exercises her rights, or the acts of those who encroach on them, be *most likely* to maximize human welfare (or something of the sort). This type of qualification will not, I think, affect the present argument, and I shall generally ignore it hereafter.

The utilitarian pattern of reasoning that I have sketched seems to clash with the idea that Mary's rights are morally defensible and thus have moral force. For it assumes that Mary's rights *make no difference* to what she and others may justifiably do, except insofar as the legal recognition of those rights changes circumstances so that certain possible courses of action have added utility or disutility. But this is not the way Mary's moral position is ordinarily viewed when it is assumed that her legal rights are morally defensible.

Suppose, for example, that a neighbor decides late at night to park his car in Mary's driveway, without obtaining her permission, in order to save himself a long cold walk from the nearest legal parking space. He might reason soundly that Mary is unlikely to be inconvenienced, since he shall move his car early the next morning. And that might turn out to be the case. Nevertheless, Mary might justifiably resent and complain of his presumption. Of course, Mary could reflect that she might have been seriously inconvenienced if an emergency had arisen during the night and she was unable to use her car. But it should not be assumed that her resentment would be justified solely by the possible inconvenience she might have suffered. For that might have happened even if she had given permission beforehand for him to use the driveway, in which case her resentment would not be warranted. Her belief is that her neighbor acted unjustifiably—that his action could not be justified simply by calculations of actual or probable utilities.

We can generalize these points as follows. Mary has the moral freedom to exercise her rights, within certain limits. Neither this freedom nor its limits can be explained by the utilitarian line of reasoning we have described. For example, Mary may act to her own disadvantage, without the prospect of compensating advantages to anyone else. Her rights also permit her some indifference to the effects of her choices upon others.

They permit her, for example, to inconvenience others while exercising her rights, without the prospect of compensating advantages to anyone, including herself. She need not act so as to maximize utility when she exercises her rights. Similarly, others may not act in certain ways without her permission, even if their doing so would maximize utility.

A utilitarian might object that he is not interested in Mary's rights as such but only in evaluation of her conduct and that of others. He might suggest that I have ignored the distinction between Mary's having rights and the conditions under which she justifiably exercises them. But I have framed my argument so as to respect that distinction. My point is not that Mary's rights completely determine what she and others may justifiably do but that her rights make a difference to the evaluation of her and others' conduct, a difference that unrestricted utilitarian reasoning cannot accept. The difference is not simple, since we cannot assume that Mary's rights are "absolute." In the present context, the difference amounts to this: from the mere fact that net utility would not be maximized by her exercising her rights, we cannot infer that her exercise of them is not justified; similarly, from the mere fact that net utility would be maximized by encroaching on her rights, we cannot infer that one is justified in encroaching on them.

One thing that complicates matters here is that Mary's rights, to be morally defensible, must have some foundation in human interests, needs, or welfare and are limited in turn by similar considerations. For this reason, utilitarian considerations are, *within limits*, relevant to a final determination of what Mary and others may justifiably do, which is bounded by a decent regard for others' welfare. Mary's decisions must give some respect to the interests of others, and what others may justifiably do is determined in part by the effects of their conduct upon people generally. Thus, despite her rights, Mary may not deny access to her driveway to someone in dire need, and others may use it without her permission if the need is pressing. But this is not to say that utilitarian reasoning *generally* determines how Mary and others may justifiably act. Let us suppose that *very substantial* utilities or disutilities outweigh the moral force of Mary's rights. We cannot infer from this that *minimal increments* of utility are sufficient to outweigh those arguments. To reason in that way would assume that Mary's rights make no difference to moral argument or, in other words, that her rights lack moral force. But, if I am right, Mary's legal rights have moral force if they are morally defensible.

It should be emphasized that I am assuming there is no moral objection to Mary's having such special control over her garage and driveway. I do not mean to suggest (and I have explicitly denied) that any arbitrary arrangements that Mary might secure under the law would have similar moral consequences. I would not suggest, for example, that if the law gave Mary comparable control over another human being—if, in other words, it regarded her as the owner of a chattel slave—then she would be morally free to decide, in a similar way, how to use that person. Even if the law regarded Mary in that way, we might reasonably deny that the legal arrangements make any difference to the way that Mary may justifiably behave, from a moral point of view. But our example is not like that. I have deliberately chosen to focus on an ordinary, mundane legal right that might plausibly be regarded as morally defensible.

It is also important to emphasize that I have not been discussing moral rights, that is, rights we are supposed to have independently of social recognition or enforcement. Nor is it suggested that Mary's rights arise of their own accord, without any foundation in fact. What is suggested, rather, is that, given the relevant facts in the social circumstances, which have to do with Mary's unobjectionably renting a house with a garage serviced by a driveway, she assumes a new moral position. She acquires rights, and her acquired rights appear to function as more or less stable moral factors with characteristic implications.

I have not claimed that there can be no utilitarian foundation for Mary's rights. It might be argued, for example, that the general welfare can be served by institutional arrangements that provide Mary with such special control over her garage and driveway. Let us now see how this argument would proceed, and what it might prove.

UTILITARIAN INSTITUTIONS

Although Bentham is widely thought to be committed to the pattern of utilitarian reasoning I have been discussing, he does not seem to deal with problems of the sort we have considered. Bentham and those who follow in his footsteps, including those wedded to normative economic analysis, are concerned with the evaluation of law and social institutions. In this connection, Bentham applies the standard of utility, not to individual acts taken separately, but rather to the rules and institutions that he thinks of as conferring rights. Those favoring economic analysis use a standard of efficiency in a similar way. They criticize, evaluate, and recommend legal rules in terms of some value that the rules are supposed to serve. These theorists assume, in accordance with The Inclusion Thesis, that rights would be conferred by institutions they regard as justified.

It does seem plausible to suppose that institutions conforming to utilitarian requirements or to the dictates of economic efficiency would incorporate rights. In the first place, when we consider possible institutions, we naturally tend to model them on those with which we are familiar, and these are generally assumed to confer rights. In the second place, and most importantly for present purposes, it seems reasonable to suppose that institutions designed to serve the general welfare or economic efficiency are capable of satisfying a *necessary* condition for incorporating rights. That is, the rules of such institutions might confer the proper range of freedom and impose the appropriate restrictions upon others' behavior that correspond to rights like Mary's. I know of no general argument that could deny this possibility.

When Bentham assumed that rights would be incorporated in utilitarian institutions, he proceeded on the assumption that rights exist whenever coercive restrictions upon behavior serve the interests of determinate individuals. It is difficult to imagine how institutions supported by the best utilitarian arguments could fail to create some useful restrictions, and it is natural to suppose that some of these restrictions would be useful by serving or securing the interests of specific persons. So, on Bentham's theory, it would seem that such institutions confer rights.

Economic theorists have not devoted much attention to the question of what it is to have a right. But it is reasonable to suppose that they have been guided by some conception of rights like Bentham's.

But we cannot pursue the basic issue here within the frame-

work constructed by Bentham. Our question is not whether
rights as Bentham conceived of them can be reconciled to
utilitarianism, nor whether rights as economic analysts conceive
of them can be reconciled with the principles of economic
efficiency. This is so for two distinct reasons.

In the first place, it could be said that Bentham took rights
a bit too seriously. He inflated their normative force into
coercive power. He imagined that, when I have a right, existing
legal rules provide for their enforcement. But enforcement is
not an essential feature of rights, not even legal rights. Rights
can be recognized by law even when no legal provisions are
made for their enforcement. Consider, for example, those civil
rights of U.S. citizens that are based upon the "equal protection
clause" of the Constitution. These rights went without enforcement for many years. The Civil Rights Acts and the Civil Rights
Division of the U.S. Department of Justice were intended as
means for securing these rights. Enforcement enhances these
rights and establishes new "secondary" rights, but it does not
create the basic constitutional rights themselves. Legal rights are
not necessarily enforced, and their enforcement need not even
be authorized. It follows that neither enforcement nor its
authorization is an essential feature of legal rights. Bentham
was mistaken. In consequence, at least part of the reason
theorists sometimes think they have for concentrating upon
legal rights while ignoring moral rights is an illusion.

In the second place, Bentham's analysis ignores the moral
force of rights under justified institutions. The question that
we face is whether utilitarianism or comparable theories can
accommodate legal rights with moral force.

This qualification is important, and it does not prejudice our
inquiry in any way that is unfair to utilitarianism or normative
economic analysis. The institutions that a utilitarian or an
economic analyst regards as fully justified are, presumably, his
best candidates for institutions that create rights with moral
force. If such a theorist regards some institutions as *justified* but
he *cannot* accommodate the moral force of legal rights conferred
by those institutions, then his theory is in trouble, faced with a
kind of incoherence. On the one hand, he wishes to claim that
the institutions he can justify would confer some rights. On the
other hand, his basic theory does not allow him to accommodate

the moral force possessed by legal rights in justified or morally defensible institutions. This is what I shall now try to show.

THE RELEVANCE OF DIRECT UTILITARIAN ARGUMENTS

The strategy of my argument is this. I shall suppose that a utilitarian or economic analyst believes that certain rights would be conferred by legal institutions that are justified by his basic normative principles. I take this to imply that the rights are to be regarded as morally defensible and thus that we can consider them as having moral force. I shall then try to show that this force cannot be accommodated by a normative position developed on the foundation of welfare or some comparable value such as economic efficiency.

For purposes of illustration, let us suppose that a utilitarian or economist believes that we can justify a set of institutions like those assumed in our example. Under the rules of those institutions, Mary has exclusive use of the garage and driveway attached to the house she is renting (though others' use of them is permitted under special circumstances, even without her permission). We shall assume, furthermore, that the freedom conferred by the rules on Mary and the obligations imposed by them on others match precisely what we should regard on reflection as the proper extent and limits of her rights when viewed from a moral standpoint. Mary is not required to worry generally about the utility of her actions or about economic efficiency when deciding how to use her garage or driveway or whether to permit others to use them. Nor are others expected to decide whether to use Mary's garage or driveway just on the basis of the utility of such conduct or its efficiency. And officials are not expected to decide on such grounds when they are called upon to apply or enforce the relevant, clear legal rules.

Unless something like this can be assumed, the idea that legal rights with moral force can be accommodated by a theory based on welfare or efficiency is defeated at the start. But the assumption appears reasonable. At least, I know of no general argument that could deny the possibility that such institutions as would be preferred by a utilitarian or by an economist might confer the proper range of freedom and the appropriate restrictions on others' behavior that correspond to the moral force of ordinary legal rights like Mary's. It should be emphasized, of course, that we are not supposing that such institutions would respect all rights that ought to be respected, including moral rights, which are independent of social recognition and enforcement, or that such institutions satisfy any other normative standards that a critic of utilitarianism or of normative economic analysis may endorse. These are concerns that a utilitarian or an economic analyst cannot be thought to share. Our strategy is to accept the normative approach of utilitarians and of economic analysts and to see where that leads us.

It must also be emphasized, however, that these assumptions do not settle the present issue. They imply only that such theories are capable of satisfying a *necessary* condition for accommodating legal rights with moral force. But our question is not whether utilitarianism or efficiency analysis could regard such institutions as justified or morally defensible. Our question is *what significance* such a theorist must attach to that fact when it comes to *evaluating conduct* in the context of those rules; for example, in determining how an official in such a system should behave.

A utilitarian or policy analyst might be thought to reason now as follows: "Institutions are justified if, or to the extent that, they promote human welfare or economic efficiency. Institutions ought to be designed so that official as well as private decisions will by and large promote such a value to the extent that this can be contrived. When that has been accomplished, conduct that is subject to the rules of those institutions can be justified only by reference to those rules. In other words, utilitarian and comparable arguments have their place, but they have no monopoly on justification. They do not always control the evaluation of conduct. When the rules are justified, they are to be followed. Their justified legal impact thus translates into moral force."

This is the approach John Rawls has suggested that a utilitarian would take to institutions that are justified on utilitarian grounds. In replying to the objection that utilitarianism allows the punishment of innocent persons, for example, he supposes that a utilitarian official who understands the utilitarian justification of the rules that he is charged with administering would abide by the rules.[8]

But the pattern of reasoning just sketched ignores some of the utilitarian considerations that are inevitably at work in particular cases that arise under such rules. For it is predictable that real social rules that are supported by the best utilitarian and economic arguments will require decisions in particular cases that would not most effectively promote welfare or efficiency. Such goals can sometimes be promoted more effectively by departing from the rules, or by changing them, than by following them. When that happens, a direct utilitarian or economic argument supports deviation from the rules.[9]

Suppose that a utilitarian official, or one who has adopted the precepts of normative economic analysis, is called upon to enforce the rules on Mary's behalf. He can understand perfectly the justification that he accepts for those rules. And his legal duty may be transparent. The rules vindicate Mary's claim, and he is legally bound to decide in her favor.

I do not see how such reasoning can settle matters for a utilitarian or economic-minded official. Suppose there are direct utilitarian or economic considerations on the other side—considerations sufficient to be appreciated by such officials, but not sufficient to surmount the justificatory threshold of Mary's rights. I do not see how our utilitarian or economic-minded official can regard these considerations as irrelevant to what he ought, ultimately, to do. He must regard them as providing arguments for deviating from existing rules, or for changing them, despite their justification. His primary aim, after all, is the promotion of welfare or efficiency. He must always consider arguments for promoting it directly, when he has the opportunity to do so. If so, he must be understood as prepared to violate Mary's legal rights—even though they are supposed to be morally defensible, from which it seems to follow that they have moral force and thus rule out unrestricted, direct, incremental utilitarian reasoning.

That is, a utilitarian official must be willing to reason as follows: "Mary's legal rights are clear, as is the utilitarian justification for allowing her to acquire such rights and to have them made enforceable by law. Even if this is an exceptional case, the same indirect utilitarian arguments continue to hold.

Utilitarian legislators would be well advised not to modify the
rules, should they have occasion to do so. These rules are as
well designed, from a utilitarian standpoint, as any such rules
can be. They cannot usefully be adjusted to take into account
every special case that may arise under them. And, taking the
utilitarian risks into account, it seems equally clear that welfare
would be better served by not enforcing Mary's rights in this
particular case." Acceptance of reasoning like this shows that
such a theorist cannot fully accept the normative implications
of his claim that Mary's legal rights are morally defensible. He
cannot regard Mary's rights as making that difference to the
evaluation of conduct that we supposed those rights do. For
such reasoning cannot justify an infringement upon Mary's
rights, though he is prepared to entertain it.

One might try to answer this objection in the following way:
"An official who faces such a decision has more utilitarian
reason to adhere to the rules than he has to depart from them.
For an official who understands the utilitarian arguments for
the rules appreciates that they assume general compliance on
the part of officials as well as private citizens. This provides him
with a general reason for believing that a departure from the
rules is likely to do more harm than good. Furthermore, in any
particular case it is likely that the direct utilitarian gains will be
seen to be outweighed by the direct utilitarian costs of departing
from the rules, resulting, for example, from frustrated expectations. It is therefore unreasonable to believe that a utilitarian
official would depart from the rules instead of enforcing Mary's
rights."

This argument requires that two points be made. In the first
place, from the fact that a sound utilitarian argument is available
for a legal rule it does not follow that utility will be maximized
by adhering to the rules in each and every case. Conditions
vary, and a sensitive utilitarian official will presumably be
flexible. In the second place, the original argument can be
understood as implying that officials *have an obligation* to comply
with morally defensible rules that establish rights—an obligation
that is not equivalent to the implications of direct utilitarian
reasoning. Like Mary's rights, this obligation is not "absolute";
it can be overridden by substantial countervailing considerations. But, given Mary's rights and this corresponding obligation,

direct, unrestricted, incremental utilitarian reasoning on the part of officials is ruled out. It is of course quite possible that direct utilitarian reasoning would yield conclusions that conform to Mary's rights; but this cannot be assumed. And the two modes of reasoning should not be confused.

A utilitarian might now reply in either of two ways. He might reject the pattern of reasoning that is entailed by talk of rights and obligations and maintain that we would be better off not to think in such terms. I do not address this issue here. My argument is meant to show certain difficulties that arise for utilitarian and comparable theories when they seek to *accommodate* rights (and obligations) under institutions they endorse.

Alternatively, a utilitarian might claim that a responsible utilitarian official would adopt a secondary principle (or perhaps a "rule of thumb") that requires him to adhere to the rules of utilitarian institutions. Such a principle, it may be said, is functionally equivalent to the idea that an official is under an obligation to adhere to the rules and to respect the rights they confer.

This line of reasoning seems, however, to concede the point at issue. To make it plausible, one must suppose that experience demonstrates that utility is best served in the long run if one reasons just as if one was under such an obligation. But systematic evidence to this effect is rarely, if ever, offered. A utilitarian who argues in this way appreciates the force of the original objection but retains the hope of *somehow* finding utilitarian arguments to meet it. He offers us no more than a promissory note, without any assurance that it can be honored.

Bentham never faced this issue squarely, and I do not think that Mill did either. They seem to assume either of two things: either that, once the rules are justified, they must be followed; or else that particular cases simply cannot arise such that the justified rules require one thing and the direct application of the utilitarian standard to those cases requires another. Bentham and Mill were, perhaps, prevented from considering such difficulties by the assumption that, once justified rules are established, the legal recognition of the rights they confer change circumstances so that certain possible courses of action have added utility or disutility. Thus, it may be thought that there is always sufficient utilitarian reason of a direct kind to

argue against deviation from justified rules. But this, as I have
already suggested, cannot be assumed. Moreover, reasoning
like this does not meet the point of the objection, which is that
once those morally defensible rights are established, certain
modes of reasoning are *illicit*.

Economists have not faced this issue squarely either. This is
because they have not generally considered the implications of
their economic "analysis" when it becomes a normative position.
They are thus faced with a significant theoretical decision.
Either they shall consider efficiency the sole fundamental basis
for normative appraisals, of conduct as well as of institutions,
in which case they must accept the consequences of the foregoing
argument. Or they must accept the idea that there are other
values to be served, beyond economic efficiency, in which case
they must entertain the possiblity of rights and obligations that
are independent of social recognition and enforcement, rights
and obligations that justified legal institutions ought to respect.

The problem I have sketched may be summarized as follows.
Normative theories that are founded on certain values, such as
welfare or efficiency, quite naturally regard legal rules or
institutions as justified if they are supported by the best arguments in those terms. But such theories do not generate any
obligation to adhere to the rules that they regard as justified.
And they cannot do so unless they are restricted for just such
a purpose.

THE RELEVANCE OF RULE-UTILITARIANISM

A type of theory that might seem to meet this objection is
"rule-utilitarianism." In its relevant forms, rule-utilitarianism
limits the application of the standard of utility to rules or social
institutions and *requires compliance* with rules that are certified
as having the requisite utilitarian justification. I do not mean to
suggest that such a theory is incoherent. But, before proceeding
further, we should distinguish two types of rule-utilitarian
theory, only one of which is directly relevant to the present
argument.

One type of rule-utilitarian theory seeks to accommodate the
idea of moral obligations (and, derivatively, moral rights). It

concerns itself with the "ideal moral rules" for a community or an "ideal moral code."[10] Another type of rule-utilitarian theory is concerned with established laws that can be defended on utilitarian grounds. It concerns itself with obligations to comply with useful social institutions. The latter, not the former, is most relevant here. For we are concerned with the question what difference it makes, from a moral point of view, to have laws and social institutions that are morally defensible. A rule-utilitarian of the first type does not address himself to this question, at least not in any direct way. But a rule-utilitarian of the second type in effect addresses himself to this question. This is the sort of rule-utilitarianism suggested (though not endorsed) by Rawls.[11]

My point about this sort of theory is that it represents a qualified utilitarian position. It does not follow from the more basic idea, common to all forms of utilitarianism, that human welfare is to be promoted. Nor does it follow from the more specific idea that social rules are to be evaluated in utilitarian terms.

What can be understood to follow from the fact that an institution can be supported by the best utilitarian arguments? If it follows that the rules must be respected (or at least that there is a moral obligation to respect them), then the utilitarian has a basis for claiming that his theory accommodates legal rights with moral force. But not so otherwise. The question may be understood as follows. If a utilitarian believes that certain rules are justified on utilitarian grounds, does he *contradict* himself by supposing that direct utilitarian arguments for deviating from the rules may be entertained? I see no contradiction here. If so, the utilitarian cannot understand the legal impact of such rules automatically to translate into moral force, not even when those rules are supported by the best utilitarian arguments. He cannot regard the morally defensible rights under *utilitarian* institutions as having moral force.

If so, The Legal Rights Inclusion Thesis must be qualified drastically, so that it becomes a morally uninteresting platitude. It cannot be understood to say that utilitarianism and comparable theories accommodate legal rights with their moral force intact, even when those rights are conferred by rules regarded as justified under such theories. It can be understood to say only that utilitarianism and comparable theories accept the possibility of justified institutions with rights that must be regarded as *merely* legal, devoid of moral force. For these theories do not allow the rights conferred by justified institutions to make the requisite difference to the evaluation of conduct that such rights are ordinarily assumed to do.

We can apply this to Rawls's argument, in which he suggested that a utilitarian official would abide by the rules of institutions he regards as justified. We can understand Rawls's argument in either of two ways. He might be taken as suggesting that regarding rules as justified on utilitarian grounds *logically commits* one to abiding by their implications in particular cases. I have just tried to show that this is a mistake. Alternatively, Rawls might be understood as proposing that utilitarians *restrict their theory* so that it applies to rules or institutions but not to conduct under them. This is, I believe, a reasonable way of reading Rawls's suggestion, and the foregoing argument implies that it is the more generous of these two alternative readings.

For nothing in the idea that welfare is to be promoted restricts the application of the standard of utility to social rules or institutions. If such a restriction is *adopted* by a theorist who sees himself as working within the utilitarian tradition, that involves the *addition* of a factor that a utilitarian is not obliged to accept, either by the constraints of logic or by the normative implications of his theory. In the absence of such a factor, a utilitarian cannot ignore direct utilitarian arguments.

Imposing such a restriction on the idea that human welfare is to be promoted is either arbitrary or else is motivated by a desire to accommodate the moral force of rights and obligations under justified rules. In its relevant forms, rule-utilitarianism represents a compromise—a recognition that the utilitarian approach is incomplete at best and, unless it is restricted, cannot accommodate the moral force of morally defensible legal rights and obligations.

Similar considerations apply to normative theories based on the goal of economic efficiency. If the moral force of legal rights and obligations under justified institutions is to be accommodated, then those theories must be restricted. And restricting them reopens general questions about the standards to be used in evaluating institutions themselves.

It may be thought that I have overstated my case. I have suggested that a utilitarian (unless he restricts his theory to accommodate objections) will evaluate conduct by means of direct utilitarian considerations—in effect, by "act-utilitarian" reasoning. But, it may be objected, from the fact that an institution is supported by the best utilitarian arguments it must be thought by a utilitarian to follow that one has reason to conform to the rules of that institution. I have ignored, it may be said, the direct practical implications that the utilitarian justification of social rules or institutions has for a utilitarian.

If this were correct, then the most that could be claimed is that utilitarianism gives rise in such contexts to *conflicting* considerations. The foregoing reasoning would not show that direct utilitarian arguments concerning conduct are *excluded* by a utilitarian justification of the institutions within the context of which that conduct may take place. It would show only that such arguments must be weighed within utilitarianism against arguments flowing from the utilitarian justification of those institutions. Then the most that could be said for utilitarianism is either that one who follows its dictates would not violate the rights it regards as justified as often as my argument implies (thought he would violate them sometimes) or else that utilitarianism is indeterminate in such cases, in which event it would not require that such rights as it regards as morally defensible ought to be respected.

If they are sound, such consequences cannot offer much comfort to the utilitarian. But are they sound? I think not. To see this, we must distinguish between (1) a reason for maintaining an institution and (2) a reason for conforming to institutional rules. It is reasonable to suppose that the utilitarian justification of an institution provides a utilitarian with a reason of type (1), that is, a reason for maintaining that institution. But we cannot assume that a reason of type (2) likewise follows. The utilitarian justification of an institution provides a reason for conforming to that institution *only if* conformity to its rules is required, in the circumstances, for maintaining that institution. But this is just what we cannot assume. For it is possible for the rules to be violated (by officials or private individuals) without threatening the institution—more precisely, without threatening its utility. In such a case, the utilitarian justification of the institution provides the utilitarian himself with no reason for conforming to its rules—not when greater utility accrues to deviation from them.

Someone might approach this issue differently. One reason why indirect utilitarian considerations, concerning rules and institutions, do not converge with direct utilitarian considerations, concerning individuals' conduct, is that real social rules must be simple enough for the practical guidance of ordinary mortals and also typically involve social costs. These costs include sanctions designed to coerce officials and private individuals into following the law when they may be tempted to act otherwise. A person might therefore reason that an official would be strongly constrained to follow rules that are predicated upon serving human welfare when those rules have been properly designed. One might suppose that a utilitarian institution would be contrived so as to make it very undesirable for an official to depart from rules that he is charged with administering. Useful sanctions might seem to insure that Mary's rights would be respected.

But we cannot assume that such expedients will do the trick. In the first place, we cannot assume that maximally useful rules, or rules supported by the best utilitarian arguments, would always be sufficiently constraining to prevent deviation from them. In the second place, someone who is guided by utilitarian considerations should not be influenced so decisively by considerations of self-interest as this suggestion assumes. He should be willing to accept a risk himself, for the sake of serving the *general* welfare more effectively, as the direct utilitarian arguments that counsel infringements on Mary's rights show possible.

Alternatively, one might assume that an official would not deviate from rules that he is charged with administering, because he would think it *wrong* to do so. One might suppose, for example, that an official would regard himself as having accepted a position of public trust, which involves obligations that he cannot in good conscience ignore. He might see himself as morally bound by his commitment to adhere to the rules as he finds them. But, if we suppose that such a factor is at work in our example, then we are assuming, in effect, the influence of *non*utilitarian arguments. If the argument suggested here is to make any difference, it must be based on the idea of an independent obligation that does not follow from the considerations already canvassed. To have recourse to such obligations, however, is to concede that utilitarian principles need supplementation before we can secure a normative theory that is capable of accommodating ordinary legal rights with moral force.

EXTENSION OF THE ARGUMENT

As we have already observed, this argument would not seem limited to utilitarianism, but concerns also the relationship of rights to other closely related theories, such as economic analysis when offered as a normative approach to law or social policy. But the considerations that extend the argument that far suggest that it must extend much further.[12] The argument would seem to concern all "goal-based" theories that satisfy two conditions: (1) the goal or goals accepted by the theory as the basis for appraising institutions are capable of being served not only through institutional design but also by the actions of individuals when their conduct falls under the scope of the institutional rules; (2) the goal or goals do not (separately or together) entail some value that demands respect for rules that are favorably appraised in relation to them. The latter condition is vague, and I am not sure what sort of goal might fail to meet it. It simply seems necessary to allow that some goals might satisfy condition (1) but would also require respect for the rights conferred by institutions that serve those goals, in the way that welfare, happiness, economic efficiency, and the like do not.

To illustrate the way the argument might be extended—imagine that we dedicate a legal system to the service of social and economic equality—a useful example, since this value is often contrasted with utility and is believed to conflict with the latter in practice. The same sorts of problems concerning rights accrue to a theory based on promoting substantive equality as attach to one based on human welfare or economic efficiency. For the rules of institutions might be contrived to serve social and economic equality as far as it is possible for rules to do, but

it would still be possible for social and economic equality to be
served (perhaps in small ways) by deviation from those rules in
particular cases. There is nothing about the basic value to be
served that requires respect for all the rights that may be
conferred by such institutions.

If we explored this issue further, we might find that a very
wide range of goal-based normative theories have the same
trouble with legal rights. We might also find that other sorts of
theories (e.g., "right-based" and "duty-based" theories) face
similar difficulties.

What all of this seems to show is that normative theories
require a more complex character than those we have considered
if they are to accommodate the moral force of legal rights under
justified institutions. Many theories fail to account for an
obligation to adhere to rules that are regarded by them as
justified. From the assumption that rules serve appropriate
values it does not seem to follow that there is the requisite sort
of obligation to adhere to them, an obligation that gives due
respect to the morally defensible rights conferred by those rules.

If a utilitarian (or other goal-based) theory of *moral* obligations
were possible, it might fill the gap just noted. It might explain
how we have moral obligations to comply with social institutions
that are predicated on serving the general welfare, for example.
We cannot assume that a utilitarian theory of moral obligations
would generate precisely this obligation, but the possibility of
a normative utilitarian theory of legal rights would be revived.

This development is ironic, for it rests the possibility of a
normative theory of *legal* rights upon the possibility of a theory
of *moral* obligations, though the former is usually thought to be
much less problematic than the latter. In any case, it brings us
round full circle. We began by noting the traditional utilitarian
attitude toward moral rights, embraced by Bentham, which is
similar to the traditional utilitarian attitude toward moral obligations (when obligations are not confused with whatever happens to be required by some sort of normative principle). Like
rights, obligations have a normative life of their own, with
implications that are neither reducible to, nor traceable by,
direct considerations of utility. It does not follow, however, that
a utilitarian theory of moral rights or obligations is impossible.

MILL'S THEORY OF MORAL RIGHTS AND OBLIGATIONS

In previous works I have offered a sympathetic reading of Mill's theory of morality and justice, in order to challenge the usual view that utilitarianism is incapable of accommodating either moral rights or moral obligations. (In recent years emphasis has been placed on rights, but obligations received more, and similar, attention a half century ago.) I would like now to summarize that argument briefly and show why it seems to fail. Considerations relevant to the main argument, concerning legal rights, apply here too.

Mill's theory is promising because (under the interpretation I have offered) his way of trying to accommodate moral rights and obligations is not a form of ad hoc revisionism motivated by the desire to evade substantive objections to utilitarianism. It is not a form of revisionism at all, but turns on a theory of the moral concepts, the relations among which establish constraints upon any normative theory. Instead of adopting (what has since been thought of as) the standard utilitarian approach to moral reasoning—instead of assuming that one is always required to promote a certain value to the maximum degree possible—Mill begins by sketching a stratified analysis of normative concepts.

Mill's general idea can be understood as follows. We can distinguish three levels of normative concepts and judgments. For present purposes, the bottom (most concrete) level concerns the rightness or wrongness, justice or injustice, morality or immorality of particular acts. The intermediate, second level consists of moral principles, which concern (general) moral rights and obligations. Judgments of right and wrong conduct at the bottom level are functions of moral rights and obligations, and of nothing else. (Since moral rights are assumed to be correlative to obligations, but not vice versa, this can be put solely in terms of obligations.) A particular act is right if and only if it does not breach a moral obligation, unless that obligation has been overridden by another obligation. But moral principles are not self-certifying; they turn upon values they somehow serve (Mill is least clear about this relation). The topmost level of normative judgments and concepts concerns the values that may be invoked to establish moral principles (which concern general moral rights and obligations). For Mill, of course, the value at work at this topmost level is human happiness or welfare. So, moral principles about general rights and obligations are supposed to have a direct relationship to the principle of utility. But judgments concerning the rightness or wrongness of particular actions have *no* such relation. Acts must be judged as right or wrong depending on whether they respect moral rights and obligations, and *never* on the basis of direct utilitarian reasoning.

This feature of Mill's reconstructed analytic theory is vital to the possibility of a utilitarian account of moral rights and obligations. It insures that Mill's theory does not collapse into act-utilitarianism. It insures, more generally, that the evaluation of conduct in his theory is not dominated by direct utilitarian considerations. Mill's way of insuring this is by conceptual analysis, which leads to the claim that moral concepts are so stratified that interactions are possible between adjacent levels but are absolutely prohibited between the top and bottom levels. Without this conceptual foundation, his theory would either collapse into act-utilitarianism or amount to just another, more or less arbitrary, revision of utilitarianism.

Mill's conceptual claims provide a necessary (though not a sufficient) condition for accommodating moral rights and obligations, if we assume that moral rights and obligations possess normative force (which Mill suggests). In the present context, that makes possible the hope that his theory will generate a moral obligation to conform to the actual rules of institutions that can be defended on utilitarian grounds, so that the theory will require respect for the rights conferred by such rules.

The success of Mill's theory thus turns upon the truth of his conceptual claims. But these seem stronger than the moral concepts can bear. It is plausible to hold that what is right or wrong is at least in part a function of moral rights and obligations (this is what is meant by the normative force of moral rights and obligations). But it is not so plausible to hold that the concepts involved *completely prohibit* the direct appeal to ultimate values, such as human welfare, when evaluating conduct. On the view I have ascribed to Mill—the one that promises a way of accommodating moral rights and obligations—someone who evaluates conduct by means of direct utilitarian arguments is guilty of a conceptual mistake. He is not reasoning unsoundly; he is reasoning *fallaciously*. But this appears excessive, to say the least; and yet nothing short of this will secure Mill's moral principles from being dominated by direct utilitarian considerations.

Consider, for example, our imaginary utilitarian official. When he takes into account the effects of his conduct on human welfare while trying to decide what to do, he does not seem to be confused or to be violating the constraints of the moral concepts. If he places too much weight upon direct utilitarian considerations, that may be a moral error, but it does not look like a conceptual mistake. As a utilitarian, it seems incumbent on him to consider the effects of his conduct on welfare. If so, we have no reason to believe that direct utilitarian considerations will not dominate his moral reasoning. Thus, we have no reason to believe that a satisfactory utilitarian theory of *moral* rights and obligations can be developed. So we have no reason to believe that a utilitarian would be obliged to respect the moral force of justified *legal* rights and obligations.

SUMMARY

A utilitarian might be assumed to reason as follows. "I will have no truck with 'moral rights,' which are figments of unenlightened moralists' imaginations. I am concerned with human welfare, with promoting it as far as possible, and I approve of social institutions to the extent they serve that purpose. Those institutions are morally defensible, and no others are. Under them, people have rights—not imaginary, toothless rights, but real, enforceable rights."

This was Bentham's attitude (though not Mill's), and it fits the normative thinking found most generally in the literature of "economic analysis." The trouble is, it ignores a central normative issue, what conduct is required or permitted by the theory that endorses those allegedly justifiable rights.

Economists might be excused for neglecting this issue—at least until it is pointed out to them—since they tend to think only about rules and regulations and to ignore how principles apply directly to individuals' conduct, perhaps because they have not approached their normative conclusions from a self-consciously normative standpoint. But utilitarians have no such excuse. As Bentham was aware, the aim of promoting some value like human welfare is as relevant to individual acts as it is to social institutions; the latter application does not rule out the former. But, unless utilitarianism is restricted, its direct application to conduct undermines respect for the very rights it wishes to endorse.

NOTES

* This is a revised version of a paper presented to the annual meeting of the American Society for Political and Legal Philosophy on January 4, 1980. An earlier version with a narrower focus, entitled "Utility as a Possible Ground of Rights," was published in *Nous*, 14 (March 1980), 17–28. In arriving at the views developed in these articles, as well as in revising them, I have been helped considerably by comments I have received from a number of individuals. These articles developed out of earlier presentations on the subject of utility and rights at the University of Texas, the University of Virginia, Colgate University, and Cornell University. On those occasions I sought to extend the utilitarian account of rights I had earlier extracted from John Stuart Mill's writings. Criticism of Mill's theory of moral rights led me to question the less controversial assumption about legal rights that is principally discussed here. I wish especially to thank John Bennett, Jules Coleman, Stephen Massey, Richard Miller, and Robert Summers for their comments on previous drafts.

1. See my "Human Rights and the General Welfare," *Philosophy & Public Affairs* 6 113–29 (1977) and "Mill's Theory of Justice," in A. I. Goldman and J. Kim, eds., *Values and Morals*, (Dordrecht: Reidel, 1978), pp 1–20.
2. See, e.g., Richard A. Posner, "Utilitarianism, Economics, and Legal Theory," 8 *J. Legal Stud.* 103–40 (1979) which also provides references to some of the relevant legal and economic literature.
3. It is sometimes suggested that economic analysis is capable of taking full account of competing normative claims, such as claims about justice or moral rights, by treating them as expressions of individuals' preferences (preferences frustrated when institutions

would be regarded by such individuals as violating moral rights or breaching other moral principles). See, e.g., Guido Calabresi and A. Douglas Melamed, "Property Rules, Liability Rules, and Inalienability: One View of the Cathedral," 85 *Harv. L. Rev.* 1089–1128 (1972). But this is inadequate. Someone who claims, for example, that slavery is morally unacceptable because it violates basic human rights may be expressing a preference against slavery, but he is doing more than that. He is claiming in this context that considerations of efficiency alone *could not justify* slavery. The question to be faced is not whether slavery will frustrate preferences but whether that claim is true. To understand this as a question about preferences (even enlarging it to include the preferences of people other than those who embrace the claim) is to look at these matters from the standpoint of economic analysis, and thus to beg the very question at issue, namely, whether economically efficient institutions can be morally unacceptable *because* they violate rights.

4. It is sometimes suggested that when we speak of "moral" rights we are referring to rights that ought to be conferred and enforced by social institutions. On this view, a utilitarian's normative theory of institutional rights is equivalent to a theory of moral rights. This notion does not affect the present argument. I believe it, however, to be mistaken. To say that rights ought to be *respected* is not to imply that they ought to be *enforced* (even by extralegal institutions). Respect for rights can simply amount to doing what the corresponding obligations require, and from the fact that one is under an obligation (even an obligation correlative with another person's rights) it does not follow that any sort of coercion, strictly speaking, is justified for the purpose of insuring obligatory performances or penalizing nonperformance.

5. For Bentham's analysis of rights, see my "Rights, Claimants, and Beneficiaries," 6 *American Philosophical Quarterly*, 173–85 (1969), and H. L. A. Hart, "Bentham on Legal Rights," in A. W. B. Simpson, ed., *Oxford Essays in Jurisprudence* (Second Series) (Oxford: Clarendon Press, 1973), pp 171–201. Bentham did accept the idea of "natural liberties," but only in the sense that one is "free" to do whatever is not restricted by coercive social rules.

6. The sort of exaggeration cautioned against here is unfortunately suggested by Ronald Dworkin's speaking of rights as "trumps" against utilitarian arguments. See his "Taking Rights Seriously," in *Taking Rights Seriously* (Cambridge, Mass.: Harvard University Press, 1978), pp 184–205. But, as Dworkin makes clear, he does not assume that rights are generally "absolute"; see, e.g., pp 191–92. My suggestion that rights have normative (or moral) force derives from Dworkin's discussion, but differs from it in several

ways. (1) I distinguish moral from legal rights and attribute moral force to legal rights only when they are morally defensible or justified. (2) The normative force of rights cannot be understood simply in terms of their relation to utilitarian arguments but must be considered more generally; my discussion attempts to allow that. (3) Dworkin's distinction between "strong" and "weak" rights corresponds roughly to the two aspects of normative force in my discussion: "strong" rights provide obstacles to the justification of others' interference, while "weak" rights provide justifications for one's own behavior. Dworkin's argument seems to rely on both aspects of the normative force of rights.

7. Dworkin seems to assume that all legal rights have moral force. See his "Reply to Critics," *Taking Rights Seriously*, pp 326–27.

8. See John Rawls, "Two Concepts of Rules," 64 *Philosophical Review* 3–32 (1955).

9. This point does not depart from the main thesis of *Forms and Limits of Utilitarianism* (Oxford: Clarendon Press, 1965), in which I argued for the "extensional equivalence" of certain principles that I called "simple" and "general" utilitarianism. The extensional equivalence argument was extended to cover a limiting case of rule-utilitarianism—a theory (dubbed "primitive" rule-utilitarianism) in which no consideration is given to such things as the complexity or cost of rules. Rule-utilitarian theories that concern themselves with ordinary, manageable social rules were explicitly excluded from the scope of that argument. Thus, *Forms and Limits* argues, in effect, that direct and indirect utilitarian arguments are *sometimes* equivalent. Along with this chapter, however, it assumes that they are *not always* equivalent.

10. See, e.g., R. B. Brandt, "Some Merits of One Form of Rule-Utilitarianism," *University of Colorado Studies, Series in Philosophy* 39–65 (1967).

11. In "Two Concepts of Rules," note 8, *supra*.

12. I owe this suggesttion to Jules Coleman.

6

UTILITARIAN JUSTIFICATIONS FOR OBSERVANCE OF LEGAL RIGHTS*

KENT GREENAWALT

David Lyons's interesting chapter provides a very helpful analysis of the scope and limits of utilitarian justifications for the creation, observance, and enforcement of legal rights. The essay tries to establish that a utilitarian cannot, consistently with his overall position, maintain a particular thesis about the relation between moral justifications and legal rights. Professor Lyons believes that few people will confortably relinquish this thesis and that the utilitarian's inability to accept it faces his own theory "with a kind of incoherence."[1] Because of the importance Lyons claims for it, we must attend very carefully to the precise relation that the utilitarian is said not to be able to accept and ask ourselves whether its rejection does involve some radical nihilism about the moral significance of legal rights. We can then begin to understand how utilitarian accounts of legal rights may differ from accounts that accept the thesis Professor Lyons regards as crucial and to assess the potential and adequacy of utilitarian accounts against our common moral sensibilities.

Briefly stated, my own view is that much less conflict exists between a utilitarian account and common moral understanding about legal rights than Lyons supposes, that utilitarian theory can, in ways that his own essay largely reveals, do a much better job of explaining the moral significance of legal rights than he acknowledges. My response assumes that the utilitarian will not accept the thesis Professor Lyons discusses but will argue that the account that can be built without it is more satisfactory than he supposes. Though I follow Lyons in concentrating on utilitarian theory, I agree with him that the questions he raises have broader relevance, touching many other goal-oriented positions about the proper ends of social institutions.[2] I also agree that insofar as various versions of restricted or rule-utilitarianism avoid the dilemmas he proposes, they tend to do so by fiat (or by debatable empirical and normative judgments). As Lyons says, the dilemmas are most sharply put for an act-utilitarian, and I address them from that perspective. Though I am skeptical that any utilitarian or broadly consequentialist account can entirely explain the moral sentiments that citizens and officials do, and should, have toward legal rights, I attempt no supplementation here, rather contenting myself with the argument that the unembellished version comes much closer to adequacy than one would gather from Lyons's essay.

The heart of his position is that utilitarians (and others with relevantly similar positions about the justification of social institutions) cannot accept legal rights that have "moral force." What Lyons means by this is that for the utilitarian legal rights have no moral authority over people, no power to determine the moral justifiability of their acts, *independent* of the effect such rights may have upon considerations of welfare, which the utilitarian regards as the basis of morally justifiable acts. Lyons claims that this denial would be strikingly at odds with ordinary understandings about the moral significance of legal rights, and that it would greatly depreciate the importance of legal rights for determination of morally justifiable acts. There may indeed by some divergence between the utilitarian position he stakes out and unreflective views about legal rights, though the divergence is no greater than that traditionally analyzed between common views of moral obligation and the utilitarian position. Whether the utilitarian position diverges very much from more carefully considered views about the moral significance of legal rights is more doubtful, since, contrary to what Lyons intimates, legal rights can be tremendously weighty factors in moral deliberations for the utilitarian.

Lyons addresses four different questions that are usefully distinguished: Can utilitarianism justify a system of legal rights? Can it account for an official's moral responsibility to enforce those rights? Can it account for the moral responsibility of others to respect those rights? Can it explain morally justifiable insistence on respect by those who hold the rights?

The first question, Lyons concedes, itself causes no difficulty for the utilitarian; but a brief summary of why utilitarianism is compatible with a system of legal rights helps us to approach the other three questions. Since human beings are largely self-interested and limited in knowledge and understanding, they need in many respects relatively clear rules for what they can do and cannot do, and they need the support of centrally organized sanctions to assure that the rules are observed by those who might benefit from breaking them.[3] Legal rights help establish for a society what one citizen can expect of another, and typically (though not always, because not every legal right is enforceable) they mark occasions for the intervention of public force. Without legal rights (especially of property and contract), economic planning of any complexity would be impossible; and we cannot imagine an advanced economic society in which they were absent.[4] Thus, it has never been a tenet of utilitarianism that the general welfare could best be promoted if individuals and government officials simply made a series of ad hoc decisions based on act-utilitarian principles; the usefulness of previously established and generally applicable norms governing classes of circumstances and conferring rights has been much too obvious to permit such a doctrine. This much is uncontroversial.

Where Professor Lyons believes that the utilitarian runs into trouble is over the import of legal rights for justified behavior. Mary's right to use her driveway freely is employed to illustrate the difficulties. I shall follow him in focusing upon legal rights whose establishment is morally defensible under a utilitarian standard and in the more stringent assumption that these rights are not ones whose legal redefinition could better serve utilitarian objectives. Even when these conditions are met, the utilitarian, according to Lyons, cannot admit the moral force of legal rights, because he will find occasions when welfare objectives will best be served by nonobservance of the rights and, as a utilitarian, will be committed in those situations to serving the welfare objectives, not respecting the rights.

This position would entail acceptance of possibilities of nonenforcement of rights that Lyons thinks would constitute a stark departure from our understanding of official roles. But it is far from clear that officials would act much differently if they did accept the utilitarian position or that their actions, even when they failed to enforce rights, would meet with sharp criticism from reflective citizens. Once the official is operating within a system in which strong expectations are (desirably) created, he has extremely powerful reasons for satisfying them, both to avoid the harmful consequences (resentment, insecurity, retaliation) that flow when individuals are denied the enjoyment of institutionally created expectations and to support the system that creates those expectations (if "rights" are too often frustrated, individuals will know they cannot be relied upon and the potential benefits of rights will be lost). Moreover, understanding his own limited capacity to make welfare calculations and the demands on his time and energy, the official may reasonably adopt the view that enforcement of guaranteed rights (which, after all, reflect in some way societal views about welfare) will more reliably promote welfare than action based upon his own fallible judgment.[5] If this analysis is sound, legal rights will make a very great difference to the morally justified acts of officials and to their perceptions of which acts are likely to be justified. Almost always acts consistent with those rights will be justified, and appear to be so, and almost always acts at odds with them will not be justified, nor appear to be so. But this influence on moral deliberations is not what Lyons means by "moral force." However modest the official is about his own judgment, however strong the utilitarian reasons for enforcement of legal rights, still on some occasions the official may be firmly convinced that nonenforcement is the welfare-producing course, and utilitarianism (not qualified by fiat) commits him to that course.

This position is less disturbing than Lyons supposes. Many officials do not, in fact, afford citizens the complete benefits of their legal rights, and their actions are thought morally defensible. Suppose Mary in Professor Lyons's hypothetical is a small-town dweller who is both something of a fanatic about legal rights and a regular vacationgoer. Every summer she visits her parents in California for the first four weeks of August, and her neighbors and the police know her home is then unoccupied.

Her nearest neighbors hold a birthday party each year on August 10 and allow guests to park in Mary's driveway, and one year Mary learns of this upon her return. Too embarrassed to speak directly to the neighbors, she calls the police the following summer from California at the time the party will be going on and asks them to make sure any cars in her driveway are moved. Even if the police will normally perform this service for homeowners, can they not justifiably refuse to act when the violation of right seems so unimportant? If Mary were seeking enforcement of a part of the traffic code designed to protect interests like hers, the part that forbids parking on a public street in a manner that blocks a driveway, the police refusal to act would fall within the generally accepted discretion of the police (and prosecutors) not to invoke the criminal process. Approval of this discretion depends partly on considerations of resource allocation, but also upon the belief that some technically criminal acts (even under ideally formulated penal provisions) simply do not warrant treatment as crimes. The resource allocation point undoubtedly applies to official initiatives to enforce private rights like Mary's right against trespass; the police should not waste their time getting the cars moved if they have better things to do. Since the police will always have something else to do, resource allocation may dispose of all practical issues, but it is important to recognize that the intrinsic inappropriateness of enforcement may also reach this far. In some circumstances, the violation of right may be so trivial and the disruption of private activities required for enforcement so considerable that officials might rightly decline to get involved, even if they had no other demands on their own time and energy.

No doubt Professor Lyons is thinking mainly of officials who need not take the initiative in this sense, whose basic responsibility is to respond impartially to claims of violations of rights by citizens. And whatever he thinks of my analysis of police responsibilities, he probably would regard it as largely beside the point. After all, the police do not deny that Mary has a right and that it was unjustifiably violated; they only refuse to get involved. Judges typically do not have this option; they are called upon to declare if a violation has taken place and, assuming they have jurisdiction over the case, must give an answer. Even judges and juries, however, in their power over remedies may be able to render less than effective enforcement. A right may be declared in court, but if actual damages are slight and the "successful" claimant is given neither an injunction nor exemplary damages because he is regarded as something of a nuisance for pressing his claim, he will (because of litigation costs) be effectively discouraged from trying the next time, and so will others in like circumstances. Such dispositions, like police non-enforcement, need not involve refusal to recognize the legal right; and perhaps it is that action that Lyons believes is especially precluded by the moral force of legal rights.

But do we really suppose that judges should never refuse to give effect to legal rights? Imagine a landlord's right to evict, a remedy that is made undeniably applicable if certain conditions are met. We shall suppose both that broad "humanitarian" exceptions written into the law would be undesirable (giving rise to too much uncertainty, too many evidentiary disputes, and too many delicate questions of line drawing) and that most landlords are humane enough not to evict in really compelling situations. In the case before the judge, however, the landlord seeks to evict a chronically ill and recently widowed tenant. The judge firmly believes that eviction at that time from her family dwelling of long standing might cause serious physical and psychological damage, but the case plainly falls outside the very limited emergency situations in which the eviction can legally be postponed. This is the rare sort of situation in which a judge might conclude that the benefits of subverting a (morally) well-drawn law outweigh the damage that will be done. While the issue may be debatable, the position that the judge should somehow avoid enforcing the law, perhaps fitting the case into a statutory exception to eviction where it plainly does not belong, is an appealing one. Since the utilitarian reasons for judicial recognition of legal rights under well-drawn laws will always be quite powerful, it will take very strong reasons on the other side to persuade the utlitarian judge to decide that welfare will be served by refusal to enforce; and when we really think hard about such situations, we may doubt that the utilitarian judge's decision not to enforce would conflict with the reflective moral judgment of most people.

If we think about citizens deciding whether to respect legal rights, is the utilitarian position less acceptable? I think not. Many legal scholars believe that as far as most contract rights are concerned, compliance with the terms of a contract is less desirable than paying damages if compliance would be uneconomical; but I shall pass over these rights and concentrate on the rights against intentional torts on which Lyons focuses and for which his view is most plausible. When we imagine a situation in which Mary (the right-holder) cares about her right, knows about violations, and resents them, we have a strong utilitarian argument against violations that she will (or may) discover, whatever other damage may be done to her interests. In those situations no slight reason of personal convenience can provide a moral justification for violation, because minimal increments in utility cannot outweigh the basic utilitarian reasons in favor of compliance. But how many of us walking in the country would feel any real moral compunction about taking a shortcut across private land, that is, committing a technical trespass, if we knew we would do no damage; were sure we would not be seen; and thought, in any event, the owner would probably not mind? And if, contrary to every reasonable expectation, we came upon the owner and he expressed his annoyance, would our embarrassment and apology be accompanied by real remorse? Professor Lyons has oversimplified the moral and legal universes in supposing that people genuinely acknowledge a substantial moral constraint against violation of any legal right they think is morally defensible. If I am right about this, again the utilitarian position is much less removed from common understanding than he leads us to believe.

Lyons may seem on strongest ground when he suggests that Mary is justified in exercising her legal rights even if that will not promote the general welfare, a conclusion that he says the utilitarian must deny. We have to be careful here about the proposition the utilitarian is committed to denying. Given human selfishness, ignorance, and irrationality, the utilitarian can certainly support institutions that create rights protecting some selfish and arbitrary actions. So he has no problem saying that from the institutional or official point of view, Mary is justified in exercises of rights that are not conducive to welfare. But the utilitarian is committed to saying that Mary has not behaved morally if she has so acted. Even here, we should remember that the utilitarian might approve some apparently arbitrary exercises of rights in the following way. Mary, realizing her deepseated, perhaps irrational, possessive feelings about her rights, knows that she will feel frustrated and resentful if they are blatantly violated; though she would suffer no tangible harm, she calculates that her discomfort if a violation is allowed will outweigh the disadvantage to the violator if he is stopped. Mary, or any other person making moral decisions on a utilitarian basis, is not precluded from treating such feelings as an aspect of welfare. Nevertheless, it is doubtful if these grounds will support all the exercises of Mary's rights that are apparently non-welfare-producing *and* seem justified. Surely she is sometimes justified even when her exercises will, in fact, have a negative effect on welfare overall. Professor Lyons has here exposed a real problem for the utilitarian, but the problem concerns the general difficulty of the position that individual actions are never morally justified unless their net effect on the general welfare is positive (or at least indifferent), not any special inability of utilitarianism to explain the moral significance of legal rights.

Professor Lyons is not an absolutist about rights. He acknowledges that moral rights can be overridden by compelling reasons, that legal rights can be subject to exceptions within the law (Mary's right does not apply if an emergency vehicle uses her driveway), and that some morally indefensible legal rights (e.g., to own slaves) do not have moral force. Although he does not take a position about the much more common instances of rights that are morally defensible in general but whose scope is less than ideal, he seems doubtful that such rights have moral force with regard to the aspects that are not morally justified. Even when legal rights have moral force, Lyons says that very strong reasons on the other side may outweigh the reasons for compliance. Yet he finds grave difficulties in a position that the scales of utility should be used to weigh the reasons for and against observing and enforcing legal rights whose scope is morally appropriate. Why he sees such grave difficulties, I am not quite sure. Though I grant that the act-utilitarian would have to deny the thesis that legal rights have moral force (in Lyons's very special sense), he can nevertheless produce, along lines imperfectly sketched here, an entirely coherent account of the relation of morality to legal rights, an account that comes much closer to reflective common understanding than Professor Lyons realizes. This account may not be fully satisfying, but we can better understand its limits and the respects in which it needs replacement or supplementation if we do not fall into the mistake of dismissing it as obviously untenable.

NOTES

* My contribution is an expansion of remarks I made as a member of the audience at the annual meeting of the American Society for Political and Legal Philosophy on January 4, 1980. Like David Lyons's essay, it has evolved somewhat since then, but remains a comment upon his essay rather than any more ambitious undertaking.

1. Lyons, "Utility and Rights," p. 120, in the present volume.
2. Many of the supporters of these other positions would, however, acknowledge that satisfying previously created expectations has some value apart from its effect on whatever goods they think should underlie the initial creation of expectations. Thus, a believer in "efficiency" or "equality" is not committed to the view that already created expectations should be disregarded whenever disregard would contribute to efficiency or equality. He may, therefore, be able to escape the dilemmas Lyons suggests more easily than the person who takes utility as an "ultimate, overriding moral principle." D. Lyons, *Forms and Limits of Utilitarianism*, 155 (1965).
3. See generally the account of H. L. A. Hart in *The Concept of Law* 181–97, (1961).
4. Even if human character could be so completely reformed that coercive sanctions would become unnecessary, a highly implausible idea, people would still need authoritative rules to direct and constrain many of their activities.
5. I am not here raising the possibility that individuals will most often come closest to judgments that are correct under an act-utilitarian standard if they deliberate wholly in other terms. I am assuming that the official remains self-consciously an act-utilitarian, but revises his initial judgment when he reflects on his limited capacity. See generally Lyons, *supra* note 3, at 67, 119, 145–49, 156–57.

7

UTILITY AND RIGHTS: COMMENT ON DAVID LYONS'S ESSAY

R. M. HARE

I must confess to a certain difficulty in handling Professor Lyons's objections to utilitarianism. He is a thoughtful, sophis-, ticated, and well-read philosopher (much better read than I am). He shows himself, not only in other writings of his, but in this very chapter, to be conversant with some possible replies to his objections. Neither the objections, nor the replies to them, nor Lyons's replies to the replies, are new—only restated in a somewhat more involved way. The argument is in its essentials an old one, going back at least to Mill and Bentham. What puzzles me is why Lyons should think his objections damaging to a careful utilitarian. And it puzzles me still more that so many people—perhaps the majority of moral and legal philosophers at the present time—should think that utilitarianism can be defeated by arguments about rights which, once the position is fully understood, have little power. The only explanation must be that they have *not* fully understood the position; so I am going to have another try at explaining it. In doing so I shall introduce only one move that is not to be found in Lyons's essay, and this move is not new either (it could be argued, but not here, that it goes back to Plato). I myself have explained it in previously published articles and shall be doing so more fully in my forthcoming book, *Moral Thinking: its Levels, Method and Point.*[1] This move is the distinction between different levels of moral thought, the intuitive and the critical. It is just possible that not seeing this distinction is what has led people to rely on such weak arguments; but I am not sure.

Sometimes, in our moral thinking, we simply apply moral principles, intuitions, feelings, reactions, dispositions (it makes no difference to the argument which of these terms we use) that we have learned or acquired in the course of our moral development. The principles in question have, for their purposes, to be fairly, but not extremely, general; that is to say, the reactions are attached to relatively broad, and perhaps not very exact, characterizations of actions and circumstances. The reason for this is that a highly specific response to highly specific situations could not be learned and, even if it could, would not be useful. Moral upbringing and development consists, in part, in the acquisition and building into our characters of responses of a fairly general sort (e.g., a repugnance toward lying or cruelty) that will be activated by situations resembling one another in certain broad features, though not necessarily features that are easily captured by a verbal description.

It is important to notice that these dispositions, though if they could be expressed they would be expressed by moral principles or universal prescriptions, are by no means the same thing as dispositions to verbalize such prescriptions. If all that someone is disposed to do is to *say* "I ought not to tell this lie" when faced with an opportunity for telling a lie, then he just does not *have* the principle (he is not a truthful person; he lacks the virtue of truthfulness).

Nor is it enough to have, for some extrinsic reason (e.g., to keep out of trouble), a constant *practice* of not lying. What is needed in addition is a firm disposition, backed up by quite strong feelings and deeply embedded in his character, to pursue truthfulness for its own sake. That is why I was sorry to see Lyons using the expression "rules of thumb." I regret having myself used this phrase, even in a different connection,[2] and it is certainly out of place here. Rules of thumb are used by engineers and others to save time and effort and get approximations to the right answers to questions of fact or practice. They do not represent the true *motivations* of those who for convenience follow them; they are not deeply engrained in their characters, do not excite compunction or remorse if broken by themselves or indignation if broken by others; they have little in common with what I am speaking of and would much better be left out of this discussion.

In most of our moral decisions we think intuitively in this way; and it is highly desirable, at least from a utilitarian point of view, that we should. It would be not only impossible for lack of time but dangerous, because of our notorious tendency to special pleading in situations of stress and temptation, to proceed in any other way. A wise act-utilitarian educator, seeking in his educative acts to promote utility (however defined) will do his best to inculcate in himself and others sound general dispositions and the feelings that go with them. If he is successful, the people so brought up will count as well brought up and will be much more likely in the course of their lives to promote utility than somebody who takes a lot of time off to do felicific calculations. But nearly all of our acts are to some degree educative, in that they have an effect on the moral attitudes of ourselves and others. So a consistent act-utilitarian will reason that it is highly probable that any act of his in relation to lying will have quite far-reaching effects on people's attitudes, including his own. It is an empirical assumption that this is likely; I believe it, but am not called upon as a philosopher to justify it. The fact that most of us believe it amply accounts for our fostering, even if we are utilitarians, of the disposition not to depart from the principle without the strongest grounds.

Some people, though I am sure that they do not include Lyons, have been superficial enough in their thinking to try to erect on this basis an argument *against* utilitarianism. It is obvious that if an act-utilitarian could justify, in terms of his own theory, acts of following and fostering the disposition, it is an argument *for* the theory to point out that we tend to do and approve of such acts—that is, it is an argument *against* those who claim that utilitarianism is at variance with our common moral notions. It would be a very inept utilitarian who was put out of his stride by the thought that his utilitarianism could often require him to follow his intuitions, as the most likely way of hitting off the optimific act, rather than do a cost-benefit analysis on the spot.

The account that intuitonists (which is what nearly all anti-utilitarians are) give of the intuitive level of moral thinking is for the most part correct: we do have intuitions, and it is right in general to follow them nearly all the time. Where the intuitionists go wrong is in neglecting the *other* level of moral thinking, which I call the critical. The intuitive level cannot in principle be self-supporting. The somewhat general principles that are the content or basis of our intuitions frequently conflict in particular cases (an inevitable consequence of their generality and the extreme variability of the world). But even if another level of thinking were not required to deal with such conflicts, it would be required in order to satisfy us that the principles embodied in our intuitions are the best ones so to embody. How are we to be sure that the people who brought us up were wise? Some people, after all, have very pernicious intuitions—that it is, for example, quite all right to discriminate against blacks. How are we to be sure that any one of our intuitions is not like that one? Those who have challenged our intuitions about what it is all right to do to dumb animals should at least have taught us to ask such questions.

I have written in the places referred to above of what goes on in critical thinking when rationally done and have tried to show that its rationality is founded on the logical properties of the moral concepts. Here I need only to put the question: *Suppose* that the rational method of critical thinking, which appraises our moral intuitions and adjudicates between them when they conflict, is utilitarian, as I think it is, what, then, must we say of Lyons's arguments and others like them? I hope to show that they become very weak.

These arguments consist essentially in appeals to received opinion. The answer to them all is to point out that the opinions in question may indeed be received ones, but that a utilitarian can easily explain both the fact that they are received and, in the case of most but not all of them, the advantages of their being received. If, as I think, the intuitive principles that nearly all of us employ are, for the most part, sound ones from the utilitarian point of view (i.e., good utilitarian reasons can be given why we should cultivate them), then critical thinking, if utilitarian, will give our intuitions a fairly clean bill of health, but will pinpoint a few that we ought to think again about (e.g., about the place of women in the home).

But before we can understand the application of all this to Lyons's argument, we shall have to make clear some distinctions that might be obscured to readers by his use of expressions like "the moral force of legal rights." This could be taken, in the writings of some natural law theorist, as meaning that no distinction can be drawn between the legal and the moral spheres; but obviously Lyons does not so intend it. It could, secondly, be taken as meaning that the according by courts and legislatures of certain legal rights is morally a good thing, can be morally justified, and so forth. Clearly, Lyons does not mean this by it, because he says that utilitarians cannot account for the moral force of legal rights, and yet allows that a utilitarian could, consistently with his theory, provide reasons why these legal rights morally ought to be accorded. Thirdly, it might be taken as meaning that, given that (as a matter of historical fact, which he is prepared to grant may be of itself morally neutral) legislatures and courts have accorded certain legal rights, individuals (including policemen and other officials) have a prima facie moral duty to preserve these rights to other individuals by respecting and enforcing the law. It seems to be this third thing that Lyons means.

If so, then this restatement enables us to clarify, but also to undermine, his thesis that utilitarians cannot give an account of the moral force of legal rights. We are then to take him as granting that utilitarians *can* give an account of why legislatures and courts *do*, and even of why they *ought* (morally) to accord certain legal rights (and therefore that in *that* sense what he calls *The Legal Rights Inclusion Thesis* is immune to the arguments in his essay); but as maintaining that in a historical situation in which they have done so, it could still be the case, according to utilitarians, that officials, policemen, and others ought to disobey the laws.

Let us, with this interpretation of his argument in mind, address ourselves to his example of Mary and her driveway. What he is then saying is that, although utilitarians can perhaps give a moral reason why Mary should be *accorded* her right to the unobstructed use of it, they cannot give any moral reason why other people, including policemen, should *respect* and *enforce* this right in cases where utility might be marginally increased by not doing so. Since we all have moral intuitions to the effect that they should, he hopes thereby to display utilitarianism as having counterintuitive consequences.

This position is, however, undermined by the separation of levels of moral thinking. At the intuitive level most of what antiutilitarians say is correct; and at that level we do not need to, and shall often be wise not to, use utilitarian considerations, even if we are act-utilitarians. For we shall know that in all but the most extraordinary cases (and Lyons's own intuitions, which incorporate a "threshold," allow him to make an exception of these) the most *likely* way of getting the optimific act is to follow our intuitions. If this is not so, then our upbringing has not been as good as it should be; for its object ought to have been to give us those intuitions, to follow which would be most likely to have this effect. If I am asked how I know that most of our existing intuitions are such as to lead us to do optimific acts on the whole, I answer that I do not know, but think it to be so. I think this because I have some experience, supplemented by that of others going back through the centuries, of how the world actually goes. I appeal neither to philosophy nor to sociology but to common knowledge (though this is open to correction by sociologists if they are to be trusted).

If anybody doubts that in the case of Mary's driveway a sensible act-utilitarian would follow these intuitions, I ask him to say what else he would do. Perhaps the policeman, instead of enforcing Mary's legal right without further ado, ought to sit down on the sidewalk in the posture depicted by Rodin, and do an hour or two's deep critical thinking; perhaps he should call up headquarters from time to time on his radio to get all the information he would require about the consequences of alternative actions, which his magical colleagues have somehow obtained?

It would be obvious to an act-utilitarian that this would not, from the viewpoint of his own theory, be the best way of proceeding, though of course policemen should be encouraged to do some critical thinking about the moral principles applicable to their vocation when there is leisure for it. And it would also be obvious to an act-utilitarian that the best moral equipment for a policeman who has to face such embarrassing situations is a firm grasp of people's rights and of the right ways to set about enforcing them. "Rights" here could mean "legal rights" or "moral rights"; the well-instructed policeman will have a good practical grasp of both (within the limits to which any man of action is subject), and of the distinction between them. And there is nothing to stop act-utilitarians from applauding well-instructed, conscientious, and in other ways virtuous policemen, and holding them up as examples to the rest of us. We too, even if we are act-utilitarians, will do right to cultivate sound intuitions and traits of character. But some policemen and others (e.g., in racist societies) have *bad* intuitions; and when we ask which are the sound ones, we shall have, in order to answer, to do come critical thinking.

I might have argued on different, but related lines that if Lyons grants, as he does grant, to the utilitarian that he can account for the moral justification of the *institution* of legal rights, then he must at the same time grant that there is a moral duty in general to respect and enforce the rights. For to have a morally justified system of legal rights but no moral duty to enforce or respect them in particular cases would be self-defeating. In other words, the moral duty to enforce and respect is part and parcel of the "moral force" of the system itself. Suppose we were to say to the legislators, "You have a moral duty to establish a system of legal rights, but *we*, the people, shall then have no moral duty to respect and enforce them"; the legislators will reasonably reply, "In that case, what is the point of our establishing the system? For if people do not acknowledge a moral duty to respect and enforce the rights, no mere legal sanctions are going to make the system work. There aren't enough policemen; and those that there are will not do their job very conscientiously if all they are thinking about is what penalties they will incur if they take it easy."

I have not used this argument, because it is effectively covered by what I have said already. According to utilitarians, a moral justification can be given, in terms of the benefits secured, for having a system of legal rights. But the benefits will evaporate if in particular cases people do not have and, except in unusual cases follow, the moral intuition that the law ought in general to be obeyed. In nearly all ordinary cases an act-utilitarian, well brought up by other act-utilitarians, can say to himself "I have a strong moral intuition that I ought to respect this legal right; it is most probable that to go against the intuition would have effects, including the most important side effect of impairing respect for law, that would make it less than optimific; so my best bet as an act-utilitarian is to follow my intuition."

I do not think I have said anything unfamiliar in this comment. But in case I have, let me summarize my defense of utilitarianism against objections based on appeals to our intuitions about the moral force of legal rights. The moral duties to which this moral force gives rise are always founded on intuitive principles (above all, on the principle that we ought, in general, to obey the law). At the intuitive level it is a sufficient justification for an act that our moral intuitions require it. But if they conflict, or if a justification is asked for having and following *those* intuitions, we have to ascend to a higher level and employ critical thinking, which is based on the logical properties of the moral concepts, and, if I am right about those properties, is utilitarian in its method. This explains why legal rights have a moral force, not only in the sense, which seems not to be Lyons's, that the according of them can be morally justified, but in the sense that there is a prima facie duty to respect and enforce them in particular cases. That there is this prima facie duty is a consequence of the facts, if they are facts, that (1) the according of the rights by legislatures and courts could be morally justified by critical thinking; (2) that the cultivation of the intuitive principle that we morally ought in cases like this to obey the law could be likewise justified; and (3) that in the case as described the probability is that to follow such intuitive principles would yield the optimific act. Lyons has not given, and I shall be surprised if he could give, any reason to suppose that all these are not facts in the case he adduces. But if they were not, then what (for Lyons as much as for a utilitarian) would have become of the legal right's moral force? Might he not have to question it, if (1) the law according the right were a bad one, or (2) the intuitive principle that we morally ought to obey the law were one that morally ought not to be cultivated, or (3) the case were such that one would obviously do best not to respect or enforce the right (Lyons himself provides some cases of this sort).

As a parting shot (but not at Lyons, because he does not here employ that kind of argument), let me insist that nobody be allowed to doctor the example, by introducing bizarre features into it, so that it becomes clearly the case that the optimific act (i.e., what it is best to do) is one that infringes Mary's rights. For, first of all, it is conceivable that bizarre problems require bizarre solutions, and Lyons rightly allows the possibility of a threshold beyond which we are allowed to disregard rights for utility's sake. And, second, the fact (if it really is a fact) that in such bizarre cases our intuitions come down in favor of respecting legal rights proves nothing; a sound moral upbringing is designed to cater for cases that are likely to occur, and a well-brought-up man will be in some perplexity if confronted in real life (not in philosophy books) with bizarre cases.

There are, on the other hand, as Lyons realizes, other perfectly ordinary cases, not bizarre at all, in which most of us would find it in accordance with our moral intuitions to infringe somebody's legal right. Lyons mentions emergency vehicles; but since these have in many jurisdictions a legal right to park where they need to, a better example is provided by my taking a shortcut between two right-of-way footpaths across my neighbor's field when out for a walk. I am infringing his legal right in so doing, but I know it will do him no harm and that he will not object. These same factors that remove the disutility of infringing the right make most of us think that I do no moral wrong in infringing it. Here too our intuitions have a threshold built into them.

If I were in a case in which it would obviously be for the best, counting in all the side effects, which are often considerable, to infringe somebody's legal rights, but in which my intuitions told me clearly and unambiguously that I ought not to do it, I might be led to question the applicability of my intuitions about rights to that case, which would have to be a very unusual one. But to anyone with a proper awareness of human fallibility it would have to be very obvious indeed (for our intuitions are on the whole reliable); and I do not expect to find myself in such a case often. I think it will be hard to find a case that does not admit of one of these two ways out: either to say, "In spite of appearances, if you count in the side effects it probably will be for the best to follow your intuitions"; or to say, "The case really is so out of the way that it does not come within the scope of your intuitions about rights." But in a difficult case it will take a wise man (a man with very good judgment about what is actually likely to ensue) to say which of these ways out is the appropriate one.

NOTES

1. See "Principles," *Proceedings of the Aristotelian Society* 73, (1972–3); and "Ethical Theory and Utilitarianism," in H. D. Lewis, ed., *Contemporary British Philosophy* 4 (London: Allen & Unwin, 1976), p. 113, and *Moral Thinking: its Levels, Method and Point* (Oxford: Oxford University Press, forthcoming).
2. R. M. Hare, *The Language of Morals* (Oxford: Oxford University Press, 1952), p. 66.

8

CAN UTILITARIANISM JUSTIFY ANY MORAL RIGHTS?

ALAN GEWIRTH

The difficulties of providing an adequate answer to the question posed in the title of this chapter stem at least in part from the complexity of its main terms. It is well known that there are many varieties of utilitarianism, and this multiplicity is further complicated when we try to fit historical utilitarian thinkers under one or another of these versions. In addition, there are different senses in which utilitarianism, in any of its variants, may be held to "justify" certain actions or policies. Also, there are many different kinds of rights and of moral rights, and there are familiar problems about the nature of rights and how their "existence" can be proved or justified. And besides all these difficulties, there is the problem of just how rights differ from utilitarian norms. For if the difference between them cannot be clearly established, then it is also difficult to accept the apparent implication of the title-question, that "utilitarianism" is one kind of thing and "moral rights" another.

While I cannot hope to deal with all these difficulties here, I shall try to make at least a dent in them by examining the chapter by David Lyons.[1] I shall use his essay as a way of bringing out and resolving some of the chief problems about the justificatory relation of utilitarianism to rights. One of my main points will be that progress on this question requires a fuller awareness of the distinction between the two relata than is displayed in Lyons's paper.

To provide an initial, neutral focus for the discussion, let us begin with the following formula for the general structure of a right (in its basic form of a claim-right): "A has a right to X against B by virtue of Y." This formula contains five main elements or variables: first, the Subject or the right-holder (A); second, the Nature of the right; third, the Object of the right, what it is a right to (X); fourth, the Respondent of the right, the person or persons who have the correlative duty to act or to forbear as the right requires (B); fifth, the Ground or justificatory basis of the right (Y). (I capitalize each of these variables in order to make more explicit their roles in the following discussion).

While the Nature of a right involves many complexities, for initial purposes we may characterize it as a justified claim or entitlement to some Object. Correlative duties are incumbent on Respondents to act or to forbear in ways required for the fulfillment of the justified claim.

I

Like other antiutilitarian theorists of rights, Lyons is confronted by what I shall call the *Utility-Rights Dilemma.* The Objects of rights either are or are not components of human goods or welfare. If they are such components, then the appeal to rights is really an appeal to utility, so that the rights theorist must be a utilitarian after all. For on this view, since the Objects of rights are goods or welfare components, they can be weighed against, and possibly be outweighed by, other components of human goods or welfare. Consequently, the obligatoriness of fulfilling any right will be contingent on a calculus whereby that action is obligatory that produces the most good, even if this involves infringing the right. If, on the other hand, the Objects of rights are not components of human goods or welfare, then the question arises as to why rights are important and wherein lies the obligatoriness of fulfilling them. If the Objects of rights are of no value, contribute nothing to human welfare, then what good are rights? I shall refer to these two alternatives, respectively, as the "welfare horn" and the "nonwelfare horn."

Lyons's position seems to fall now on one side of this dilemma, now on the other. On the one hand, he seems to uphold the nonwelfare horn. For he defines utilitarianism as "the theory that the only sound, fundamental basis for normative (or moral) appraisal is the promotion of human welfare" (p. 107). Since he holds that rights provide a basis for moral appraisal different from utilitarianism, this definition suggests that rights are not concerned with "the promotion of human welfare." A similar conclusion is suggested by Lyons's assertion that "rights . . . have a normative life of their own, with implications that are neither reducible to, nor traceable by, direct considerations of utility" (p. 132). In keeping with this assertion, when he refers to his right to life, he says that in acting so as to save it, "I need not show that my life is valuable or useful . . ." (p. 111).

On the other hand, Lyons also seems to uphold the welfare horn of the dilemma. Thus, referring to his example of Mary's rights to the use of a private driveway and garage that she has rented, he says that "Mary's rights, to be morally defensible, must have some foundation in human interests, needs, or welfare and are limited in turn by similar considerations" (p. 117). Hence, he goes on to admit that "*very substantial* utilities or disutilities outweigh the moral force of Mary's rights" (p. 117), even though it is not the case that "minimal increments of utility are sufficient to outweigh" (p. 117) these rights. (Here and in all other quotations from Lyons, the emphases are in the original).

Apart from his seeming to straddle both sides of the Utility-Rights Dilemma, Lyons's position confronts several difficulties. If morally defensible rights "must have some foundation in human interests, needs, or welfare" (p. 117), then how are they different from utilitarian norms, which are concerned with "the promotion of human welfare"? Lyons's answer is quite unsatisfactory. As we have seen, he says that the moral force of rights, in such a case as that of Mary's driveway, is outweighed only by "very substantial utilities or disutilities," but not by "minimal increments of utility." (p. 117). A utilitarian, however, could completely accept this distinction. He would say that Mary's rights, like any others, consist in, or at least have as their Objects, certain components of welfare, and their moral force, the obligatoriness of actually fulfilling them, is contingent on their relation to other components of welfare with which they may conflict. The rights must be fulfilled only when these other components (Lyons's "minimal increments of utility") do not outweigh the welfare components of the rights. But when the other components consist in "very substantial utilities or disutilities," or in what Lyons also calls "pressing needs" (p. 117), the rights must give way to these. Hence, so far as he has been able to show, he fully accepts the welfare horn of the Utility-Rights Dilemma, so that on his position moral rights are not in principle distinct from utilitarian norms in general. Thus, he is really a utilitarian after all.

Lyons strenuously tries to avoid this upshot. He denies that "utilitarian reasoning *generally* determines how Mary and others may justifiably act" (p. 117). He insists that once morally defensible rights are established, utilitarian "modes of reasoning are *illicit*" (p. 126). But he fails to show that or how this is so. He correctly denies that all rights are necessarily absolute (although he does not consider the possibility that some rights may be absolute); and, so far as he has shown, this denial entails that rights may be overridden by certain utilities.

At one point Lyons explicitly tries to differentiate his position on moral rights from utilitarianism. He says: "Why should we suppose that arguments based on moral rights diverge from welfare considerations? The answer has to do with the normative character of rights. If I have a right to do something, this provides *an argumentative threshold* against objections to my doing it, as well as a presumption against others' interference. Considerations that might otherwise be sufficient against my so acting, in the absence of my having the right, or that might justify others' interference, are ineffective in its presence. . . . I call this argumentative threshold character the *normative force* of moral rights" (p. 111). So far, however, Lyons has not shown either that moral rights are different from welfare considerations or what aspect of rights gives them the "normative force" he ascribes to them. The example he provides of the right to life is of little help, and indeed it confuses the issue. He says that his right to life "entails that I may act so as to save it and that others may not interfere, even if these acts or the results would otherwise be subject to sound criticism. I need not show that my life is valuable or useful, and the fact that my defending it would have bad overall consequences or is otherwise objectionable does not show that my defending it is wrong, or that others' interference is not wrong" (p. 111).

One trouble with this statement is that it obscures what Lyons later admits, that moral rights "must have some foundation in human interests, needs, or welfare and are limited in turn by similar considerations" (p. 117). It is irrelevant to say that he "need not show that my life is valuable or useful" (p. 111). Of course he doesn't have to show this, for it is obvious that his life has enormous value for him. But isn't it equally obvious that his right to life has at least some of its "foundation" in this value and hence in his "interests or welfare"? Moreover, when he says that he may act to save his life even if "my defending it would have bad overall consequence or is otherwise objectionable" (p. 111), how does this square with his subsequent admission that "*very substantial* utilities or disutilities outweigh the moral force of" (p. 117) certain rights? Suppose that the person whose life is involved has gone on a murderous rampage and can be stopped only by being killed. In this case, does he still have the right to life, and is it still morally permissible for him to act to save it even if his defending it would have such "bad overall consequences" for "human welfare"? (p. 111).

A related way in which Lyons tries to differentiate moral rights from utilitarian norms is through the contrast between a general maximizing criterion and the specific "difference" rights make. He says that according to utilitarianism, "Mary is fully justified in exercising her legal rights only when and in a manner in which she can promote human welfare to the maximum degree possible . . ." (p. 115). But this pattern of reasoning "seems to clash with the idea that Mary's rights are morally defensible and thus have moral force. For it assumes that Mary's rights *make no difference* to what she and others may justifiably do. . . . She need not act so as to maximize utility when she exercises her rights" (p. 116).

Now this reference to "maximizing" is indeed important in differentiating rights from utilitarianism. But as Lyons uses it and related notions, it does not succeed in making the desired differentiation. For one thing, much of the point of his story about Mary consists in the great utility of her having a private garage and driveway, so that the normative "difference" made by her having the right to these is, in his story, justified by its impact on her needs or welfare. One wonders if he would claim the same justification and hence the same normative "differ-ence" if the person who had rented the garage and driveway, and hence had the "right" in question, were a member of a criminal gang or a millionaire who used his car for driving to assignations. For another thing, as we have seen, Lyons does not hold that Mary's rights are "absolute"; on the contrary, *"very substantial* utilities or disutilities outweigh the moral force of Mary's rights" (p. 117), while "minimal increments of utility" do not. This distinction seems to invoke the very criterion of maximizing utility that Lyons officially wishes to reject or at least to differentiate from reasoning about rghts.

These difficulties in Lyons's position are more basic than the one he ascribes to the utilitarian view of rights, for they bear on the very possibility of distinguishing reasoning about rights from utilitarian calculation. He holds that a utilitarian official must always be prepared to violate any legal right if his doing so will "promote human welfare," so that he "cannot regard Mary's rights as making that difference to the evaluation of conduct that we supposed those rights do" (p. 124). But how distinct is this from Lyons's own position? To be sure, he may be interpreted as holding that the utilitarian official is prepared to violate Mary's rights even if "minimal increments of utility" will result thereby, whereas Lyons holds that only *"very substantial* utilities or disutilities outweigh the moral force of Mary's rights." But Lyons has given us no way of measuring utilities so as to distinguish between "minimal" and "substantial" increments. Moreover, the utilitarian may well hold that in his own meas-urement of utilities he must give an important place to the regularized expectations authorized by Mary's legal rights as well as by the "pressing needs" subserved by her having these rights. Consequently, his utilitarian calculus will allow infringing her rights only when the utilities gained by the infringement are greater than what she derives from fulfillment of her needs and expectations. How different is this from Lyons's position?

One of the main sources of Lyons's difficulties is that he is quite hazy about two of the elements of moral rights distin-guished above: their Nature and their Ground. He does not make clear what constitutes moral rights and what it is about them that gives them their normative force or obligatoriness.

Thus, he does almost nothing to counterbalance his utilitarian-sounding admission that moral rights "must have some foundation in human interests or welfare" by indicating any further Ground that would differentiate moral rights from utilitarian norms. The definition he provides for "moral rights" is merely negative: that they "exist independently of social recognition and enforcement" (p. 108), they simply "do not depend on social recognition or enforcement" (p. 108). Well, then, what do they depend on? What is their Ground or justifying basis? Apart from his unhelpful (to his antiutilitarian thesis) admission just cited, Lyons provides no answer to this question.

II

So far as Lyons has been able to show, then, moral rights (and morally defensible legal rights) are not appreciably different from utilitarian norms. I now want to establish that there are indeed important differences. Some of the distinctions I shall use for this purpose are quite familiar. But, as Lyons's difficulties attest, the distinctions must be put into a more general theoretical framework if they are to do the required job. Since I have elsewhere developed the relevant considerations in some detail, I shall present the main points here in summary and somewhat dogmatic form while referring the reader to some other writings of mine for fuller arguments on these matters, as well as for the necessary qualifications and elucidations.[2]

It must be kept in mind that the points to be presented here are not only conceptual but also normative, in that they involve requirements for individual action and social policy. These requirements, in turn, derive from a rationally justified moral principle, which I have called the Principle of Generic Consistency (*PGC*). The *PGC* is addressed to every actual or prospective agent; its main precept is: "Act in accord with the generic rights of your recipients as well as of yourself." (I shall explain the meaning of "generic rights" below). It is this principle that provides the ultimate Ground or justifying basis of moral rights and that shows why the most important of these rights must belong equally to all prospective agents as their Subjects.

The difficulties we found in Lyons's position were focused primarily on the Objects of rights, where he was confronted by the Utility-Rights Dilemma. The *PGC* shows how this dilemma is to be avoided. The Objects of moral rights are indeed components of human goods or welfare, so that to this extent the welfare horn of the dilemma must be accepted.[3] But from this it does not follow that we are committed to a utilitarian weighing of the Objects of rights against other goods or interests. The main reasons for this, stemming from the Ground of moral rights, are that the Objects in question are much more determinate and that the Subjects of moral rights must be viewed distributively, not collectively or aggregatively.

The *PGC* establishes that all prospective purposive agents have equal rights to the necessary conditions of human action and of successful action in general. These conditions are necessary goods in that they are what any person must have if he is to be able to act either at all or with some chances of success in achieving the purposes of his actions. Because they are such necessary goods, the conditions in question are the generic features of all action and successful action in general, and the rights to them are, correspondingly, *generic rights*. These necessary goods are of two kinds: freedom and well-being, where freedom consists in controlling one's behavior by one's unforced choice while having knowledge of relevant circumstances, and well-being comprises the substantive general abilities and conditions needed for fulfilling one's purposes. The components of such well-being fall into a hierarchy of three kind of good: *basic, nonsubtractive,* and *additive.*

Basic goods are the essential preconditions of action, such as life, physical integrity, and mental equilibrium. Nonsubtractive goods are the abilities and conditions required for maintaining undiminished one's level of purpose-fulfillment and one's capabilities for particular actions, while additive goods are the abilities and conditions required for increasing one's level of purpose-fulfillment and one's capabilities for particular actions. Examples of nonsubtractive goods are not being lied to or stolen from; examples of additive goods are self-esteem and education. I have elsewhere shown that the rights to these necessary goods of action—that is, basic, nonsubtractive, and additive rights— underlie or constitute all of the more general moral rights, especially those now called human rights, and that all prospective agents have these rights equally.[4]

It is because the *PGC* establishes that the Objects of moral rights are the necessary goods of action, and that their Subjects are all prospective agents equally, that it avoids the difficulties raised by the Utility-Rights Dilemma. We saw that, according to Lyons, moral rights (and morally defensible legal rights), because they "must have some foundation in human interests, needs, or welfare," (p. 117) may be outweighed by "very substantial utilities"; and, so far as he was able to show, this subjected moral rights to a utilitarian calculus. The problem arose because, lacking an adequate conception of the Ground of moral rights, Lyons was unable to defend some familiar contrasts between utilitarianism and moral rights. His essay indicates that he is indeed aware of these contrasts. But it is a matter, not only of his intentions, but also of his ability to fulfill them in the light of problems like the Utility-Rights Dilemma.

Let us briefly recall some of the contrasts between moral rights and utilitarianism in order to see how the *PGC* is able to explicate and defend them. These contrasts bear on all five of the elements of a right distinguished above. In the formula, "A has a right to X against B by virtue of Y," the *PGC* shows that the Nature of a moral right involves not only that it is a justified claim or entitlement had by A but also that it is his own moral property,[5] something that belongs individually to him, so that he can justifiably control his having its Object and can justifiably demand of other persons, the Respondents, that by appropriate actions or forbearances they respect his having its Object. The reason why the right is his moral property is given by the Ground or justifying basis of moral rights, and this in turn refers also to the Objects of the rights in the way indicated above. The primary Objects of moral rights consist in the necessary goods of action, freedom, and well-being; and the *PGC* and the arguments leading to it show that all prospective agents equally have rights to these goods because they need them in order to act either at all or with any chance of success in achieving their purposes. The primary Subjects of moral rights, then, are not simply persons, let alone sentient beings; they are prospective agents, persons who have the ability to control their behavior by their unforced choice with knowledge of relevant circumstances in order to achieve their purposes. (By a Principle of Proportionality, other beings, such as children, fetuses, mentally deficient persons, and animals can be shown to have moral rights in lesser degrees).[6] The *PGC* shows that moral rights belong equally to all prospective agents.

On all these points, utilitarianism differs sharply. The Ground or justifying basis on which it ascribes goods to persons is not their own individual needs or requirements for agency, so that these goods belong to persons as their own moral property. Rather, the criterion of utilitarian ascription of goods is primarily aggregative rather than distributive: what it requires is the maximizing of utility, that allocation of goods that will promote the greatest total or average utility. Bentham's egalitarian dictum, "Everybody to count for one, nobody for more than one,"[7] provides not for equal distribution of goods among persons but only for impartial consideration of persons as loci of goods in adding up the total amount of goods. Nor is the utilitarian calculus advanced appreciably toward equality by its traditional emphasis, found at least beginning with Hume, on the diminishing marginal utility of money and other goods. For the utilitarians go on to recognize that the need for incentives sharply limits the degree to which equal distribution may serve to maximize utility.[8] The primary emphasis is still aggregative, not distributive.

There is a similar contrast with regard to the Subjects or possessors of rights. Although utilitarianism agrees with the doctrine of moral rights, in opposition to organicist theories, that the possessors of goods or utilities are individual persons, utilitarianism does not specify these as prospective agents; on the contrary, it makes the ultimate possessors or Subjects of rights to be the collective whole of all humans or even of all sentient beings. For it is the requirements of maximizing utility and hence of what it diffusely calls the "general welfare" that are the primary Ground and Subject of utilitarian judgments. In its results, consequently, utilitarianism may coincide with organicist theories much more closely than with theories of moral rights. For what is required in order to maximize utility overall may infringe the individual's own entitlements or rights to the goods he needs for his own possibilities of action or of successful agency.

These considerations also involve a contrast with regard to Objects. Whereas the Objects of moral rights consist primarily in the necessary goods required for agency, the goods or values dealt with in utilitarianism are much more diffuse and eclectic. In the utilitarian calculus all utilities or even all preferences enter indiscriminately, at least in the first instance, and hence it is possible that large amounts of some small good will outweigh a basic good of one distinct individual.

On the basis of these contrasts, we can see how Lyons's difficulties with the Utility-Rights Dilemma are to be avoided. Although the Objects of moral rights are components of human goods or welfare, this does not entail that they enter into a utilitarian calculus. For the Objects in question are not goods or utilities indiscriminately but rather the necessary goods of action; and what the *PGC* requires is not that these be maximized regardless of the particular Subjects to whom they may belong, but rather that they be had by each of the individual prospective agents whose moral property they are.

It is indeed true that, while some individual moral rights are absolute,[9] most are not. But it is important to emphasize that the criteria for the overriding of rights derive not from a utilitarian calculus but rather from the same distributive moral principle or Ground as justifies the having of moral rights in the first place. Each propsective agent has a right to the basic and other necessary goods of action, and this right cannot be overridden or outweighed by considerations about the aggregation or maximizing of goods. Hence, even if the removal of basic goods from one person A would result in many other persons' having many more goods and thus in a larger sum total of goods, this removal is prohibited by the *PGC*. Each person's right to the basic goods must first be fulfilled; the distributive criterion is primary. This primacy, moreover, is not a matter of arbitrary preference; it has deep theoretical justification in the rational basis of morality itself.[10]

When the *PGC* justifies the overriding of some right, the overriding must be only by another right, not merely by considerations of goods, values, or interests as such. It is because all prospective agents have equal moral rights that a right of one person may override the right of another person. The overriding considerations or Grounds consist in the moral rights of *other* propsective agents, and the point of the overriding is to help to equalize or at least to protect certain basic rights—rights to basic goods—when some persons lack them or are threatened with losing them. For the *PGC* establishes that what is rationally justified and required is the equality of generic rights, not the maximization of their Objects without regard to which persons are entitled to them.

A primary criterion set by the *PGC* for the overriding of some rights by others consists in the degrees of necessity of various goods for action. Since the primary Objects and Grounds of moral rights comprise the necessary goods of action, one right *R* overrides another right *S* if the good that is the Object of *R* is more necessary for action than is the good that is the Object of *S*. For example, A's nonsubtractive right not to be lied to is overridden by B's basic right not to be murdered when these rights conflict so that both cannot be fulfilled. Here it is not a utilitarian calculus about overall utility but rather the comparative bearing of rights on the individuals' needs of action that justifies the overriding of one personal right by another. A similar point applies to more complex social issues of taxation, when some persons' additive rights to wealth and income are overridden by other persons' basic rights to subsistence and other essential needs. In such cases the application of the criterion of degrees of necessity for action requires a context of institutional rules.

This way of distinguishing between moral rights in terms of their Objects' degrees of necessity for action may bear some resemblance to Lyons's distinction between "very substantial utilities" and "minimal increments" of utility. But the distinctions are different from one another because of all the contrasts indicated above about the Objects, Subjects, and Grounds of moral rights as between the *PGC* and utilitarianism. Simply by calling the Objects in question "utilities," Lyons obscures the difference between the objects of utilitarian norms and the Objects of moral rights consisting in the necessary goods of action. And by his failure to provide a Ground for moral rights and to indicate their specific Subjects, he is unable, contrary to his intentions, to ward off the absorption of his "utilities" into a utilitarian calculus. The upshot is that the *PGC*'s distinctions, unlike Lyons's, do not lend themselves to the utilitarian aggregative weighing that the Utility-Rights Dilemma held to be entailed by its welfare horn.

It must also be noted that when the *PGC* authorizes the possible overriding of some persons' less necessary rights by other persons' more necessary rights, this does not contradict the idea that the overridden rights are the moral property of the individuals who have them. There would be a contradiction only if the moral property in question were held to be absolute or if the relation of rights to the varyingly necessary goods of action were overlooked.[11] What the *PGC* requires, however, is that the generic rights (but not necessarily all the results of exercising the rights) be equalized among all prospective agents. The Ground or justifying basis of these moral rights, then, is found not only in the necessary goodness of their Objects but also in the rational egalitarian principle of distribution that affects their Subjects. For utilitarianism, on the other hand, the justifying basis of actions and policies is found in the maximization of goods taken indiscriminately.

From these considerations emerges a related shortcoming of Lyons's analysis. His central contention turns on the familiar distinction between act- and rule-utilitarianism; he holds that rule-utilitarianism may "accommodate" moral rights (or morally defensible legal rights) while act-utilitarianism cannot, and that a utilitarian official in his individual actions or conduct would, to be consistent, have to follow the requirements of act-utilitarianism rather than those of rule-utilitarianism. Thus, Lyons says: "It does seem plausible that institutions conforming to utilitarian requirements or to the dictates of economic efficiency would incorporate rights" (p. 119). He adds: "I know of no general argument that could deny this possibility" (p. 119).

What Lyons fails to see here is that the difficulties he correctly attributes to the act-utilitarian view of rights also infect rule-utilitarianism. Even if the rules of utilitarian institutions confer rights, the rules in question cannot take adequate account of the rights because of the oppositions between moral rights and utilitarianism with regard to the various elements indicated above. Utilitarian rules would confer rights for utilitarian Grounds or reasons, focused on the requirements of maximizing utility, and not because of each person's own needs of agency. Hence, the rules' ascription of rights is derivative and calculative in a way in which the *PGC*'s ascription is not. Since the primary aim of utilitarian rules is to maximize utility overall, the way in which rights get distributed is always worked out with a view not simply to the individual person's needs of agency but rather to the production of the greatest total or average amount of goods. Thus, it is always possible that *rules* as well as *actions* justified by the utilitarian calculus may require removing rather than protecting goods that belong to individuals as a matter of their moral rights, when such removal serves to maximize utility overall. The calculus may require using some persons only as means for others, without regard for the former's own rights.

It follows that only in a certain limited sense can utilitarianism be held to justify any moral rights. A distinction must be drawn between *essential* and *accidental* justification. To justify something *X* is to show or establish that it is correct, valid, or required. When *X* receives an essential justification, its correctness is established from Grounds or premises that are directly appropriate to *X*. But when *X* receives an accidental justification, the Grounds or premises from which its correctness is established are not directly appropriate to *X* but consist rather in considerations that are conceptually or causally external to *X*. For example, the assertion that there are five thousand persons at a certain public gathering is accidentally justified if it is based only on the assurance given by an entrepreneur who has a personal stake in its being believed that so many persons are present; the assertion that there is a fire nearby is accidentally justified if it is based only on the sight and sound of a fire truck racing down the street. Even if each of these assertions turns out to be correct or true, the Grounds on which they are made or accepted are not adequate bases of justification. In contrast, an essential justification of the first assertion would be based on some such method as a direct count, and of the second assertion on the actual seeing of the flames or smelling of smoke.

Utilitarian justifications of moral rights are only accidental, not essential, because the aggregative Grounds on which they are based are not directly appropriate to the distributive allocation of the necessary goods of agency to each individual prospective agent. As a consequence, even if the utilitarian calculation comes out in such a way as to justify rules or institutions that require that each prospective agent be given control over these goods for himself, this is an accidental result. Unlike the requirements of the *PGC*, it is not based directly on what each individual must have in order to fulfill his needs of agency.

Moral rights when based on utilitarian justifications or Grounds are hence precarious, for the utilitarian calculus, being aggregative rather than distributive in its Ground or criterion, may, *whether it is applied to acts or to rules*, come out against certain individuals' having the relevant goods. The case is otherwise, however, when moral rights are justified by the *PGC*. This is so for several reasons. First, as indicated above, the *PGC*'s justifications are essential, not accidental, so that they do not admit the influence, for the allocation of moral rights, of considerations that may be antithetical to each individual's needs of agency. Second, the *PGC* allows rights to be overridden only by other rights, not by considerations of general utility whose contents may not include the necessary goods of action. In cases of such overriding, the criterion of degrees of necessity for action assures that basic rights, whose Objects are the essential preconditions of action, will not be infringed for the sake of other goods or utilities even when the aggregate of these latter, summed for a larger number of persons, can be somehow shown to add up to more overall utility than do the basic goods of a few or even one prospective agent. The *PGC* does not permit, for example, the actual or highly probable infliction of cancer on a few persons, such as certain industrial workers, even if a "cost-benefit analysis" may show that the "costs" of preventing the infliction outweigh its "benefits."[12] The overriding of some rights by others raises other problems, including conditions of severe disaster or catastrophe. I have tried to deal with some of these issues elsewhere.[13]

The overriding of some rights by others may also require reference to an institutional context of legal rules. Such a context provides the proximate Ground of what Lyons calls "morally defensible legal rights," in contrast to moral rights per se. It must be noted, however, that the legal order itself must be justified by the *PGC* in ways that involve what I have called the "indirect applications" of the principle.[14] In general, a legal order is justified when it serves to protect the generic rights that derive from the direct applications of the *PGC*. Legal rights that derive from a morally justified legal framework, such as, in Lyons's example, Mary's right to the exclusive use of her garage and driveway, are justified in a related way. Although a fuller discussion would have to deal with such rights specifically, the criteria in question are provided by the *PGC* in the ways already indicated above.

III

The contrasts drawn above between the *PGC* and utilitarianism may be further elucidated by comparing two different structures of normative argument. The structure of the *PGC* contains three main elements, in the following order:

1. Necessary goods or action-needs of individuals.
2. Rights as individuals' moral property in the fulfillment of these needs.
3. Duties of other individals or of government to act or to forbear with a view to securing these rights.

The structure of utilitarian rights also contains three main elements, in the following order:

1. Utilities or goods in general, or general utility.
2. Duties of individuals or of government to maximize these utilities.
3. Possible rights of individuals consequential on, or productive of, this maximization.

From these two sequences it can be seen that while rights provide the basis of duties for the *PGC*, the relation is the reverse for utilitarianism. Rights are justified by utilitarianism only insofar as they may be instrumental to fulfilling the duties incumbent on all individuals and on government to promote or maximize general utility. Thus, while the *PGC* makes primary the rights needed to provide for each individual the necessary goods of action, utilitarianism gives rights a role subordinate to the maximizing of overall utility. We have already noted the implications of this contrast.

In attributing the above sequence to utilitarianism, I am referring to its overall conceptual structure, not to more restricted contexts involving only legal rights and duties. It is in such a more restricted context that Bentham says that the law that confers a right on one party imposes a duty or an obligation on some other party.[15] He is here dealing directly only with legal rights and duties, not with moral ones. In contrast, he uses what seems to be the moral "ought" in passages where the requirements of the principle of utility are directly presented, such as the following: "Of an action that is conformable to the principle of utility, one may always say either that it is one that ought to be done, or at least that it is not one that ought not to be done."[16] "It has been shown that the happiness of the individuals of whom a community is composed, that is, their pleasures and their security, is the end and the sole end which the legislator ought to have in view."[17] In such passages the moral "ought" has the status assigned to it in the second step of the utilitarian sequence listed above.

It should also be noted that the utilities or goods listed in the first step of the utilitarian sequence are not viewed, at least initially, as the moral property of determinate individual persons. The locus of these goods is initially more diffuse; they pertain to, or consist in, the "general happiness" or "general utility." The word "general," like the word "common" in "common good," is ambiguous as between aggregative and distributive meanings. In the former meaning, "general utility" and "common good" signify the sum total of utilities or goods in some group or community, without any implication about how these goods are to be distributed among the individuals composing the group. In the distributive meaning, "common good" signifies that the good in question is equally common to, equally had by, all the members of the group. For Bentham, the primary meaning is aggregative; thus, he says that "the interest of the community" consists in "the sum of the interests of the several members who compose it."[18] This aggregative meaning entails that the rights of individuals are given the subordinate status noted above.

In certain respects, John Stuart Mill's sequence of argument may seem closer to that of the *PGC* than to utilitarianism. He declares that the primary Object of moral rights is security, "the most vital of all interests," "the most indispensable of all necessaries, after physical nutriment," "the very groundwork of our existence."[19] He here suggests the kind of qualitative differentiation among various Objects of rights that the *PGC* recognizes in distinguishing between basic, nonsubtractive, and additive rights. Mill's statements about security also suggest that persons have moral rights simply in virtue of their basic needs, and hence independently of the requirements of social utility or the general welfare, especially where these are viewed as aggregative maximizing conditions.

Nevertheless, despite his emphasis on the connection between rights and the basic needs of individuals, Mill retains the utilitarian derivation of rights from general utility. Thus, he says: "To have a right, then, is, I conceive, to have something which society ought to defend me in the possession of. If the objector goes on to ask, why it ought? I can give him no other reason than general utility."[20]

Why did Mill give this answer? Why didn't he say simply that society ought to defend me in the possession of my rights because their Objects are "the very groundwork of [my] existence"? It might be thought that the following two questions must be distinguished: First, why (or with what justification) does an individual have any rights? Second, why should society defend these rights? Nevertheless, if the second question is given Mill's utilitarian answer, this seems to suggest a possible opposition or at least difference between "general utility" and the basic needs of individuals. Mill's general utilitarian position admits this contrast. And by his utilitarian answer to the justificatory question of why society should defend an individual's possession of his rights, Mill falls into the utilitarian position of subordinating individual rights to general utility.

A similar contrast is found in Mill's theory of liberty. Just as he said that the Objects of rights are basic needs of individuals, so he held that the Ground or justifying basis of individual liberty is "the permanent interests of a man as a progressive being." And he connected this with "individuality as one of the elements of well-being."[21] On the other hand, when he came to the question of whether individual liberty may be interfered with, the justification he offered consisted not in the interests of individuals but rather in "the general interests of mankind," "whether the general welfare will or will not be promoted."[22] Thus, in final analysis Mill too follows the utilitarian sequence rather than that of the *PGC*.

The utilitarian sequence has a significant implication for the status of moral rights in their relation to duties. For whereas in the *PGC*'s sequence, duties are derivative from rights, in the utilitarian sequence rights are derivative from duties. It is important to see the basis of each of these derivations. Since the rights dealt with in the *PGC*'s sequence are claim-rights, to which duties are *correlative*, in what sense can it be that duties are *derivative* from rights in that sequence? The answer is that duties are correlative with rights precisely because they are derivative from rights. That is, the ground of one person B's having a duty toward another person A is that A has a right that B act or refrain from acting toward A in the way that is required if A is to have the Object of the right. For example, it is because A has a basic right to life that B has a duty to refrain from killing him; it is because A has a nonsubtractive right that promises made to him be kept that B has a duty to keep his promise to A. The relation of "because" here is both conceptual and teleological. The duty exists for the sake of the right, not conversely. It is not the case that the Ground of A's having a right against B is that B has a duty to A. The right generates the duty, not conversely.

The existence of the right can indeed by inferred from the existence of the duty, as correlativity requires. But two qualifications must be noted. First, just as it is only claim-rights but not "liberties" or "privileges" (in Hohfeld's sense) that entail correlative duties,[23] so it is only strict duties but not looser duties of generosity or charity that entail correlative rights. Second, the validity of inferring claim-rights from strict duties is not antithetical to the unique grounding of the latter in the fomer. The relation is analogous to that of parents and children: each is logically correlative with the other, so that the past or present existence of parents can be inferred from the existence of children; yet in the causal sequence the latter are derivative from the former, but not conversely.

In the utilitarian sequence, on the other hand, rights are derivative from duties. Rights have no prior, independent status or Ground in the action-needs of individual persons. On the contrary, what is primary is the good of maximal utility. Duties derive from the moral requirement of contributing as effectively as possible to this maximization. Rights arise, if at all, as ways of helping to fulfill these duties, or as results of the fulfillment. The right is for the sake of the duty and its utility-maximizing purpose, not conversely. Hence, if any right proves antithetical to such fulfillment, the right must be overridden.

It is worth noting that this derivative, subordinate role of rights is also found in the organicist idealist tradition. The structure of argument presented by Bernard Bosanquet, for example, contains four main elements, in the following order:

1. The common good.
2. Social positions or functions as instrumental to the common good.
3. Duties to fulfill the requirements of positions.
4. Rights as powers instrumental to the performance of duties.

According to Bosanquet's sequence, the common good is the ideal fulfillment of every "real self" as a member of a community that promotes the good life. Individuals have "positions" or "functions" insofar as they can make unique contributions to such a life. The conditions of these positions constitute duties or obligations that are incumbent on individuals for the sake of the positions. This is especially the case insofar as the conditions of the positions require enforcement. Rights, finally, are powers instrumental to the performance of duties, so that rights arise in virtue of social positions. "All rights, then, are powers instrumental to making the best of human capacities, and can only be recognized or exercised upon this ground. In this sense, the duty is the purpose with a view to which the right is secured, and not merely a corresponding obligation equally derived from a common ground; and the right and duty are not distinguished as something claimed by self and something owed to others, but the duty as an imperative purpose, and the right as a power secured because instrumental to it."[24]

There are, of course, many differences between the utilitarians' "general utility" and the idealists' "common good," although Bosanquet also uses a kind of aggregative language when he refers to that "which would promote the best life of the whole" as the "maximization of our being."[25] But the utilitarians and idealists have in common that, in contrast to the *PGC*, they assign a subordinate role to the rights of persons, making them derivative from, because instrumental to, duties toward the social whole. This contrast has many further implications for the status of human rights as well as for the whole question of the proper relation of rights to social duties and responsibilities. I cannot go further into this question here. But it is the derivative position of rights that differentiates utilitarianism from principles like the *PGC* that directly base rights on the action-needs of persons. And it is because of this difference that utilitarianism can provide only accidental justifications for moral rights.

APPENDIX: REPLIES TO SOME CRITICISMS

My essay "The Basis and Content of Human Rights" was published in NOMOS XXIII: *Human Rights* (1981) together with three sets of comments by Richard B. Friedman, Martin P. Golding, and Arval A. Morris. Because that essay and the issues raised by the comments also figure in my present paper in this volume of NOMOS, and because the issues are, I believe, of considerable independent importance, I have thought it worthwhile to present the following response.

In my essay, and more fully in my book *Reason and Morality*, I argued that every actual or prospective agent must hold, on pain of contradiction, that he has rights to freedom and well-being because these are the necessary conditions of his action and of his successful action in general. The rights are, so far, prudential, not moral, in that the justifying ground on the basis of which the agent claims them for himself consists in his own agency-needs as required for his pursuit of his own purposes. Only through a subsequent step do the rights become moral, where a "moral" judgment or claim is defined as one whose maker is concerned to uphold the interests of other persons as well as of himself. This further step is accomplished by showing, through the principle of universalizability, that the agent must admit that all other prospective agents have the rights he claims for himself.

The main argument for every agent's having to hold that he has the prudential rights to freedom and well-being is as follows. As an agent, he regards the purposes for which he acts as good on whatever criteria (not necessarily moral ones) are involved in his purposes. Hence, he must regard his freedom and well-being, the necessary conditions of his acting for purposes, as necessary goods, so that he implicitly accepts (1) "I must have freedom and well-being" (where this "must" is practical-prescriptive and not merely a dispassionate means-end locution). Now suppose the agent were to deny or reject for himself the statement (2) "I have rights to freedom and well-being." Then, because of the correlativity of rights and strict "oughts," he would also have to deny (3) "All other persons ought at least to refrain from removing or interfering with my freedom and well-being." By virtue of denying (3), the agent would have to accept (4) "It is not the case that all other persons ought at least to refrain from removing or interfering with my freedom and well-being." Hence he would also have to accept (5) "Other persons may (i.e. It is permissible that other persons) remove or interfere with my freedom and well-being." And by virtue of accepting (5), the agent would have to accept (6) "I may not (i.e. It is permissible that I not) have freedom and well-being." But (6) contradicts (1) above. Since every agent must accept (1), he must reject (6). And since (6) is entailed by the denial of (2), it follows that every agent must reject that denial; so that he must accept (2) "I have rights to freedom and well-being."

Professor Golding presents two main objections to this argument. First, he holds that the very idea of a prudential right does not make sense; he says, "I must confess I haven't grasped" what the term means (p. 169). Now I find this somewhat surprising. At least since Kant (if not Hobbes and Plato) the idea of a prudential "ought" has been familiar in philosophy. It signifies the requirements a person must fulfill (or thinks he must fulfill) with a view to furthering his own self-interest or achieving his own purposes. Such an "ought" is prudential because its justificatory basis or criterion is prudential, consisting in the person's self-interest or achieving his own purposes. Why, then, shouldn't this also be the case with the term "a right" (used in the substantive rather than the adjectival sense)? A prudential right, then, is, or is set forth as, a justified claim or entitlement whose justificatory basis or criterion is likewise prudential, in that it is based on a person's furthering his own self-interest or the conditions of his fulfillment of his own purposes. It is in this sense that I have held that every agent must hold that he has prudential rights, i.e. rights to have the necessary conditions of agency. He bases this claim on his own agency-needs, not on the needs or purposes of other persons, including the persons to whom he addresses his right-claim.

It is indeed the case that right-claim imply demands or requirements on other persons, that they at least not interfere with the claimant's having the Objects to which he claims a right. But this is also true of prudential "oughts"; in fact, because these *are* requirements that are based on the speaker's own self-interest or his pursuit of his own purposes, they also imply demands on his part that other persons at least not interfere. In this regard, prudential "oughts" as uttered by some person on his own behalf are at least partially correlative with prudential right-claims.

That this concept of a prudential right makes perfectly good sense can be seen in several other related ways. It is well known that there are legal rights as well as moral ones, the initial difference between these being that they are grounded, respectively, in legal and in moral justificatory bases or criteria. And as I have shown in some detail, there are also intellectual or logical rights grounded in intellectual or logical justificatory bases or criteria (*Reason and Morality*, pp. 69–71). Hence, since prudence—the agent's self-interest or pursuit of his own purposes as such—is a quite distinct basis of normative discourse and valuation, it also provides a distinct justificatory basis of rights and right-claims. This is not to say that all such rights are conclusively valid or definitive, any more than legal rights are. But there are at least prudential right-*claims*, in that prospective agents hold that they are entitled at least to non-interference with the necessary conditions of their agency. In all these different contexts, moreover, the expression "a right" is not equivocal, any more than the word "good" is equivocal when it is applied with different criteria to different kinds of objects. In each case the rights in question are, in Hohfeld's classification, claim-rights in that they are, or are set forth as, justified claims or entitlements entailing correlative duties to forbear or assist.

A further reason why the concept of a prudential right should not provoke in Golding the shock of nonrecognition is that many of the traditional objections to rights-talk (and hence to the concept of a right) have been based on the view that rights as standardly asserted or claimed are egoistic or self-centered. Thus Marx wrote: "the so-called right of man . . . are simply the rights of a member of civil society, that is, of egoistic man, of man separated from other men and from the community. . . . None of the supposed rights of man, therefore, go beyond the egoistic man, man as he is, as a member of civil society; that is, an individual separated from the community, withdrawn into himself, wholly preoccupied with his private interest and acting in accord with his private caprice."[26] While there is much in this criticism that I do not accept, it shows that at least the *concept* of prudential rights, of rights as being founded on self-interest or the agent's pursuit of his own purposes, is far from novel.

A very large part of Golding's failure to understand the concept of a prudential right stems from his apparent belief that all rights are moral ones. He correctly notes that the starting-point of my argument is morally neutral so that it applies to all agents, including, as he puts it, "the prudent, self-interested agent who is a rational amoralist" (p. 167). From this, Golding concludes that the prudent moralist "does not use" such terms as "rights": "the term 'a right' does not occur in his basic language. The amoralist, so to speak, does not play in the moral ballpark" (pp. 167–168). The error Golding makes here is that of thinking that the concept of rights occurs only "in the moral ballpark." Strictly interpreted, this would rule out not only legal rights (which differ in important respects from moral ones) but also intellectual as well as prudential rights. He does not see that prudence also supplies, at least for each prudent agent (including the amoralist), a justificatory (although not moral) basis or criterion on which the agent may set forth various right-claims.

Golding says that "before the prudent amoralist can begin to speak the language of rights at all," a certain addition is required: an appeal to "mutual cooperation and mutual under-takings" (p. 169). He gives as an example a case where "a group of prudent amoralists want to accomplish a task that requires their mutual cooperation" (p. 168), so that they "agree" on certain rules on the basis of which they claim "rights." But Golding is simply mistaken if he thinks that explicit or even tacit agreement on rules or other normative considerations is a necessary condition for the assertion of rights. As I have shown in some detail in *Reason and Morality* (pp. 74–75), right-claims may be addressed to persons with whom one has, or has made, no such agreements. Familiar examples are the claims of rights made by slaves against their masters, the claims made by South African blacks against the exponents of apartheid, and so forth. The whole modern and contemporary drive for human rights in countries whose rulers disavow or violate them is proof that "mutual cooperation and mutual undertakings" are far from being necessary conditions of the intelligibility of right-claims.

In my discussion of the argument presented above (from the agent's regarding his freedom and well-being as necessary goods to his holding that he has rights to them), I gave three reasons why the argument is valid only when it proceeds by the dialectically necessary method, whereby the agent uses first-person discourse from within his own conative standpoint in purposive action. Golding maintains that none of these three reasons succeeds in establishing that the prudential amoral agent must use rights-language or claim rights for himself. But here too Golding is mistaken, largely from the same cause as before: that he confines all rights to moral ones.

I shall take up each of the three points in turn. First, when the agent says, "My freedom and well-being are necessary goods," this statement of his is prescriptive in that "it carries *his* advocacy or endorsement" (p. 128; emphasis added); that is, he is advocating that *he* have freedom and well-being. On this point, Golding says that he does not see how this statement prescribes anything *for someone else*. Does the agent have a 'moral gun' in his recipient's back?" (p. 170; emphasis added). Here, Golding makes two false assumptions: that all prescriptive language must be "moral," and that it must always prescribe *"for* someone else" besides the speaker. In the first instance, the agent is advocating for himself. He is also prescribing *to* other persons. But there is this difference between prescribing *to* and prescribing *for* other persons: the latter, unlike the former, suggests that the other persons recognize or accept the prescription or rules on which it is based or at least the authority of the prescriber. This is indicated by Golding's example of the patron in a restaurant telling the waiter he wants a cup of coffee (p. 170). But when the agent advocates his having freedom and well-being and hence prescribes *to* other persons that they at least not interfere with his having these necessary goods, he is not necessarily assuming that the other persons will accept his demand or normative rules on which it is based, any more than slaves who claim the right to freedom necessarily assume that their masters will recognize their authority to make the claim. All the agent can strictly assume is that the other persons also accept the criteria of deductive and inductive reasoning and that, as prospective agents, they have the same general conative motivations as characterize all agents. Hence, they are capable of understanding and respecting his prudential right-claim; but there is, so far, no assurance that they will in fact comply with it (see *Reason and Morality,* pp. 74–75). Further steps are needed for this purpose.

Second, when I say that the agent's statement about the necessary goods must imply a claim on his part against other persons, Golding objects that this would constitute "an abandonment of moral neutrality by the amoralist," so that his demand that other persons not interfere with his freedom and well-being "is not a claim being made as a matter of right" (p. 171). This objection is incorrect, because the right-claim the agent makes against other persons is not yet a *moral* one, so that in making it he does not abandon moral neutrality.

The third point at issue here concerns my contention that the agent, by virtue of holding that freedom and well-being are necessary goods for him, must hold that these goods are due to him, so that he is entitled to them from within his own conative standpoint in purposive agency. Since Golding recognizes no standpoint for right-claims other than a moral one, he says: "I frankly am at a loss to understand what 'due to' could possibly mean here. I cannot see how any entitlement enters into the picture, even on—and perhaps especially on—a prudential criterion" (p. 171). Golding is unaware that prudential criteria as well as moral criteria may serve to ground right-claims. The agent's prudential standpoint in purposive action provides for him a ground of entitlement such that, from within this standpoint, he regards as his due whatever is required for his being an agent (see *Reason and Morality*, pp. 68–73). It is simply arbitrary to reject such a prudential basis as a ground for right-claims and to hold that they are confined to moral criteria, just as it would be obviously false to hold this in the case of "oughts."

I turn now to Golding's second main objection to my argument. This objection is in two parts. First, in my argument as spelled out above, he holds that "it is far from certain" that step (6) ("I may not have freedom and well-being") "really does contradict" step (1) ("I must have freedom and well-being").[27] His reason for doubting that I have established a genuine contradiction, as my argument requires, is that the "must" in (1) is "a nonnormative 'must'," while the "may" in (6) is "the normative 'may' of moral license" (p. 172). But here, Golding is wrong on both counts. The "must" in (1) is normative: it sets forth a practical requirement which the agent endorses because of his conative attachment to the generic features of his action (see *Reason and Morality*, p. 79). It is irrelevant to say, as Golding does, that this "must" "is hardly prescriptive *for* some other person"; rather, it is prescriptive *to* other persons in that it sets forth a requirement at least of other persons' non-interference with the agent's freedom and well-being. And the "may not" in (6) is also normative, but it is not the "may" of "*moral* license"; rather, it sets forth as permissible the precise negation of what (1) sets forth as normatively necessary or mandatory. Its criterion is prudential, not moral. Indeed, as is required if (1) and (6) are to contradict one another, the criteria of the 'must' and the 'may' are the same, consisting in the agent's own requirements for agency (see *Reason and Morality*, page 81).

In the other part of his second main objection, Professor Golding makes a very acute point. He distinguishes between strong and weak denials of a rights-claim, where a weak denial does not entail "that some other rights-claim or normative claim is true" (p. 172). He then says that when the agent denies (2) "I have rights to freedom and well-being" and hence also denies (3) "All other persons ought at least to refrain from removing or interfering with my freedom and well-being," he is not thereby logically required to accept (4) "It is not the case that all other persons ought at least to refrain from removing or interfering with my freedom and well-being." For, Golding holds, the prudent amoralist agent should be construed as at most making a weak denial of (2), so that he is not logically committed to accept (4). Indeed, "the prudent amoralist neither asserts nor denies any rights-claim . . . because the terminology of 'rights' is not part of his vocabulary" (p. 173).

The first thing I want to say about this objection is that it is precisely the same as one I presented against myself in *Reason and Morality* (p. 89):

> This objection is that the agent need make no right-claim or 'ought'-judgment at all, either positive or negative. He need not accept either statement (3) given above or its negation (4), for he might be an amoralist who disavows for himself all uses of moral or deontic concepts. Thus, in refusing to assert such a judgment as (2) "I have rights to freedom and well-being" and hence also (3) "All other persons ought at least to refrain from interfering with my freedom and well-being," the amoralist agent would not thereby have to accept (4) "It is not the case that all other persons ought at least to refrain from interfering with my freedom and well-being." . . . For, as an amoralist, he would deny that concepts like "ought" and "right" have any valid application, at least in his own case. . . . (Hence, any statement he might make) would not involve him in the contradictions elicited above, for these all depended on the agent's having to accept the negative "ought"-judgment (4).

This objection raises the following very important question: Can a prudent amoralist agent logically dispense with, or reject for himself, all normative concepts, including deontic ones like "ought" and "rights"? It is Golding's affirmative answer to this question that underlies most of his criticisms of my whole argument. His objection, and my own just given, would be conclusive if the answer to this question were indeed affirmative. But, in fact, the answer is negative. I have shown this in some detail in *Reason and Morality,* pp. 89–95,[28] and the reader is invited to consult the extensive argument I have presented there. (Indeed, the whole section entitled "Generic Rights and Right-Claims," pp. 63–103, deals in detail with the issues discussed in this Appendix.)

I have space here to present only the barest summary of the argument. First, if something Z threatens the prudent amoralist's basic well-being (for example, his life) and he believes both that the necessary and sufficient condition of his avoiding Z is his doing X and that he can do X, then he will accept for himself such a prudential and prescriptive 'ought'-judgment as (7) "I ought to do X." He must accept this "ought" for himself because it signifies the practical requirement which he must acknowledge because of his commitment to maintaining his basic well-being and hence the necessary condition of his being an agent. He could reject this "ought" only if he were not even minimally rational or conatively normal, but this would contradict the idea that he is a prudent agent. Hence, every agent, even an amoralist, must accept for himself the use of a deontic concept setting forth a practical requirement for his action based on his own prudential purpose.

Now by virtue of his accepting (7), the agent must also accept (8) "I ought to be free to do X." For without at least the negative freedom of absence of interference, he cannot carry out the requirement he has accepted in (7), that he do X. And, because of the meaning of "free," (8) in turn entails (9) "All other persons ought at least to refrain from interfering with my doing X." Hence, the rational amoralist agent must also accept (9). Since, moreover, one sole reason for which he accepts the requirement that he do X is that this is the necessary and sufficient condition of preserving his basic well-being, (9) here entails (10) "All other persons ought at least to refrain from interfering with my basic well-being." Here, as before, the "ought"-judgments (9) and (10) are prudential ones in that they are concerned to further the interests or purposes not of the judgments but rather of the agent who addresses the judgments to those subjects.

In this way, then, I have argued that every agent, including the prudent amoralist, must accept for himself the use of the deontic concept "ought," not only a self-directed one as in (7), but also other-directed ones as in (9) and (10). From these, in turn, it follows that he must accept for himself the concept of a right. For in (10) he holds that noninterference with his basic well-being is a requirement whose fulfillment is owed to him by all other persons because of the necessity of such noninterference for his continuing to be at least a prospective agent capable of achieving his purposes. Although not all "ought"-judgments entail or are correlative with rights-judgments, the correlativity holds when the person making the "ought"-judgment regards it as setting for other persons duties that they owe to him. For when duties are owed to him, he has a right to their performance or to compliance with them. Now the agent regards in this way the "ought"-judgment that other persons ought at least to refrain from interfering with his basic well-being. For he does not view the judgment as stating merely an obligation that has some general ground not related to himself; rather, the "ought" in question prescribes the fulfillment of what is necessary to his being a purposive agent.

To see how this point logically involves the concepts of "due" and "owed," we must first recall that these concepts are not confined to specific transactions or relationships; they also apply to the sphere of general rights, such as those of freedom and well-being. Also, these concepts, as well as "rights," are not antithetical to the purview even of the prudent amoralist, because their criterion is here prudential, not moral. We must next note that there is a more general reason, deriving from the nature of rights, as to why he must use such deontic concepts. Every claim-right is based on a Justifying Ground which establishes that the Subject's having a certain Object is required or mandatory, and that for this reason other persons have correlative duties which they owe to the Subject. Whenever there is such a Justifying Ground, the concept of a claim-right is logically called for. Now for any agent as such, including the prudent amoralist, there is a Justifying Ground which consists in the conditions needed for his being an agent, these conditions including especially his basic well-being. So long as he is an agent and intends to continue to be one, the necessary conditions of his being an agent constitute for him the Justifying Ground for requirements whose fulfillment by other persons he must regard as owed to him, because these conditions are constitutive of the very standpoint from which he proceeds as an agent. Hence, every prospective agent must hold or accept that he has a right to these conditions.

It will not do to say that the prudent amoralist agent accepts no Justifying Grounds. For, as we have seen, he must accept the idea of requirements both on his own actions and on those of other persons so long as he is even minimally rational and conatively normal. And the idea of a requirement logically involves the idea of a Justifying Ground as the basis of the requirement.

What follows from this point is that there is a strict "ought," in the sense of what is due or owed, in the prudent amoralist's statement (10) "All other persons ought at least to refrain from interfering with my basic well-being." Hence, (10) entails (11) "I have a right to basic well-being." This is, of course, an essential part of (2) "I have rights to freedom and well-being." That the prudent amoralist logically must accept the remainder of (2) can be shown by the same sorts of arguments as led to his having to accept (11). Thus even an amoralist must accept that he has prudential rights to freedom and well-being.

What I have tried to establish by this argument, then, is that the prudent amoralist logically cannot dispense with, or reject for himself, all normative concepts and, more specifically, deontic concepts like "ought" and "rights," because he must use these concepts to express the requirements—justified from his prudential standpoint—that must be satisfied if he is to fulfill his own needs of purposive agency. In all this he remains, so far, within his own prudential context; he can use these concepts without having to accept moral criteria. This disposes of the remainder of Golding's objection.

Both Richard Friedman and Arval Morris raise questions about the equal distribution of human rights according to my theory with its Principle of Generic Consistency. Friedman contends that I have not shown why a rational prudent agent "*must* stake his claim to rights to freedom and well-being on the ground of their necessity," as against "a wide variety of possible and indeed well-known grounds for rights," including "individual merit of desert" (pp. 152–153)—grounds that would logically support an unequal rather than equal distribution of rights. And Morris similarly asserts that I am "committed to an elitist conception of human rights" because my theory assigns rights not simply to all "humans" as such but rather to "persons" who are agents, and it holds "that the degree of human agency present in a human being at any given time determines the number and character of human rights that the human being has at that time" (pp. 160, 161).

I have dealt with this question in considerable detail in *Reason and Morality* in the whole section entitled "The Criterion of Relevant Similarities" (pp. 104–128), and much more briefly in "The Basis and Content of Human Rights" (pp. 130–131, 133–134). Friedman is mistaken when he says that I have not shown why a rational agent must base his claim to the generic rights "on the ground of their necessity." Although he does not explain the meaning of this phrase, I assume he is referring to characteristics that necessarily belong to all agents equally, as against more specific, unequally distributed characteristics that are not necessarily had by all agents. In "The Basis and Content of Human Rights" (p. 130), I wrote: "There is one, and only one, ground that every agent logically must accept as the sufficient justifying condition for having the generic rights, namely, that he is a prospective agent who has purposes he wants to fulfill." The reason for this is that if the agent were to hold the position that he has these rights only for some more restrictive reason R (such as merit, race, or profession), then he would contradict himself. For, according to this position, if the agent were to lack R, he would have to accept for himself, "I do not have the generic rights"; but it has previously been shown that every agent *must* accept for himself, "I have the generic rights." Since this latter statement logically must be accepted for himself by every agent, he can avoid contradicting himself only by giving up the position that his rights are grounded on some criterion R that is more restrictive than his simply being a prospective purposive agent. And since this latter characteristic belongs equally to all agents, the distribution of the generic rights that follows from it is likewise an equal one.

Although it is true, as Morris points out, that humans differ in their abilities of agency, this does not entail an unequal distribution of the generic rights. For the ground on which each agent claims the generic rights for himself is not simply that he has the abilities of agency, but rather that he is a prospective agent who has purposes he wants to fulfill; and this "is an absolute quality, not varying in degree" (*Reason and Morality,* p. 123). "It is not the generic features or abilities of action as a whole that directly lead an agent to hold that he has rights to freedom and well-being; it is rather that aspect of the features or abilities whereby he pursues purposes he regards as good. . . . In relation to the justification for having the generic rights, then, being an agent is an absolute or noncomparative condition. Wherever there is an agent—a person who controls or can control his behavior by his unforced choice with knowledge of relevant circumstances in pursuit of purposes he regards as good—there is an implicit claim to have the generic rights. This claim on the part of the agent is not affected by degrees of practical ability or agency" (ibid., p. 124).

While tragic cases like Karen Anne Quinlan do indeed have a marked decrease in the generic rights because of their total lack of the abilities of agency, and there is a similar proportionality for mentally deficient persons who do not have the abilities of agency to the extent indicated in my above definition of an agent, such proportionality or degrees of having the generic rights do not pertain to persons who fulfill the above definition. The definition, and hence the characteristic of being an actual or prospective agent, applies to all normal humans, i.e. persons who can control their behavior in the ways indicated. (See also *Reason and Morality,* pp. 140–145).

Morris also has another objection to my theory, but it is based on the mistaken view that the agent, according to my argument given above, holds that his claim to the generic rights is "morally justified" (p. 164). As I have emphasized in my reply to Golding, however, the agent adduces only prudential, not moral, grounds for his right-claim. The moral justification for human rights occurs only in the subsequent step, when the agent recognizes that the ground on which he claims the rights for himself also applies to all other prospective agents. I have discussed this sequence in *Reason and Morality,* pp. 145–147.

NOTES

1. A shorter version of the present chapter was presented at the annual meeting of the American Society for Political and Legal

Philosophy held January 3–4, 1980, in Phoenix, Arizona. It was written as an invited commentary on David Lyons's essay, "Utility and Rights," an expanded version of which is printed in this volume of *Nomos.* All quotations from Lyons are from this chapter.

2. Alan Gewirth, *Reason and Morality* (Chicago: University of Chicago Press, 1978); "The Basis and Content of Human Rights," *Nomos XXIII: Human Rights*, ed. J. Roland Pennock and John W. Chapman (New York: New York University Press, 1981), pp. 119–147) "Starvation and Human Rights," in K. E. Goodpaster and K. M. Sayre, eds., *Ethics and Problems of the 21st Century* (Notre Dame, Ind.: University of Notre Dame Press, 1979), pp. 139–59; "Human Rights and the Prevention of Cancer," 17 *American Philosophical Quarterly* 117–26 (1980); "Are There Any Absolute Rights?" 31 *The Philosophical Quarterly* 1–16 (1981).

3. It is sometimes argued that the Objects of rights need not be goods or interests of the Subjects of the rights. For example, S. I. Benn says: "I may have rights that are not to my advantage. A right to drink myself to death without interference would not be logically absurd" ("Rights," *Encyclopedia of Philosophy*, ed. Paul Edwards [New York: Collier-Macmillan, 1967], vol. 7, p. 196). For similar arguments, see George P. Fletcher, "The Right to Life," 13 *Georgia L. Rev.* 1372–75 (1979).

These arguments can be answered in at least two ways: assertorically and dialectically. Assertorically, a distinction must be drawn between particular and general Objects of rights. For example, freedom is a general Object and a good, but some particular uses of freedom may not be good. The controverted proposition would then say that the Objects of moral rights are general goods (see my reference below to "generic rights"). Dialectically, the controverted propoition would say that when any person *claims* that he has a right to X, it must be the case that he *thinks* X is a good, at least for himself.

The relation of rights to goods also raises more general questions about deontological theories that hold, for example, that the duty to respect the rights of persons has nothing to do with whether anyone stands to benefit thereby. For a version of such a theory, see H. L. A. Hart, "Are There Any Natural Rights?" 64 *Philosophical Review* 175–91, at 180–82 (1955); and Hart, "Bentham on Legal Rights," in A. W. B. Simpson, ed. *Oxford Essays in Jurisprudence* (Second Series) (Oxford: Clarendon Press, 1973), pp. 171–201. I have briefly discussed this issue in *Reason and Morality*, pp. 75–77. For a more general discussion of deontological moral theories, see A. Gewirth, "Ethics," *Encyclopedia Britannica*, 15th ed. (1974), vol. 6, pp. 976–98, at pp. 990–94.

192 ALAN GEWIRTH

4. See Gewirth, *Reason and Morality*, chs. 3–4; also "The Basis and Content of Human Rights," note 2, *supra*.

5. I borrow this expression from H. L. A. Hart, "Are There Any Natural Rights?" 64 *Philosophical Review* 182 (1955).

6. See *Reason and Morality*, pp. 121–25, 141–45.

7. See J. S. Mill, *Utilitarianism*, ch 5. (Everyman's edition), p. 58.

8. See Hume, *Enquiry Concerning the Principles of Morals*, ed. L. A. Selby-Bigge, sec. III, part ii, pp. 193 ff.; J. Bentham, *Theory of Legislation*, ed. C. K. Ogden (London: Routledge and Kegan Paul, 1928), p. 104; H. Sidgwick, *Principles of Political Economy* (London: Macmillan, 1901), pp. 519 ff.; Sidgwick, *Elements of Politics* (London: Macmillan, 1919), pp. 160 ff.

9. I have argued for this in "Are There Any Absolute Rights?" and "Human Rights and the Prevention of Cancer," note 2, *supra*.

10. See *Reason and Morality*, esp. pp. 135, 145–50, 164–69, 183–87, 200–206.

11. Examples of these positions can be found in Robert Nozick, *Anarchy, State, and Utopia* (New York: Basic Books, 1974), pp. 28–33, 170, 173, 238; and Judith Jarvis Thomson, "Some Ruminations on Rights," 19 *Ariz. L. Rev.* 49 ff. (1977).

12. See "Human Rights and the Prevention of Cancer," note 2, *supra*.

13. See "Are There Any Absolute Rights?" note 2, *supra*.

14. *Reason and Morality*, pp. 200–201, 272 ff.

15. J. Bentham, *Introduction to the Principles of Morals and Legislation* (New York: Hafner, 1948), ch. XVI, sec. xxv, pp. 224–25n.

16. *Ibid.*, ch. I, sec. x, p. 4.

17. *Ibid.*, ch. III, sec. i, p. 24.

18. *Ibid.*, ch. I, sec. iv, p. 3. Cf. *ibid.*, ch. IV, sec. v, pp. 30–31.

19. J. S. Mill, *Utilitarianism*, ch. V (Everyman's edition), p. 50.

20. *Ibid.*

21. J. S. Mill, *On Liberty*, chs. 1, 3 (Everyman's edition), pp. 74, 114.

22. *Ibid.*, chs. 4, 5, pp. 132, 150.

23. See W. N. Hohfeld, *Fundamental Legal Conceptions* (New Haven: Yale University Press, 1964), pp. 36 ff.

24. Bernard Bosanquet, *The Philosophical Theory of the State*, 4th ed. (London: Macmillan, 1951), pp. 187–201. The quotation is from p. 195.

25. *Ibid.*, p. 174. See also p. 170.

26. Karl Marx, "*On the Jewish Question*" in *The Marx-Engels Reader*, ed. Robert C. Tucker, second edition (New York: W. W. Norton & Co., 1978), pp. 42, 43.

27. In his restatement of my argument Golding uses letters instead of numbers. To bring his restatement into line with my own presentation of the argument given in the text above, I have changed

his letters to the corresponding numbers for the various steps. It should also be noted that the argument given in this Appendix differs slightly from the one given in "The Basis and Content of Human Rights" (p. 129), but the changes make no substantive difference. In the quotation given below from *Reason and Morality*, p. 89, I have also changed the numbers to make the various steps uniform with the version given in this Appendix.

28. I have also discussed this question in detail elsewhere: "Must One Play the Moral Language Game?" *American Philosophical Quarterly* 7 (1970): 107–118.

9

RIGHTS, UTILITY, AND CIVIL DISOBEDIENCE

RICHARD E. FLATHMAN

For a considerable period, much of the disputation between utilitarians and their critics took the following form. Utilitarians claimed their theory was encompassing and systematic. They argued that its basic principle is foundational of all morality (and perhaps the entirety of our normative experience), and they claimed that any principle, practice, institution or judgment that could not be defended by (perhaps even derived from) reasoning based on that principle was thereby shown to be unacceptable. Critics responded by calling attention to features of our moral experience that everyone, including utilitarians, firmly believe to be fully justified and attempted to show that utilitarians could not, consistent with the basic tenets of their theory, justify those features. Utilitarians then responded that the critics either inadequately grasped the utilitarian principle and utilitarian reasoning or misunderstood the features of moral experience in question (or both). They then proceeded to argue that, properly understood and applied, their theory accounts for whatever is justified in the beliefs, practices, or arrangements in question. Much of this debate was not only piecemeal in the manner suggested but proceeded in terms of purpose-built examples and counterexamples.

In considerable part, Professor Lyons's essay and this rejoinder to it fit this familiar (and somewhat unsatisfying) pattern. The oft-repeated charge that utilitarianism cannot consistently accommodate a salient and widely valued feature of moral experience, that is, moral rights, is extended by Lyons to encompass legal rights as well. (Or rather legal rights that possess what Lyons calls "normative force." I find this notion somewhat obscure, but because, so far as I can see, nothing in my counterargument turns upon his use of it, I will not take it up). This is an interesting claim because while Bentham and perhaps some other utilitarians have embraced the conclusion that "moral rights" is a defective notion, all utilitarians known to me have insisted that they could give an (indeed the only) adequate account of and justification for legal rights. My counterargument will be in part an attempt to show that Lyons gives inadequate attention to the fact that legal rights are part of a system or practice of authority. Focusing on the significance of this fact for moral and political reasoning, I suggest, allows the utilitarian improved (as against Lyons's account) purchase on legal rights.

In recent years, however, the discussion has deepened in salutary ways. Critics have argued (sometimes by reviving arguments of a yet earlier period) that the very foundations of utilitarianism are defective. Various utilitarians have begun to rejoin in kind by reworking basic aspects of the utilitarian position. Professor Lyons has recently contributed importantly to this process by giving us sympathetic and sensitive reconstructions of J. S. Mill's version of the theory. A brief comment such as this will not permit of any very conclusive discussion of these deeper issues. But my rejoinder will reflect the more recent discussions in at least one respect, namely that it will draw on Lyons's interpretation of the basics of Mill's theory as part of arguing against Lyons's claim that utilitarianism cannot accommodate legal rights.

I

Lyons concedes that non-act-utilitarian utilitarians can justify institutions, including the institution known as legal rights. That is, in principle they can, consistent with the basics of their theory, conclude that the institution known as legal rights has a justified place in at least some societies under at least some circumstances. The difficulty arises when utilitarians must bring this general judgment about the institution to bear on particular decisions about conduct within the setting of that institution. Qua utilitarians, they are committed to maximizing the general welfare (or some such foundational value). They find the institution of legal rights justified because, as a generalization, having the institution contributes to this most fundamental of objectives. But there is no logic by which this generalization can of certainty be carried over to particular questions that arise within the confines of the institution. Circumstances might arise in which encroaching upon a right contributes more to the general welfare than respecting or enforcing it; if and when they do, and even if the contribution of the violation is only marginally greater than that of respecting the right, consistency with their basic principle requires utilitarians to violate the right. Attempts by rule-utilitarians to block this inference are "either arbitrary or else . . . motivated by a desire to accommodate the moral force of rights and obligations under justified rules."[1]

There is an all but standard type of utilitarian rejoinder to arguments such as Lyons's. Such objections, the rejoinder goes, depend upon an overly narrow identification of the act in question and hence on an artificially restricted assessment of the consequences of the conduct for the general welfare. Critics impute to the utilitarian an almost total lack of peripheral moral vision. When this error is corrected, when the utilitarian is credited with ordinary capacity to appreciate the radiations of the conduct and their consequences for the general welfare, it will be evident that the utilitarian judgments will encompass everything that is defensible in our considered moral judgments.

Owing to the fact that Lyons's example relies heavily on the conduct of an official, a rejoinder of this type is readily available. Officials as such act by virtue of their authority. If the persons who hold offices act in ways that exceed their authority, their acts are *ultra vires* and rightfully have no official consequences whatever. It is a conceptual fact, moreover, that the legal rights of persons in society set limits on the authority of all officials. Save for highly exceptional and conceptually discombobulating circumstances (such as those that stymied the U.S. Supreme Court in the Japanese internment cases), it is a conceptual impossibility for an official to violate a legal right and yet act *intra vires*.

Recognizing this, if Lyons's official wants to act officially, he will have a conclusive reason for respecting rights. If he fails to respect them, he can expect that his superiors, whether a higher administrative official or a court, will annul his attempted act.[2] Qua official acting within a legal system that includes legal rights, Lyons's agent, whether of utilitarian or some other persuasion, *must* respect rights.

Strictly speaking, then, Lyons's example is incoherent. The reasoning he assigns to the leading character in his philosophical mini-drama is excluded by the role which that character has been assigned in the play.

Later on, I will try to show that this critique of Lyons's example comports nicely with his own account of the place of conceptual considerations in Mill's version of utilitarianism. But first I explore somewhat further the implications of my argument to this juncture.

Lyons might rejoin that my line of analysis shows that the trouble with utilitarianism is even wider than his story was intended to illustrate. If utilitarianism cannot accommodate respect for rights in particular cases, and if such respect is a condition of the exercise of authority, then my analysis shows not that utilitarians must respect rights but rather that they have the same problem with authority that they have with rights. All cases in which utility requires officials to violate rights will also be cases in which utility requires those "officials" to exceed their authority. Authority is just another deontic notion, and it will no more withstand the acids of utilitarianism than will rights. It appears that utilitarians can justify institutions such as rights and authority but cannot logically commit themselves to respecting the demands of either in day-to-day practice.[3]

We can and should concede that in an ultimate sense utilitarianism must subordinate both authority and rights to the general welfare. Presumably, this is an implication of the doctrine that the general welfare is the criterion by which institutions should be justified or disjustified. Our initial counterargument nevertheless helps us to see the complex, and the complexly interwoven, character of the situation presented by

Lyons's example and the corresponding complexity of utilitarian (or any other) reasoning that is genuinely reasoning concerning that situation. Let us imagine that Lyons's official does indeed believe that there is a good utilitarian justification for the institution of authority. As with the comparable belief about rights, the possibility of which Lyons concedes to the Millian utilitarian, this belief does not entail the view that persons who are officials may never justifiably exceed their authority or that those who subscribe to that authority must always obey laws and commands that are invested with it. But in any nontrivial sense, holding this belief does presuppose knowing in at least a rough sort of way such distinctions as those between authority and power; between the exercise of authority and the choices and actions of merely private persons; between a law or command and counsel, advice, moral exhortations, expressions of opinion, and the like. It also involves the view that maintaining and respecting these distinctions promotes the general welfare. Actions that erode or engender confusion concerning these distinctions may be justifiable in particular cases, but the justification must be responsive to the considerations on the basis of which the distinctions—and hence the institution of authority— are judged to be valuable.

It does not follow that intelligent, well-informed, rational, utilitarian officials will always decide to stay within their authority and hence always decide to respect all rights that will be affected by their actions. It is evident, however, that there are substantial, properly weighty considerations in favor of doing so, considerations that are conceptually connected with, but not exhausted by (that stand in internal relations to), the rights in question and the reasons that support *them*. These considerations, I should immediately add, hold not only for utilitarians who are also officials but for any utilitarians who believe that the institutions of authority and rights are justified by utilitarian criteria.

The traditional way of stating this type of argument is that violating rights produces side effects that must be considered in assessing the utility of the violation. But is is essential to emphasize two features of the argument that are not always noticed. The first is that some of these side effects, including some that utilitarians with the beliefs I am positing must regard

as in some measure harmful to the general welfare, are necessary, not contingent. *All* violations of legal rights by officials are
also and necessarily *ultra vires*. Thus, the familiar complaint that
utilitarianism leaves it to chance whether important institutions
such as rights and authority should be respected is at least
qualified. The utilitarian may decide that this or that violation
of rights, these or those *ultra vires* acts, are on balance justified
in particular circumstances. But for a utilitarian who knows
what rights and authority are, there is nothing contingent about
the fact that violating a right is an *ultra vires* act. And if the
same utilitarian believes that rights and authority are institutions
that contribute importantly to the general welfare, there is
nothing contingent about there being weighty reasons against
such acts.

The second point to emphasize is that the non-contingent
character of the relationship between authority and rights, while
especially manifest, is hardly unique to those two institutions.
Any number of institutions and more or less institutionalized
arrangements impose duties and obligations, requirements, and
limitations on those who occupy the statuses and play the roles
of which the institutions largely consist. Numerous of these are
interwoven one with the other in ways that are parallel to or
more or less strongly analogous with the relations between state
authority and legal rights. In all such cases the proper charac-
terization of acts done by persons occupying these statuses and
roles, and the appropriate descriptions of the consequences of
those acts, will be given at least in part by the institutional
positions and relations in question. In many cases there will also
be noncontingent "side" effects that will require consideration
by any utilitarian who believes that the institutions contribute
to the general welfare. No utilitarian can deny that parents have
definite duties, that there are more or less clearly defined
proprieties and improprieties in playing the parental role. In
many cases the proper, the conceptually settled, identification
of acts that commit those improprieties themselves entail iden-
tifications of the consequences of those acts. It is the moral duty
of parents to provide food, clothing, shelter, and many other
things for their children. A parent's refusal to provide (or to
make every effort to provide) for their children is not just
wrong in some generalized, flattened-out sense, it just is the

breach of a specific duty. In some cases, moreover, the consequences of breaching that duty will have to be described, not
merely (!) as harmful or as causing pain and suffering, but as
violating a right of the child. Even if this description of the
consequences is thought to be inappropriate (perhaps because
of doubts about ascribing *rights* to children), it will be conceptually requisite to describe the consequences as child neglect.[4]
No utilitarian can object to this description of the consequences.
Any utilitarian who thinks that the institution of parenthood
contributes to the general welfare will have to regard the fact
that child neglect is a consequence of a course of actions as a
weighty reason against it.

II

A very large number of examples of the kind of conceptualizations and interwoven conceptual relations I have been discussing abound. Questions about the general welfare do not
typically arise in a setting of facts so close to being "brute" (in
the notional sense in which some philosophers use that term of
art) that all we can, or need, say about them is that they will
produce some number of units of pain, pleasure, happiness, or
some other highly abstract property. We have a vastly richer, a
vastly more differentiated and particularized normative vocabulary. To eschew this vocabulary, to restrict ourselves to the
thin abstractions imputed to utilitarians, is to misdescribe and
to misunderstand the actions and consequences with which we
purport to be dealing. Questions about the general welfare are
delineated, given distinctive shape and specificity, by the conceptualizations in which they are put.

This understanding, of course, is close to the one that Lyons,
correctly in my judgment, attributes to Mill in respect to rights,
obligations, and justice. In contrast to G. E. Moore's view that
there is no significant differentiation among moral questions,
that all such questions reduce to the common denominator of
determining which action or course of action will "promote
intrinsic value [a flattened out abstraction if there ever was one]
to the maximum degree possible," Mill begins at the other end.
He considers, in effect what forms of judgment must be

accommodated by a moral theory and then applies his basic
values within the resulting constraints."[5] I take the phrase
"forms of judgment" to be shorthand for the kind of established
conceptualizations and conceptual relations that are represented
by legal authority and legal rights, parental duty, and child
neglect. And I take the expressions "must be accommodated"
and "within the resulting constraints" to indicate that in Lyons's
view Mill understood both the deeply settled character of the
conceptualizations, the strong sense in which these are given,
and the noncontingent character of the relations. Mill may or
may not have fully appreciated the extent to which, the number
of cases in which, moral issues are structured in these ways. But
he appreciated it in respect to rights, obligations, and justice;
and his acceptance of the conceptualizations, Lyons seems to
think, was consistent with his larger utilitarian theory.

The last point is presumably an expression of Lyons's view
that Millian utilitarians can justify institutions.[6] But Lyons does
not find this position satisfactory, does not believe it entitles
Mill to claim that he has accounted for rights and obligations.
As a utilitarian, Mill's basic value is the general welfare. He may
think of himself as applying that value within the constraints of
the institution of rights and obligations. But when he does so
concretely, when he takes up questions about particular rights
or obligations in specific circumstances, he will always be obliged
to ask whether respecting that right or discharging that obligation will in fact maximize the general welfare. If it does not,
if even a minimal addition to the general welfare is achieved by
violating the right or the obligation, then the right or the
obligation will have to be violated. This means, as Lyons sees it,
that Mill cannot accommodate "the common understanding"[7]
of rights and obligations.

Lyons's conclusion here obviously depends as much on his
account of this "common understanding" as on his understanding of Mill's utilitarianism. His several formulations of it[8] vary
somewhat, and he does not here defend them at any length.
Lacking space to take them up in detail that would be necessary
to assess his accounts adequately, I will instead conclude with
some further remarks about authority, inviting the reader to
consider the extent to which the two notions are parallel and,
to that extent, whether my remarks put into question both

Lyons's account of rights and his conclusion that Mill's utilitarianism cannot accommodate them.

III

Imagine that someone claims to believe that authority is in
principle a justifiable institution by utilitarian criteria and also
to believe that a particular instance of that institution, say, the
authority of the government under which he lives, is in fact
justified by those criteria. He claims, that is, to subscribe to that
authority. At the same time, however, he insists that it is both
conceptually and normatively proper for him to obey admittedly
intra vires laws and commands only when doing so, in the
circumstances under which the question of obedience arises in
practical form, maximizes (in his judgment) the general welfare.
This combination of views, most of us would hold, is incoherent;
the last claim contradicts, and as a practical matter nullifies, the
claims that precede it.

It might be thought that this incoherence could be avoided
in one of only two ways. Our utilitarian must either commit
himself to the view sometimes known as legal absolutism or he
must forthrightly embrace philosophical anarchism. Either the
authority of a law is a sufficient, a conclusive reason for acting
as the law requires, or it is irrelevant to the question of how to
act and acts must be chosen and justified on their (directly
utilitarian) merits.

Neither legal absolutism nor anarchism, however, seem to me
to map the "common understanding" of this matter. Many
people see merits to the institution of authority and recognize
that subscription to it commits them to treating the authority of
laws or commands not only as a relevant but as a weighty,
indeed ordinarily a decisive, reason for acting as the laws and
commands require. But they also believe that they ought to
subject the content of laws and commands to critical scrutiny.
A not inconsiderable number, moreover, hold that one is
sometimes morally justified in disobeying substantively objectionable laws while continuing to avow, both sincerely and
cogently, subscription to the authority of the government that
promulgated the law.

The views just sketched will be recognized as the rudiments of the theory of civil disobedience. This theory, it seems to me, addresses the same question (albeit in the setting of a different institution) that Lyons raises about the compatibility of Mill's utilitarianism with legal rights. Just as Mill claims to understand and to accept as justified the institution of rights and obligations as they present themselves in the societies about which he is thinking, so civil disobedients claim to understand and to accept as justified the institution of authority as it presents itself via the governments under which they live. Just as Mill recognizes that accepting rights and obligations as justified commits him (means that he is rationally required) to treat them as weighty, ordinarily decisive reasons for action, so civil disobedients take the same view of the practical import of their acceptance of authority. But neither Mill nor civil disobedients regard the institutions in question as self-justifying. Rights, obligations, and authority are justified on some ground or other. (Of course the ground need not be utilitarian). Further, both Mill and civil disobedients hold out the possibility, at once logical or conceptual and normative, of appealing to that ground as a reason for not drawing the practical inferences that (they not only concede but insist) are strongly supported by the reasoning that justifies the institution. Lyons's view that this feature of Mill's theory vitiates Mill's claim to understand, account for, and genuinely to accept rights and obligations implies, by parity of reasoning, that civil disobedients cannot, consistent with their theory, claim to understand, account for, and genuinely accept salient features of authority.

I do not want to overstate Lyons's position. His view of rights is importantly different from the absolutist's view of legal authority and law. He allows that there can be cogent, convincing justifications for encroaching upon undoubted and undoubtedly defensible rights and that one can accept and act upon such justifications without contradicting or abandoning one's belief that the institution of rights, and the particular right in question, have a convincing general justification. His objection seems to be that the utilitarian reaches this conclusion, as it were, too easily; that the reasoning by which the utilitarian justifies encroachments deprives rights of the distinctive standing they in fact have in the common understanding.

I am inclined to agree with this conclusion as regards act-utilitarianism (which, as Lyons points out, does not settle the question whether act-utilitarianism is the theory we ought to adopt). But the conclusion seems wrong concerning the more complex, conceptually sensitive mode of utilitarianism he finds in J. S. Mill. Let us return to the theory of civil disobedience to see whether it can help to arbitrate this disagreement.

Civil disobedients, including utilitarian civil disobedients, do not merely avow or claim, abstractly as it were, to respect authority. They take some pains to show that their commitment to authority has substance, carries specifiable significance or import for their thought and action. The several versions of the doctrine pursue this objective in varying ways, but most of them do so at least by:[9]

1. Treating questions about subscription and obedience, non-subscription and disobedience as distinct and distinctively important questions—questions that require serious concern and sustained, reflective attention. (We might say that civil disobedients show their sense of the distinctive importance of these questions precisely by elaborating a notion of *civil* disobedience).

2. Accepting that there are circumstances in which well-grounded adverse judgments about the substantive merits of laws and commands do not provide a sufficient justification for disobedience. The familiar distinction between a single unjust or otherwise objectionable law and a recurring pattern of such laws is perhaps the most dramatic manifestation of this view, but in almost all versions of the theory it is accompanied by less categorical maxims counseling restraint and circumspection when deciding whether to engage in civil disobedience.

3. Accepting a variety of constraints on the modes of conduct that will be employed in the course of disobedient action. Among the more important of these are that the action will be done openly, not conspiratorially, and without the use of physical violence.

4. Insisting that well-founded adverse judgments about laws and commands do not deprive officials of the authority to attach and enforce legal sanctions for disobedience to

them. Well-grounded adverse judgments about laws and commands, in other words, do not themselves (directly) deprive the latter of their authority. The only implication that follows immediately from such judgments is that the obligation to obey them, which ordinarily follows (the civil disobedient insists) from the fact of their authority, is called into question as a conclusive reason for obeying them. It remains a reason for obedience to which serious-minded persons must give considerable weight (which it does not do, for example, for the anarchist or the revolutionary). But if the judgment that the laws are strongly objectionable conjoins with a number of other judgments about matters such as the likely consequences of the acts of disobedience, including the likely effects of acts of disobedience on the viability of the practice of authority, that judgment is accepted as contributing to a justification for disobedience.

We may observe, in passing, that on this understanding of the matter justifying civil disobedience will not be notably easy. Leaving that point aside, we must recognize that some of these commitments will have to be modified or discarded if we are to construct a theory of civil disobedience to, or "civil encroachment upon," individual rights.[10] I cannot detail the necessary modifications here. The general point that emerges from the discussion, however, seems sufficiently clear. If there are good reasons for the belief that institutions such as rights and authority are justified, and if a particular moral decision is made in the context of such an institution, then the reasons for the belief are relevant to, have bearing upon, that decision. Persons who accept those reasons (and who are acting rationally) will therefore recognize their bearing and give consideration to them in making their moral decisions. They may not find them conclusive, (dispositive) in this case or that. Where they do not find them conclusive, they will explain (at least to themselves) why they do not. That is, they will present the considerations that block or qualify the conclusion that, in their view, the reasons ordinarily support. Their doing so does not deny that the reasons are *reasons*, does not deprive them of that standing. (If it did so, presenting the counterreasons would be irrelevant.

Or rather it would be a contradiction in terms to describe it in this way, the notion of a counterreason obviously presupposing that the consideration countered is a reason).

Because the reasons continue to have standing, they will count as considerations bearing upon the manner in which the persons ought to implement the conclusions they have reached concerning the practical question that set them to reasoning. That is, the considerations will bear upon the further practical questions attendant upon the initial question and judgment. There are many ways to disobey a law. The decision to do so civilly is a decision supported by the reasons (among others) that justify the institutions of authority and law. There are many ways to violate a person's rights. The manner in which one does so, and the consequences of doing so, will (should) be influenced by the grounds on which one thinks that rights are justified.

We are discussing a possible understanding of the relation between justifications for institutions and justifications for actions taken in the setting of institutions that the actors believe to be justified. The understanding is exemplified by, acting on it has been instantiated in, the theory and practice of civil disobedience. Available formulations of that theory elaborate the understanding, giving it the kind of detail that allows us to understand and assess its assumptions and implications. The actual practice of civil disobedients has established, in my judgment, that the theory has definite practical significance, that those who understand, accept, and act upon its tenets act differently, and with importantly different consequences for institutions, from those accepting the major alternative understandings.

As noted, the theory and practice of civil disobedience to authority cannot be simply or mechanically applied to the theory of rights. It is my hope, however, that the discussion has shown important parallels between the issues theorists and practitioners of civil disobedience have addressed and the vital issues in the theory of rights that Lyons discusses in his essay. Whether the understanding developed by civil disobedients is correct concerning any of those issues, it seems undeniable that it has an important bearing upon them.

The theory of civil disobedience, of course, is not a logical adjunct of, indeed stands in no determinate relationship to, utilitarianism. As Lyons recognizes, however, the problem of working out the relation between justifications for institutions and justifications for actions taken in the setting of institutions is not a problem specific to utilitarianism. Let us assume that Lyons is correct that Mill's version of utilitarianism is capable of justifying the *institution* of rights. Let us further assume that the theory of civil disobedience provides a basically satisfactory understanding of the relation between the justification for institutions and justifications for particular actions within the setting of institutions. Specifically, it shows that well-grounded and genuine respect for the institution of authority is compatible with refusals to obey particular commands of authority under certain circumstances. On these assumptions, we need only one further premise to reject Lyons's conclusion that Mill's theory cannot accommodate well-grounded, genuine respect for *particular* rights. That premise, of course, is that the understanding we have found in the theory of civil disobedience is compatible with Mill's form of utilitarianism (or the other way around). I will not attempt a systematic argument for this premise here. I suggest, however, that some of the virtues Lyons finds in Mill's theory, sensitivity to the complexity and the normative import of the conceptual and institutional settings in which moral reasoning occurs, are also virtues that go far to explain both the theoretical appeal and the practical importance of civil disobedience. Perhaps a theory of civil encroachment on rights would contribute importantly to the theory of rights and at least to this aspect of the dispute between utilitarianism and its critics.

NOTES

1. David Lyons, "Utility and Rights," p. 128 of this volume.
2. Lyons recognizes that an official might be punished for *ultra vires* acts and says rightly that the self-interested desire to avoid this fate cannot and ought not to be relied upon in reasoning about how the official ought to act. *Ibid.*, pp. 130–31. My argument, however, does not rely on self-interest in this sense.
3. If this were literally true, it would be less than clear that utilitarianism could justify institutions. Can the justification for an institution be devoid of implications for justified action within the

setting of that institution? Strictly, Lyons's argument here is a retraction of his concession that certain species of utilitarian can justify institutions.

4. Of course there can be disagreements about the facts—about whether the parent made a genuine effort to provide for the child, about whether the provision was in fact adequate, and so forth. The resolution of these disagreements will influence the question of how the consequences of the act should be characterized. But there is no reason to think that these disputes will pit utilitarians against non- or antiutilitarians.

5. This quotation from an earlier version of Lyons' essay does not appear in the version herein published. But see pp. 133–35 [Editors]

6. Actually, the passage we quoted from Lyons just above might be read as expressing a different view. If "forms of judgment" are institutions, and if certain of these "must be accommodated" by a moral theory (including utilitarianism), if the basic values of any theory must be applied within the constraints of those institutions, it would appear that there would be no question of justifying the institutions. (Compare in this respect Robert Nozick's view that natural rights place inviolable "side-constraints" on all decisions, actions, policies, and institutions and the familiar charge that Nozick's theory of rights is without foundations). The institutions would be "given" in some stronger sense than has been implicit in our discussion above. (Perhaps they would be given in the sense that Wittgenstein seems to have in mind when he speaks of "What has to be accepted, the given, is—so one could say—*forms of life.*" *Philosophical Investigations*, 3d ed. trans. by G. E. M. Anscombe (New York: The Macmillan Company, 1971) p. 226e. And this might plausibly be taken to mean that the determination that a person has a right, or that the parent's act was a breach of duty, would be morally dispositive. As we see below, however, if this is a correct reading of the passage, Lyons does not stick with this stronger view.

7. Lyons, *op. cit.*, p. 133.

8. See Lyons esp. *op cit.*, pp. 133–35.

9. The summary that follows is taken, with minor modifications, from my *The Practice of Political Authority* (Chicago: University of Chicago Press, 1980), pp. 121–22.

10. Numerous moral and political philosophers have been receptive to the doctrine of civil disobedience to authority. If it is true that there are important parallels between the "logic" of authority and the "logic" of rights, why have they taken such a sharply contrasting

position concerning seemingly well justified (or the possibility of well justified) violations of rights? If it is because they think more highly of the institution or practice of rights than of authority, I for one would agree with them. But then they should not present their much more stringently deontological views about rights as grounded in the "logic" or the "common understanding" of the notion of a right.

10

UTILITY AND SKEPTICISM

GEORGE P. FLETCHER

Lyons's thesis provokes little disagreement. We hardly need to be convinced of the popular view that utilitarianism cannot readily accommodate rights that insulate decisions from the direct appeal to utilitarian considerations. If there is merit in maintaining an ongoing tension between utilitarian and deontological moral theories, then today we should seek arguments to keep the utilitarian perspective alive. I shall offer a modest argument for reconciling utilitarianism with legal rights that, as Lyons says, have normative force. But first we need to clarify the apparatus that underlies Lyons's claim that utilitarianism cannot accommodate these rights.

First, we need to get straight about three ideas that generate problems for utilitarians who insist on judging every action by appealing to their first principle of value maximization. These ideas are (1) legal rights, (2) moral rights, and (3) legal rights with normative force. The distinction between legal and moral rights must strike most readers as uncontroversial, for we are accustomed to thinking in the positivistic framework cast so convincingly by Hobbes and Bentham. The assumption, which remains unchallenged even in Dworkin's critique of positivism, is that lawmaking agencies can enact enforceable rules of law. These enforceable laws supposedly entail or confer rights on individuals, but since the rights thus conferred might be morally objectionable, we call them "legal rights" in order to reserve normative judgment. In order to distinguish these neutral rights from those we wish to endorse, we need an additional term.

Mill appeals to the notion of moral rights to explain why a validly enacted law might be unjust; a law is unjust, Mill argues, if it deprives someone of that to which he or she has a moral right.

This conventional dichotomy between legal and moral rights fails to exhaust the world Lyons wishes to describe, for he finds it important to introduce another term of moral approval, namely the notion of "rights with normative force." All moral rights, he says, have normative force; but not all legal rights can claim that "the force is with them." Yet as an empirical guess, Lyons claims that at least some legal rights must have this special force behind them, and these normatively appealing rights are precisely those that pose a problem for the utilitarians, for they purport to insulate actions from utilitarian assessment. Yet we lack a convincing argument to restrain legal officials from piercing this insulation and applying their first principle of utility maximization.

Lyons's strategy in introducing the third category of normatively appealing rights is not as transparent as Mill's reasons for speaking of moral rights. Obviously, Lyons wishes to hold back the term "moral rights" from some rights that enjoy normative force. All moral rights have normative force, but to avoid redundancy, we should assume the converse is not true. We are left, then, with the intriguing question of why some rights with normative force fail to qualify as moral rights.

As an aside, let me say that I regard this entire manner of speaking as differing markedly from the discourse of lawyers. There might be some cases in which a lawyer opposing the recognition, say, of a constitutional right to welfare, might say that the right is merely moral. But no intelligent advocate would ever concede that the right he or she was asserting was merely legal. Not even Shylock would claim that his rights under his bond with Antonio should be acknowledged regardless of their merit. Admittedly, there are some procedural rights whose arbitrariness would hardly make sense unless one could appeal to a statutory definition. "I have a legal (or statutory) right to file the appeal within seven days of judgment," the lawyer might claim. Here the appeal to statutory authority functions primarily to stave off the suggestion of arbitrariness in the well-defined time limit. It goes without saying that lawyers arguing for the recognition of substantive rights would never qualify their claims by alleging that the right was moral or that it enjoyed normative force. This point comes through even more clearly in the rhetoric of duties. To label a duty as moral sometimes counts as an argument against its legal recognition. In the cases on the duty to render aid to persons in distress, for example, judges argue that the defendant has a moral duty, but, of course, moral duties are different from those duties that ought to be recognized in the legal system. This is the Kantian way, and even judges in our tradition have enjoyed its influence.

This point is important, for Lyons has a picture of moral and legal rights as though they existed on the same plane and share a common subject matter. Moral rights beckon for admission into the temple of the law, and sometimes progressive judges let them. This way of thinking ignores the Kantian insight that law and morality have different realms. To argue for a moral duty in the Kantian tradition is to make a point against, rather than for, legal recognition of the duty.

But let's stick to Lyons's terminology born of three centuries of academic English positivism. This is not language of lawyers or of judges, but of critics properly coining new terms to account for the phenomena of the legal system. Lyons's new term is "rights with normative force." One puzzle that attends this innovation is how the normative force could attach to the right itself rather than to the exercise of the right. Consider the range of rights generated by the contemporary trend to legalize abortion, all private sexual activity, and the use of marijuana. Now I suppose this trend is, by and large, sound; but I am not sure that the right to abort a fetus or the right to commit adultery accordingly enjoy normative force. Before assessing an abortion or an extramarital affair, we should want to know something about the circumstances. Legalization in these fields hardly suggests the belief that people who exercise their newly acquired rights always do the right thing. The circumstances are so varied and so complex that whether we apply a utilitarian or a competing moral standard, we are hard-pressed to decide whether conduct under particular circumstances is right or wrong. These are spheres of conduct in which the better—the happier—society is one in which people decide these difficult moral issues for themselves. If these are examples of rights with normative force, then we should underscore an important ambiguity in Lyons's notion of good law. If individuals have the right to make difficult decisions that affect their own lives (as well as the lives of fetuses), then these rights might be normatively sound in one of two senses:

1. They are sound, for by and large we expect people to exercise their rights soundly. For utilitarians, this means they are likely to exercise their rights to maximize the general welfare.
2. They are sound, for the issues are so complex that we reduce error in the long run by decentralizing decision making and allowing people closest to the moral controversy to decide by and for themselves what they should do.

Lyons responds to the first of these possibilities. Identifying it as a form of rule-utilitarianism, he argues persuasively that in particular cases the direct appeal to utility will prevail over judgments of utility in the long run. The rule-based right will yield in any case in which the direct appeal to utility undermines the general rule.

Yet so far as I can tell, Lyons does not consider the second possibility. This alternative rests not on rule-utilitarianism but on skepticism about our capacity to assess and to maximize utility. Economists share this skepticism when they claim that as a matter of subjective preference, utility does not lend itself to interpersonal comparison. Lawyers express the same skepticism about the objective maximization of utility when they argue for the decentralization of decisional competence. Individual rights to decide complex moral matters might derive precisely from skepticism. It is not that we believe that decentralized decision making will maximize utility, but rather that decentralization might be the least dangerous strategy for structuring power in a morally divided society.

For the economist, this should be familiar ground, for the analogue of the first interpretation is central planning; the analogue of the second is the free market. Both central planning and the free market appeal to utilitarian standards of justification. The dispute between them turns largely on epistemological questions: Is the planner or the consumer aided by the mechanism of the market, in the better position to act for the common good? The analogy with economic theory falls short, for there is no analogue in decentralized moral decision making to the hidden hand of the market. But the two fields share the assumption that the person closest to the decision is most likely to make the right, value-maximizing decision. Indeed, proponents of the common law urge the same principle in advocating case-by-case development of the law as superior to legislation.

The question remains whether the second interpretation— the argument born of skepticism—qualifies as utilitarian justification of rights. Two versions of the skeptical argument need to be distinguished. According to the first version, analogous to the economist's rejection of the interpersonal comparison of utility, the skepticism is complete. There is no way of knowing what might maximize utility. In that case, we might favor letting individuals decide complex moral matters for themselves. But the argument for individual rights in this case would not be utilitarian. The recognition of rights would reflect a rejection of centralized decision making and a commitment to individual liberty as a nonutilitarian value.

The second version of the skeptical argument resembles the thinking of lawyers rather than that of skeptical free market economists. In defending judicial development of the law, lawyers often argue that the person closest to the problem is most likely to make the right decision. Judges, therefore, are more likely to make a sound decision than legislators, further removed from the details of the social conflict. This way of thinking reflects only a partial skepticism. It is possible to make the right decision. Yet some are more likely to make the right decision than others. For present purposes, let us assume that the "rightness" of the decision is measured in criteria of utility.

The notion that some people "are more likely to make the right decision" is missing from Lyons's arsenal of utilitarian arguments. Yet this argument, borrowed from the thinking of lawyers about institutional competence, provides a modest utilitarian defense of legal rights with normative force. The argument would be that in some situations, such as abortion, divorce, and other family matters, the individual confronted with the moral question is most likely to make the best decision. It follows that the individual should have the right to resolve the moral quandary for himself or herself.

This modest argument obviously needs refinement. The suggestion is offered here only to stimulate reconsideration of the utilitarian position.

PART III

INTERNATIONAL REDISTRIBUTION

11

HUMANITY AND JUSTICE IN GLOBAL PERSPECTIVE

BRIAN BARRY

This chapter has three sections. The first argues that considerations of humanity require that rich countries give aid to poor ones. The second argues that considerations of justice also require transfers from rich countries to poor ones. The third picks up the distinction between aid and transfer and argues that, when we get into detail, the obligations imposed by humanity and justice are different, although not incompatible.

I. HUMANITY

1. Introduction

What is it to act in a way called for by humanity? A humane act is a beneficent act, but not every beneficent act is a humane one. To do something that helps to make someone who is already very happy even happier is certainly beneficent, but it would not naturally be described as an act called for by considerations of humanity.

The *Oxford English Dictionary* defines humanity as "Disposition to treat human beings and animals with consideration and compassion, and to relieve their distresses; kindness, benevolence."[1] In this essay I shall understand by "humanity" the relief of distress. As a matter of usage, it seems to me that the *OED* is right to put this before the more extended sense of kindness or benevolence in general. In any case, it is this notion that I want to discuss, and the word "humanity" is the closest representation of it in common use.

There are three questions to be dealt with. First, is it morally obligatory to behave humanely, or is it simply laudable but not morally delinquent to fail so to act? Second, if it is morally obligatory, what implications does it have, if any, for the obligations of rich countries to aid poor ones? Third, if (as I shall suggest) rich countries have a humanitarian obligation to aid poor ones, on what criterion can we determine how much sacrifice the rich countries should be prepared to make?

2. The Obligation of Humanity

I shall begin my discussion by taking up and considering the argument put forward by Peter Singer in his article "Famine, Affluence and Morality."[2] Singer puts forward a simple, clear, and forceful case for a humanitarian obligation for those in rich countries to give economic aid to those in poor countries. The premises of his argument are as follows. The first is "that suffering and death from lack of food, shelter, and medical care are bad."[3] The second is given in two alternative forms. One is that "if it is in our power to prevent something bad from happening, without thereby sacrificing anything of comparable moral importance, we ought, morally, to do it."[4] The other, and weaker, form is that "if it is in our power to prevent something very bad from happening, without sacrificing anything morally significant, we ought, morally, to do it."[5] He goes on to say that "an application of this principle [i.e., the second version] would be as follows: if I am walking past a shallow pond and see a child drowning in it, I ought to wade in and pull the child out. This will mean getting my clothes muddy, but this is insignificant, while the death of the child would presumably be a very bad thing."[6] All that has to be added is that the application of the second premise is unaffected by proximity or distance and "makes no distinction between cases in which I am the only person who could possibly do anything and cases in which I am just one among millions in the same position."[7] If we accept these premises, we are committed, Singer claims, to the conclusion that people in the rich countries have a moral obligation to help those in the poor countries.

For the purpose of this chapter, I am going to take it as common ground that one would indeed be doing wrong to walk past Peter Singer's drowning child and do nothing to save it. This of course entails that, at least in the most favorable cases, duties of humanity must exist. In the space available, it hardly makes sense to try to argue for a complete theory of morality from which this can be deduced, and in any case I myself am more sure of the conclusion than of any of the alternative premises from which it would follow. Anyone who disagrees with the claim that there is an obligation to rescue the child in the case as stated will not find what follows persuasive, since I certainly do not think that the case for international aid on humanitarian grounds is *stronger* than the case for rescuing the drowning child.

3. Does the Drowning Child Case Extend to International Aid?

The extension of the drowning child case may be challenged along several lines. Here I can only state them and say briefly why I do not think they undercut the basic idea that the case for an obligation to save the drowning child applies also to giving international aid. The appearance of dogmatism is purely a result of compression.

The first argument is that the child may be supposed not to be responsible for his plight (or at any rate it may be on that supposition that the example gets to us) but that countries are responsible for their economic problems. My comments here are two. First, even if it were true that the death by disease and or starvation of somebody in a poor country were to some degree the result of past acts or omissions by the entire population, that scarcely makes it morally decent to hold the individual responsible for his plight; nor, similarly, if his predicament could have been avoided had the policies of his government been different.

Let us move on to consider another way in which a challenge may be mounted to Singer's extension of the argument for a duty to aid from the case of the drowning child to that of famine relief. It may be recalled that Singer explicitly made the shift from one case to the other via the statement that niether proximity nor the one-to-one relation between the victim and the potential rescuer makes any moral difference. Clearly, if this claim is denied, we can again agree on the duty to rescue the drowning child but deny that this is an appropriate analogue to the putative duty of people in rich countries to aid those in poor ones. A number of philosophers have tried to drive a wedge between the cases in this way, but I have to say that I am not very impressed by their efforts. The argument for proximity as a relevant factor is that, if we posit a duty to rescue those near at hand, we keep the duty within narrow bounds and thus do not let it interfere with people's life plans; but, if we allow the duty to range over the whole of mankind, it becomes too demanding. Although some people see merit in this, it appears to me that it is invoked simply because it provides a way of arbitrarily truncating the application of the principle so as to arrive at a convenient answer. I shall go on later to agree that there are limits to what people can be required to sacrifice. But I see no ethically defensible reason for saying that, if we can't (or can't be required to) do anything we might, we should simply contract the sphere of operation of the principle that we are obliged to relieve suffering. Perhaps we should channel our limited humanitarian efforts to where they are most needed, which, if we live in a relatively rich country, is likely to be outside its boundaries.

Singer also made it explicit that, if the case of the drowning child were to be extended to international aid, one would have to rule out the one-to-one relation between the rescuer and the potential rescuee as a morally relevant factor. Attempts have been made to do so, but they likewise seem to me to lack merit. If there are several people who could save the drowning child, it is sometimes said that none of them is particularly responsible for saving it. But if the child drowns because none of them saves it, they are all, I would suggest, morally responsible for its death. Conversely, suppose that several people are drowning at some distance from one another and there is only one person around to save them. It has been argued that since that person cannot do his duty, if that is defined as saving all those whom he might save (assuming that he could save any one of them but cannot save more than one), no such duty exists. The obvious reply to this is that the duty has been incorrectly defined: the duty in this case is to save one, and his duty is not affected by the fact that there are others who cannot be saved.

Finally, it might be accepted that the case of the drowning child would extend to international aid if the aid would do any good, but then denied that it will. The main lines of this argument are two. The first is the one from waste and inefficiency: aid does not get to the right people; development projects are a disaster; and so on. But I would claim that even if waste is endemic in aid to poor (and probably ill-organized) countries, the difference it makes to health and nutrition is sufficient to make it worth giving if only part of it gets to the people it is supposed to get to. And if, as is all too true, aid in the past has often been inappropriate, the answer is not to withold aid but to make it more appropriate: no more massive dams, electricity-generating stations, or steel mills, but cheaper, less complex, and more decentralized technology.

The second line of argument is the neo-Malthusian: that the only effect of aid in the long run is to lead to population increase and thus to even more suffering. I agree that if this is the only effect of aid, the humanitarian case for it falls to the ground. But it is clear that economic development combined with appropriate social policies and the widespread availability of contraception can actually reduce the rate of population growth. The implication is thus that aid should be given in large amounts where the social and political conditions are right, so as to get countries through the demographic transition from high birthrate and high death rate to low birthrate and low death rate as rapidly as possible.

Where ideological or religious dogmas result in pronatalist government policies or rejection of contraception by the population, one might conclude that aid would be better withheld, since the only foreseeable effect of economic improvement will be to increase numbers. But can we really be so sure that attitudes will not change? The election of a relatively young and doctrinally reactionary pope does not encourage hopes of any early change in official doctrine. But even without any change at that level, it is striking how, in the developed countries, the practices of Roman Catholics have altered dramatically in just a couple of decades. For example, in the Province of Quebec, which had for more than two centuries a birthrate close to the physical maximum, with families of more than 10 children quite common, has now one of the lowest birthrates in North America.

4. How Far Does the Obligation Extend?

If we accept the conclusion that the rich have some obligation on humanitarian grounds to provide economic aid to the poor, the next question is, How much sacrifice is required? In my view, no simple and determinate criterion is available. This is a problem of the obligation of humanity in general, not a peculiarity of the international context. In the standard case of rescuing someone in danger of drowning, the usual guidance one gets from moral philosophers is that the obligation does not extend to risking one's life, though it does require that one suffer a fair amount of inconvenience. However, the decision in such cases, like that of Singer's drowning child, characteristically has clear and finite limits to its implications. But, given the failure of most people or governments in rich countries to give much aid, it would clearly be possible for individuals to give up a high proportion of their incomes without risking their lives and still leave millions of savable lives in poor countries unsaved. Thus, the question of limits is pressing.

There is an answer that is, in principle, straightforward. It is the one embodied in Singer's claim that one is obliged to help up to the point at which one is sacrificing something of "comparable moral importance." This is, of course, a maximizing form of consequentialism. If you say that pains and pleasures are what is of moral importance, you get Benthamite utilitarianism (in the traditional interpretation, anyway); if you say it is the enjoyment of beauty and personal relationships, you get G. E. Moore's ideal consequentialism; and so on. The trouble with this is, needless to say, that most of us do not see any reason for accepting an obligation to maximize the total amount of good in the universe.

Singer's weaker principle that we should give aid up to the point at which we are sacrificing anything of moral importance seems to me useless: for a Benthamite utilitarian, for example, even getting one's trousers muddy would be in itself an evil—

not one comparable to the death of a child, but an evil none the less. Even Singer's chosen case would therefore be eliminated on this criterion, let alone any more strenuous sacrifices.

5. Conclusion

I conclude, provisionally and in the absence of any plausible alternative, that there is no firm criterion for the amount of sacrifice required to relieve distress. This does not mean that nothing can be said. I think it is fairly clear that there is a greater obligation the more severe the distress, the better off the potential helper would still be after helping, and the higher the ratio of benefit to cost. What is indefinite is where the line is to be drawn. In the words of C. D. Broad, in what may be the best single article in philosophical ethics ever written, "it is no objection to say that it is totally impossible to determine exactly where this point comes in any particular case. This is quite true, but it is too common a difficulty in ethics to worry us, and we know that we are lucky in ethical questions if we can state upper and lower limits that are not too ridiculously far apart."[8]

What, in any case, are we talking about here as the range? We could perhaps wonder whether the level of aid from a country like the United States should be 3 percent of GNP (the level of Marshall aid) or 10 or 25 percent. But, unless we reject the idea of an obligation to aid those in distress altogether, we can hardly doubt that one quarter of 1 percent is grotesquely too little.

II. JUSTICE

1. The Concept of Justice

"Are we not trying to pack too much into the concept of justice and the correlative concept of rights? The question whether it is *wrong* to act in certain ways is not the same question as whether it is *unjust* so to act."[9] I think the answer to Passmore's rhetorical question is in the affirmative. We should not expect to get out of "justice" a blueprint for the good society—nor should we wish to, since that degree of specificity would inevitably limit potential applicability. Surely it ought to be possible for a just society to be rich or poor, cultivated or philistine, religious or secular and (within some limits that are inherent in justice itself) to have more or less of liberty, equality, and fraternity.

Up to this point, I have studiously avoided any reference to justice. I have been talking about the obligation to relieve suffering as a matter of humanity. The fact that the obligation is not derived from justice does not make it a matter of generosity, nor does it entail that it should be left to voluntary action to adhere to it. It is an obligation that it would be wrong not to carry out and that could quite properly be enforced upon rich countries if the world political system made this feasible. And the core of the discussion has been the claim that the obligation to help (and a fortiori the obligation not to harm) is not limited in its application to those who form a single political community.

It is of course open to anyone who wishes to do so to argue that, if the rich have a properly enforceable obligation to give, this is all we need in order to be able to say that the rich must give to the poor as a matter of justice. I have no way of proving that it is a mistake to use the term "just" to mark out the line between, on the one hand, what is morally required and, on the other, what is praiseworthy to do but not wrong to omit doing. All I can say is that such a way of talking seems to me to result in the blunting of our moral vocabulary and therefore to a loss of precision in our moral thinking. Justice, I wish to maintain, is not merely one end of a monochromatic scale that has at the other end sacrifice of self-interest for the good of others to a heroic or saintly degree. Rather, it points to a particular set of reasons why people (or societies) may have duties to one another and to particular features of institutions that make them morally condemnable.[10]

I shall return to the distinction between humanity and justice in Section III, where I shall be able to refer to the results of my discussions of each of them. My plan is to analyze justice under two heads. The first is justice as reciprocity; the second, justice as equal rights. These are both familiar ideas, though I shall give the second a slightly unfamiliar twist. Justice as reciprocity

I will discuss in three aspects: justice as fidelity, justice as requital, and justice as fair play.

2. Justice as Fidelity

The notion of justice as fidelity is that of keeping faith. In addition to covering contract and promises, it extends, in a rather indefinite way, to meeting legitimate expectations not derived from explicit voluntary agreement. Clearly it is an essentially conservative principle and tends if anything to operate contrary to the interests of poor countries, insofar as they often find themselves in the position of seeking to renegotiate disadvantageous deals with transnational corporations within their territories.

3. Justice as Requital

Justice as requital is also a basically conservative principle but can, on occasion, have revisionist implications vis-à-vis justice as fidelity. No simple rule governs what happens when they conflict. Henry Sidgwick, with characteristic caution, said that we have two standards of justice, as the customary distribution and as the ideal distribution, and added that "it is the reconciliation between these two views which is the problem of political justice."[11] I shall not take up that challenge here, but explore the possible implications of justice as requital for international distribution.

The idea of justice as requital is that of a fair return: a fair exchange, a fair share of benefits from some common endeavor, and so on. The most obvious application in the relations between rich and poor countries is whether poor countries are getting fair prices for their exports and paying fair prices for their imports. This, of course, raises the obvious question of what the criterion of a "fair price" is. Suppose, however, that we say, minimally, that it is the prevailing world price. Then it seems clear that, even on this criterion, many poor countries have legitimate complaints about the transfer pricing of transnational corporations. For example, when in the late 1960 the Andean Pact countries (Bolivia, Colombia, Ecuador, and Peru) started taking a serious interest in the pricing policies of transnational corporations operating within their territories, they found overpricing of imports to be the norm, sometimes by factors of hundreds of percent, and, less spectacularly, underpricing of the value of exports.[12] This enabled the companies to attain rates of return on capital of often more than 100 percent while at the same time evading government limits on repatriation of profits. Since the Andean Pact countries have been politically independent for a century and a half and have relatively sophisticated bureaucracies compared with most countries in the Third World, it is inconceivable that similar practices do not obtain in other, more vulnerable countries.

When we turn to the structure of world prices itself, the criterion of justice as requital becomes less helpful. The countries of the Third World, as part of their demands for a "New International Economic Order" have demanded an "Integrated Program" of commodity management that would be designed to push up the prices of raw materials in relation to manufactured products.

The success of The Organization of Petroleum Exporting Countries (OPEC) is, of course, significant here in providing a dazzling example of the effectiveness of a producer cartel. Oil, however, seems to be unique in that it is so cheap to extract and worth so much to consumers. This means that it has always, since the days of the Pennsylvania oilfields, yielded enormous economic rents. The only question has been who captured them. And clearly, until 1973, the Middle Eastern oil producers were getting only a small proportion of the economic rent.

Other commodities are not like oil. It may indeed be possible to push up the prices by restricting supply, but substitution or recycling is likely to set in. From the long-run point of view of the world, this pressure toward conservation would be desirable, no doubt, but the point is that it does not spell a bonanza for the raw material producers.

Clearly, this is only scratching the surface, but I think that it is, at any rate, important to keep in mind that, even if commodity prices could be raised substantially across the board, this would not make most poor countries *appreciably* better off; and it would make some, including the important cases of India and Bangladesh, worse off. Whatever conclusion one wishes to draw, therefore, about the applicability to world prices of justice as requital, the implications are not going to be such as to solve the problem of poor countries that are also resource poor.

4. Justice as Fair Play

We still have to see if any redistributive implications flow from the third branch of justice as reciprocity: justice as fair play. The idea here is that if one benefits (or stands to benefit) from some cooperative practice, one should not be a "free rider" by taking the benefits (or being ready to take them if the occasion arises) while failing to do one's part in sustaining the practice when it is one's turn to do so. Thus, if others burn smokeless fuel in their fireplaces, pack their litter out of the backcountry, or clean up after their dogs, it is unfair for you to refuse to do the same.

The principle of fair play has a potentiality for underwriting a certain amount of redistribution from rich to poor insofar as one practice that might be regarded as prospectively beneficial to all concerned would be the practice of helping those in need. If such a practice existed, it would operate analogously to insurance, which is a contractual way of transferring money from those who have not suffered from certain specified calamities to those who have. The principle of fair play would then hold that it would be unfair to be a free rider on a scheme of helping those in need by refusing to do your part when called upon.

The invocation of this notion of what the sociobiologists call "reciprocal altruism" may appear to provide a new way of distinguishing the drowning child case from that of international aid. Perhaps what motivates us in agreeing that there is an obligation to rescue the child is an unarticulated contextual assumption that the child belongs to our community (however widely we may conceive that "community") and that there are norms within that community calling for low-cost rescue from which we stand to gain if ever we find ourselves in need of rescue. Such feelings of obligation as we have in this case can therefore be adequately explained by supposing that they arise from the application of the principle of fair play. It was, thus, an error to have taken it for granted that an acknowledgment of an obligation to help in the drowning child case must show that we accepted a general principle of an obligation to aid those in distress.

I believe that the objection is formally valid. That is to say, it is possible by invoking the principle of fair play to underwrite the obligation to rescue the drowning child without committing oneself to a universal obligation to rescue. One could respond to this by arguing that the conclusions in Section I of this essay can be reinstated by deriving universal obligations from the existence of world community. I shall consider this argument below. But before doing so, I should like to follow an alternative and more aggressive line.

The point to observe is that, although we may indeed be motivated to agree that we ought to rescue the drowning child by considerations of justice as reciprocity, it does not follow that we are motivated solely by those considerations. Suppose that you are briefly visiting a foreign country, with an entirely alien culture, and have no idea about the local norms of rescue. Would you, if you came across Singer's drowning child, have an obligation to wade in and rescue it? I think that most people would say yes in answer to that question. And, clearly, those who do are acknowledging obligations of humanity as distinct from obligations of justice.

None of this, of course, is intended to suggest that the difficulties in moving from a general obligation of humanity to an obligation on the part of rich countries to give economic aid to poor ones is any less problematic than it appeared earlier. But it does fend off a possible challenge to the move from the drowning child case to the universal obligation to aid. The view I want to maintain is that the answer in the drowning child case is overdetermined where the duty of fair play also underwrites rescue. The strength of the obligation depends upon the circumstances, but it never disappears. Both psychologically and morally, the obligation to aid would be strongest if there were an explicit and generally observed agreement among a group of parents to keep an eye on one another's children: humanity, fidelity, and fair play would then coincide and reinforce each other. The obligation would be perhaps a little less strong but still very strong in a small, stable, and close-knit community with a well-developed tradition of "neighborliness," since the obligation of fair play would here have maximum force. It would be less strong if the norm of rescue were more widely diffused over a whole society, and would of course vary according to the society. (New Zealand would rate much higher than the United States on the strength of the norm of helping strangers within the society, for example.) And, finally, in the absence of any established practice of aiding strangers that would give rise to obligations of fair play, there is still, I am suggesting, an obligation of humanity that does not in any way depend upon considerations of reciprocity.[13]

I have been taking for granted that the existence of a practice of rescue does give rise to an obligation to play one's part. This can be questioned. Somebody might say: "Why should I cooperate with the scheme if I'm willing to renounce any benefits that might be due to me under it?[14] But the cogency of the objection depends upon the existence of stringent conditions of publicity: it must be possible to make this known to all those in the scheme, and it must be remembered perhaps for decades. (This is essential, since many transfers to those in need are going to be predominantly from the young and middle-aged to the old, so it would undermine the integrity of any such cooperative scheme if people could change their minds about its value as they got older.) Neither condition is generally met. Consider a practice of rescuing the victims of accidents—drowning swimmers are the usually cited case. If this practice exists in a whole society, it is not feasible for those who wish to opt out to notify everybody else in advance. And how many could be counted on to be strong-minded enough to wave away a would-be rescuer when they were in need of help themselves? Even if they could, in many cases the rescuer has to incur the trouble and risk in order to get there (as with rescuing a swimmer) or the victim may be unconscious and thus incapable of spurning help.

It is crucially important to notice, however, that the principle of fair play is conditional; that is to say, it stipulates that it is unfair to be a free rider on an actually existing cooperative practice, and that it *would* be unfair to free ride on other mutually beneficial practices if they did exist. But it does not say that it is unfair for a practice that would, if it existed, be mutually beneficial, not to exist.

As anyone familiar with Rawls's theory of justice will have been aware for some time, we are here on the edge of deep waters. For one strand of Rawls's theory is precisely the notion of justice as reciprocity that is embodied in the principle of fair play. According to Rawls, a society is a scheme of social cooperation, and from this fact we can generate, via the notion of fair play, principles of justice. But, clearly, any actual society simply generates whatever is generated by its actual cooperative practices. If it provides retirement pensions out of social security taxes, it is unfair to be a free rider on the scheme by dodging your share of the cost. And so on. But if I am right about the applicability of the principle of fair play, the most Rawls can say about a society that does not have such a scheme is that it suffers from collective irrationality in that it is passing up a chance to do itself some good. He cannot, I suggest, employ the principle as a step in an argument that such a society is unjust.

I make this point because Charles Beitz, in the last part of his admirable book, *Political Philosophy and International Relations*,[15] has argued, within a Rawlsian framework, for a global difference principle. That is to say, income should be redistributed internationally so that the worst-off representative individual in the world is as well off as possible. Beitz acknowledges that he is taking for granted the general validity of Rawls's theory and is simply arguing from within its basic premises for the dropping of Rawls's restriction on the application of the two principles of justice to societies. I have been suggesting that, even within a society, one cannot use the fact that it is a cooperative scheme to argue that it is unfair not to have more extensive cooperation, though not to do so may be collectively irrational. But the international scene presents two further difficulties. First, I think that Rawls is broadly right in (implicitly) denying that the whole world constitutes a single cooperative partnership in the required sense. Second, I do not think that international redistribution can plausibly be said to be advantageous to rich as well as poor countries. Rawls is therefore probably correct in deducing from his system only nonaggression, diplomatic immunity, and the like as mutually advantageous to countries and thus, on his side of the principle of fair play, just. If I am right, however, they are simply collectively rational and give rise to duties of fair play only to the extent that they are instantiated in actual practice.

Beitz's argument for extending the Rawlsian difference principle is in essense that the network of international trade is sufficiently extensive to draw all countries together in a single cooperative scheme. But it seems to be that trade, however multilateral, does not constitute a cooperative scheme of the relevant kind. Trade, if freely undertaken, is (presumably) beneficial to the exchanging parties, but it is not, it seems to me, the kind of relationship that gives rise to duties of fair play. To the extent that justice is involved it is, I would say, justice as requital, that is, giving a fair return. Justice as fair play arises not from simple exchange but from either the provision of public goods that are collectively enjoyed (parks; defense; a litter-free, or unpolluted, environment; and so on) or from quasi-insurance schemes for mutual aid of the kind just discussed. Trade in pottery, ornamentation, and weapons can be traced back to prehistoric times, but we would harldy feel inclined to think of, say, the Beaker Folk as forming a single cooperative enterprise with their trading partners. No more did the spice trade unite East and West.

To the extent that we are inclined to think of the world as more of a cooperative enterprise now, this is, in my judgment, not because trade is more extensive or multilateral, but because there really are rudimentary organs of international cooperation in the form of United Nations agencies and such entities as the International Monetary Fund (IMF) and the World Bank. But the resulting relationships clearly fall short of those of mutual dependence found within societies. And my second point comes in here to draw attention to the fact that the extent of increased cooperation that would really be mutually beneficial is probably quite limited. In particular, redistribition on the insurance principle seems to have little appeal to rich countries. In the foreseeable future, aid to the needy is going to flow from, say, the United States to Bangladesh rather than vice versa. The conditions for reciprocity—that all the parties stand prospectively to benefit from the scheme—simply do not exist. One could, of course, again retreat behind the "veil of ignorance" and argue that, if people did not know to which society they belonged, they would surely choose something like a global difference principle—or at any rate a floor below which nobody should be allowed to fall. And this seems plausible enough. (I have argued it myself in an earlier work.[16]) But this move clearly points up even more sharply than in the case of a single society the degree to which inserting the "veil of ignorance" takes us away from the sphere of the principle of fair play.

5. Justice as Equal Rights

In his well-known article, "Are There Any Natural Rights?"[17] H. L. A. Hart argued that special rights must presuppose general rights. Before people can act in ways that modify their, and others', rights (paradigmatically by promising), they must, as a matter of elementary logic, have rights that do not stem from such modifications. Putting this in terms of the present discussion, we can say that justice as reciprocity needs a prior assignment of rights before it can get off the ground.

Now we might try to solve the problem of sanctifying the status quo. We could, in other words, simply declare that we are going to push the principle of justice as the fulfillment of reasonable expectations to the limit and say that whatever rights somebody now has are to be taken as the baseline in relation to which all future developments must satisfy the requirements of fidelity, requital, and fair play. If we note that the conservation of value is akin to the Pareto principle, we may observe that this would give us the Virginia school of political economy, especially associated with James Buchanan.

I have criticized his approach elsewhere,[18] and I shall not repeat my criticisms here. But it is surely enough for the present purpose to draw attention to the fact that on the principle of the unquestioned justice of the status quo, the most grotesque features of the existing allocation of rights would be frozen in place forever unless those who suffered from them could find some quid pro quo that would make it worth the while of, say, a shah of Iran or a General Somoza to accept change. But that would be, if it could be found, an improvement in efficiency arising from the reallocation of the existing rights. It would not face the real problem, which was, of course, the injustice of the initial allocation of rights.

Hart's answer to his own question is that the general right that is presupposed by any special rights is an equal right to liberty. He does not give any explicit argument, as far as I can see, for its being equal. But I take it the point is that since a general right is something that is necessarily anterior to any act giving rise to a special right, there is simply no basis for discriminating among people in respect of general rights. In order to discriminate, one would either have to do so on the basis of some quality that is obviously irrelevant to the assignment of rights (e.g., skin color) or on the basis of something the person has done (e.g., made a promise) that provides a reason for attributing different rights to him. But then we get back to the original point, namely that such a differentiation in rights entails that we have an idea of the proper distribution of rights without the special factor adduced. And that must, it seems, be an equal distribution.

In this essay I want to take this idea and apply it to the case of natural resources. I shall suggest that they fit all the requirements for being the subjects of a general right and that therefore everyone has an equal right to enjoy their benefits.

As Hillel Steiner has remarked, "Nozick rightly insists that our commonsense view of what is just—of what is owed to individuals by right—is inextricably bound up with what they *have done* . . . [but] unlike other objects, the objects of appropriative rights . . . are *not* the results of individuals' past actions. . . . Appropriative claims, and the rules governing them, can have nothing to do with desert."[19] Consider, for example, Bruce Ackerman's fable of the spaceship and the manna. One of the claimants, "Rusher," says: "I say that the first person who grabs a piece of manna should be recognized as its true owner" and, when asked for a reason, says, "Because people who grab first are better than people who grab second."[20] That, I think, illustrates my point. What exactly is supposed to be the virtue of getting there first, or even worse, in merely having some ancestor who got there first?

The position with regard to countries is parallel to that of individuals. Today the basis of state sovereignty over natural resources is convention reinforced by international declarations such as votes of the United Nations General Assembly in 1970, 1972, and 1974 to the effect that each country has "permanent sovereignty over natural resources" within its territory.[21] It is easy enough to see the basis of the convention. It has a transcendent simplicity and definiteness that must recommend it in international relations. For, in the absence of a "common power," stability depends heavily on conventions that leave the minimum amount of room for interpretation. Within a municipal legal system, by contrast, it is possible to introduce and enforce complex rules limiting the rights of individual appropriation (e.g., restricting the amount of water than can be drawn off from a river) and transferring a portion of the economic rent from the property owner to the state. Moreover, in the absence of a "common power" it is a convention that is relatively easy to enforce—at any rate easier than any alternative. For a state may be presumed, other things being equal, to be in a better position to control the appropriation of the natural resources of its own territory than to control those of some other country.

In practice, of course, things are not always equal, and many Third World countries have found that controlling foreign companies that own their natural resources is no easy matter: an unholy alliance of multinational corporations and their patron governments (for most, this is the United States) stand ready to organize international boycotts, to manipulate institutions such as the World Bank and the IMF against them; and, if all else fails, go in for "destabilization" on the Chilean model. The problem is exacerbated when a country seeks to gain control of the exploitation of its own natural resources by expropriating the foreign-based companies that have been there, often long before the country became independent. For the issue of compensation then arises, and this is likely to be contentious, not only because of the possibility of dispute about the current value of the investment, but also because the country may claim compensation for inadequate (or no) royalties paid on extraction in the past, a claim that (as we noted above) falls under the head of justice as requital.

However, as far as I am aware, no body of opinion in either the North or the South is adverse to the principle that each country is entitled to benefit exclusively from its own natural resources, and to decide whether they should be exploited and, if so, at what rate and in what order. And even the practice has come a long way in the last twenty years. The OPEC is of course the outstanding illustration, but the same pattern of improved royalties and more control over the amount extracted and the way in which it is done obtains also in other countries and other commodities.

It would hardly be surprising if, when the principle of national sovereignty over natural resources has been so recently and precariously established, Third World countries should be highly suspicious of any suggestion that natural resources should in future be treated as collective international property. They may well wonder whether this is anything more than a cover for the reintroduction of colonialism. I do not see how such doubts can be allayed by mere assertion. Clearly, everything would depend on the principle's being applied across the board rather than in a one-sided way that lets the industrialized countries act on the maxim "What's yours is mine and what's mine is my own." So far, that is precisely how it has been used, as in the proposals of American chauvinists such as Robert Tucker that the United States should be prepared to occupy the Saudi Arabian oilfields by military force in order to maintain the flow of oil at a "reasonable" price, so that Americans can continue to use up a grossly disproportionate share of the world's oil. Since the United States, if it used only domestically produced oil, would still have one of the world's highest per capita levels of consumption, the effrontery of this proposal for the international control of other countries' oil would be hard to beat.

If the Third World countries were too weak to do anything more than hang on to the present position of national sovereignty over natural resources, we would, it seems to me, have to regard that as the best outcome that can be obtained. It is clearly preferable to the earlier setup, in which countries with the power to do so controlled the natural resources of others. For, although the distribution of natural resources is entirely arbitrary from a moral point of view, it has at any rate the kind of fairness displayed by a lottery. That is presumably better than a situation in which the weak are despoiled of their prizes by force and fraud.

In spite of these forebodings about the potential misuse of the principle that natural resources are the joint possession of the human race as a whole, I think it is worth pursuing. For it is scarcely possible to be satisfied with the present situation from any angle except that of extreme pessimism about the chances of changing it for the better rather than for the worse. The overwhelming fact about the existing system is, obviously, that it makes the economic prospects of a country depend, to a significant degree, on something for which its inhabitants (present or past) can take absolutely no credit and lay no just claim to its exclusive benefits, namely its natural resources—including in this land, water, minerals, sunlight, and so on. The claims of collectivities to appropriate natural resources rest, as do those of individuals, on convention or on law (in this case, such quasi-law as the United Nations resolutions cited above). No doubt, the point has been impressed on people in the West by examples such as Kuwait, the United Arab Emirates, or Saudi Arabia, and it may be that such small numbers of people have never before become so rich without any effort on their own part, simply as a result of sitting on top of rich deposits. But I see no coherent way of saying why there is anything grotesque about, say, the case of Kuwait, without acknowledging that the fault lies in the whole principle of national sovereignty over natural resources. If it were simply a matter of a few million people hitting the jackpot, things would not be bad, but of course the obverse of that is countries that have poor land, or little land per head, and few mineral resources or other sources of energy such as hydroelectric power.

Obviously, some countries are richer than others for many reasons, and some, like Japan, are among the more affluent in spite of having to import almost all their oil and the greatest part of many other natural resources. What, then, about the other advantages that the people in the rich countries inherit—productive capital, good systems of communications, orderly administration, well-developed systems of education and training, and so on? If the point about special rights is that someone must have done something to acquire a special right, what have the fortunate inheritors of all the advantages done to give them an exclusive claim to the benefits flowing from them?

The answer that the defenders of property rights normally give at this point is that, although the inheritors have done nothing to establish any special rights, those who left it to them did do something (namely, help to create the advantages) and had a right to dispose of it to some rather than to others. The special rights of those in the present generation thus derive from the use made by those in the previous generation of *their* special rights.

I cannot, in this already long chapter, undertake here to ask how far this answer takes us. We would have to get into questions that seem to me very difficult, such as the extent to which the fact that people who are no longer alive wanted something to happen, and perhaps even made sacrifices in order to insure that it could happen, provides any basis in justice for determining what those now alive now should do. I shall simply say here that I regard any claims that those now alive can make to special advantages derived from the efforts of their ancestors as quite limited. First, the inheritance must itself have been justly acquired in the first place, and that cannot be said of any country that violated the equal claims of all on natural resources—which means almost all industrial countries. Second, the claims to inheritance seem to me to attenuate with time, so that, although the present generation might legitimately derive some special advantages from the efforts of the preceding one, and perhaps the one before that, the part of what they passed on that was in turn inherited from their predecessors should, I think, be regarded as by now forming part of the common heritage.

Obviously, making this case out would require elaboration beyond the space available. But I do want to emphasize that what follows constitutes, in my view, a minimalist strategy. That is to say, whatever obligations of justice follow from it represent the absolutely rock-bottom requirements of justice in international affairs. To the extent that other advantages can be brought within the net of the principle of equal rights, the obligations of rich countries go beyond what is argued for here.

6. International Institutions

It would be ridiculous to spend time here on a blueprint for a scheme to put into effect the principle that I have been advancing. Its implementation on a worldwide scale, if it happens at all, is going to occur over a period measured in decades and, indeed, centuries. It will depend on both fundamental changes in outlook and on the development of international organs capable of taking decisions and carrying them out with reasonable efficiency and honesty.

The history of domestic redistribution is, I think, very much to the point here in suggesting that there is a virtuous circle in which the existence of redistributive institutions and beliefs in the legitimacy of redistribution are mutually reinforcing and have a strong tendency to become more extensive together over time. When Hume discussed redistribution in the *Enquiry*, the only form of it that he considered was "perfect equality of possessions."[22] The notion of continuous redistribution of income through a system of progressive taxation does not seem to have occurred to him. The Poor Law did, of course, provide a minimum of relief to the indigent, but it was organized by parishes and it is doubtful that the amateurish and nepotistic central administration of the eighteenth century could have handled a national scheme. The introduction of unemployment and sickness benefits and old age pensions in one Western European country after another in the late nineteenth century and early twentieth century was made possible by the development of competent national administrations.

At the same time, these programs constituted a political response to the extension of the suffrage, or perhaps one might more precisely say a response to conditions that, among other things, made the extension of the suffrage necessary for the continued legitimacy of the state. A certain measure of redistribution was the price the privileged were prepared to pay for mass acceptance of their remaining advantages. Once in place, however, such programs have shown a universal tendency to take on a life of their own and to grow incrementally as gaps in the original coverage are filled in and the whole level of benefits is gradually raised. Indeed, it has been found in cross-national studies that the best predictor of the relative size of a given program (say, aid to the blind) within the whole welfare system is the amount of time the program has been running compared with others. In the long run, the programs seem to generate supporting sentiments, so that even Margaret Thatcher and Ronald Reagan propose only reductions of a few percentage points in programs that even thirty years ago would have seemed quite ambitious.

I do not want to drive the comparison with the international arena into the ground, but I think that, if nothing else, reflecting on domestic experience ought to lead us to look at international transfers from an appropriate time perspective. The United Nations Organization obviously has a lot wrong with it, for example, but its administration is probably less corrupt, self-serving, and inefficient than that which served Sir Robert Walpole. If one takes a time span of thirty years, it is, I suggest, more remarkable that the network of international cooperation has developed as far as it has than that it has not gone further. And in the realm of ideas the notion that poor countries have claims of one sort or another to aid from rich ones has moved from being quite exotic to one that is widely accepted in principle. At any rate in public, the representatives of the rich countries on international bodies no longer deny such a responsibility. They merely seek to evade any binding commitment based on it. But in the long run what is professed in public makes a difference to what gets done because it sets the terms of the discussion.

7. International Taxation

It is not at all difficult to come up with proposals for a system by which revenues would be raised on a regular basis from the rich countries and transferred to the poor ones. Accordingly, no elaborate discussion is needed here. If any such scheme ever gained enough momentum to be a serious international issue, economists and accountants would no doubt have a field day arguing about the details. There is no point in anticipating such arguments, even in outline here. However, the relative brevity of treatment here should not lead to any underestimation of its importance. It is in fact the centerpiece of what is being put forward in this essay.

Now, broadly speaking, two alternative approaches are possible. One would be to take up each of the aspects of international justice that have been discussed—and whatever others might be raised—and to base a system of taxes and receipts upon each. This would be messy and endlessly contentious. The alternative, which is, I predict, the only way in which any systematic redistribution will ever take place, if it ever does, is to have one or two comprehensive taxes and distribute the proceeds according to some relatively simple formula among the poor countries.

The most obvious, and in my view the best, would be a tax on the governments of rich countries, assessed as a proportion of gross national product that increases with per capita income, the proceeds to be distributed to poor countries on a parallel basis of negative income tax. Gross national product reflects, roughly, the use of irreplaceable natural resources, the burden on the ecosphere, and advantages derived from the efforts of past generations, and past exploitation of other countries. Ideally, this tax would be supplemented by a severance tax on the extraction of mineral resources and a shadow tax on the value of land and similar resources. (States could be left to collect the money by any means they chose. But their aggregate liability would be assessed by valuing the taxable base and applying the set rate). This would certainly be required to take care of some glaring inequities that would still otherwise remain. But the simple system of transfer based on gross national product would be such an advance over the status quo that it would be a mistake to miss any chance to implement it by pursuing further refinements.

I believe that any other kinds of general tax, that is to say, taxes not related specifically to some aspect of justice, should be rejected. For example, a tax on foreign trade, or on foreign trade in fossil fuels has been proposed.[23] This is so obviously arbitrary that it is hard to see how anyone can have considered it worth mooting. It has the manifest effect of penalizing small countries and countries that export (or import, if one believes that the tax on exports of fossil fuel would be shifted forward) coal and oil. It conversely has an absurdly favorable effect on very large countries that import and export little in relation to the size of the GNPs and are relatively self-sufficient in energy derived from fossil fuels. No doubt the State Department loves it, but why anyone else should be imposed on is a mystery to me.

I have assumed without discussion that resources transferred

to satisfy the requirements of justice should go straight to poor
countries rather than being channeled through international
agencies and dispensed in the form of aid for specific projects.
I shall spell out the rationale for this in the next section. But I
will simply remark here that nothing I have said about justice
rules out additional humanitaran transfers. And these would
appropriately be administered by international organizations.
The basis for raising such revenues for humanitarian aid would
very reasonably be a progressive international shadow income
tax, since this would perfectly reflect ability to pay. We might
thus envisage a dual system of international taxation—one part,
corresponding to the requirements of justice, going directly to
poor countries to be spent at their own discretion; the other
going to the World Bank or some successor organization less
dominated by the donor countries.

III. THE RELATIONS BETWEEN HUMANITY AND JUSTICE

1. Introduction

I have been arguing that both humanity and justice require
a substantial expansion in the scale of economic transfers from
rich countries to poor ones. I should now like to show that, as
the two rationales are very different, so are their practical
implications. This point is, I think, worth emphasizing because
those who pride themselves on the possession of sturdy Anglo-
Saxon "common sense" tend to conclude that, if we agree on
the humanitarian obligation, we are wasting our breath in
arguing about claims of injustice—claims for the rectification
of alleged unrequited transfers from poor to rich countries in
the past that are hard to assess and impossible to quantify or
involving more or less abstruse doctrines about the nature of
justice in the contemporary world. If we recognize the case for
action on simple and straightforward humanitarian grounds,
the idea goes, shouldn't we concentrate on putting into place
the appropriate aid policies, rather than allow ourselves to get
sidetracked into fruitless wrangles about justice? In this context
it is often said that the demands made by the countries of the
South are "symbolic" or "ideological" and have the effect only

of making more difficult the real, practical task of negotiating actual concessions by the countries of the North. The question that seems to me of more import is the following: If an obligation of humanity is accepted, under whatever name, how much difference does it make whether or not the kinds of claims I have been discussing under the heading of "justice" are also conceded?

2. Rights and Goals

The answer is, I believe, that it makes a great deal of difference. Putting it in the most abstract terms, the obligations of humanity are goal-based, whereas those of justice are rights-based.[24] I would once have expressed the distinction between humanity and justice as one between an aggregative principle and a distributive principle.[25] I now, however, regard that distinction as less fundamental than the one I wish to mark by talking of goal-based and rights-based obligations. The point is that humanity and justice are not simply alternative prescriptions with respect to the same thing. Rather, they have different subject matters.

Humanity, understood as a principle that directs us not to cause suffering and to relieve it where it occurs, is a leading member of a family of principles concerned with what happens to people (and other sentient creatures)—with what I shall call their well-being, intending to include in this such notions as welfare, happiness, self-fulfillment, freedom from malnutrition and disease, and satisfaction of basic needs. Justice, by contrast, is not directly concerned with such matters at all. As well as principles that tell us what are good and bad states of affairs and what responsibilities we have to foster the one and to avert the other, we also have principles that tell us how control over resources should be allocated. If we understand "resources" in a very wide sense, so that it includes all kinds of rights to act without interference from others, to constrain the actions of others, and to bring about changes in the nonhuman environment, then we can say that the subject matter of justice (at any rate, in modern usage) is the distribution of control over material resources. At this high level of generality, it is complemented by the principle of equal liberty, which is concerned with the control over nonmaterial resources. To put it in a slogan, which has the advantages as well as the disadvantages of any slogan, humanity is a question of doing good; justice is a question of power.

When the contrast is stated in those terms, it might seem that bothering about justice is indeed a waste of time and that the bluff Anglo-Saxon advocates of commonsensical utilitarianism have the best of it after all. Why, it may naturally be asked, should we care about the distribution of *stuff* as against the distribution of *welfare*? Isn't this simply commodity fetishism in a new guise?

The easy but inadequate answer is that the concept of justice is, of course, concerned not only with old stuff but the kind of stuff that has the capacity to provide those who use it with the material means of well-being: food, housing, clothing, medical care, and so on. This is correct as far as it goes and shows that being concerned with justice is not irrational. But it is inadequate because it leaves the supporter of justice open to an obvious flanking movement. His opponent may reply: "You say that the only reason for concern about the distribution of the things whose proper allocation constitutes the subject matter of justice is that they are the means to well-being. Very well. But are you not then in effect conceding that your "deep theory" is goal-based? For what you are saying is that we really are ultimately concerned with the distribution of well-being. We simply take an interest in the distribution of the means of well-being because they are what we can actually allocate. But this means that justice is a derivative principle."

There are two lines of response open at this point. One is to concede that criteria for the distribution of resources are ultimately to be referred to the goal of well-being, but at the same time to deny that if follows from that concession that we can cut out the middleman (or put in the Michelman) and set out our principles for the allocation of resources with an eye directly on the well-being they are likely to produce. Or, more precisely, we may say that among the constituents of well-being is autonomy, and autonomy includes the power to choose frivolously or imprudently. Thus, on one (admittedly controversial) interpretation, Mill's talk of justice in Book V of *Utilitarianism* and his presentation of the "simple principle" of *On*

Liberty in terms of rights is all consistent with an underlying utilitarian commitment if we allow for the importance to people of being able to plan their own lives and make their own decisions.

I think that this is by no means an unreasonable view and has more to be said for it than is, perhaps, fashionable to admit. Anyone who wishes at all costs to hold up a monistic ethical position is, I suspect, almost bound to finish up by trying to make some such argument as this. But I think that it is, nevertheless, in the last analysis a heroic attempt to fudge the issue by using the concept of autonomy to smuggle a basically foreign idea into the goal-based notion of advancing well-being.

The alternative is to deny that, in conceding that control over resources is important only because of the connection between resources and well-being, one is thereby committed to the view that principles for the distribution of resources are derivative. According to this view, there simply are two separate kinds of question. One concerns the deployment of resources to promote happiness and reduce misery. The other concerns the ethically defensible basis for allocating control over resources. Neither is reducible, even circuitously, to the other. When they conflict, we get hard questions, such as those involved in the whole issue of paternalism. But there is no overarching criterion within which such conflicts can be solved, as is offered (at least in principle) by the idea that autonomy is an important, but not the only, ingredient in well-being.

As may be gathered, this is the position that I hold. In what follows, I want to show what difference it makes to employ an independent principle of justice in considering issues of international distribution. To make the discussion as clear as possible, I shall draw my contrast with a principle of humanity understood in the kind of pretty straightforward way exemplified in Section I of this chapter. The contrast would be softened the more weight we were to give to autonomy as a component in well-being. Note, however, that even those who might wish to emphasize the importance of individual autonomy are likely to doubt the value to individual well-being of autonomy for states; yet it is precisely the question of autonomy for states that is going to turn out to be the main dividing line between humanity and justice at the international level.

3. International Applications

The point is one of control. The rich countries already mostly concede, at least in verbal declarations, that they have a humanitarian obligation to assist the poor countries economically. The importance to the future of the world of their beginning to live up to those declarations can scarcely be overestimated. I trust that nothing in this chapter will be taken as disparaging humanitarian aid. To the extent that it does in fact relieve problems of poverty, disease, malnutrition, and population growth it is, obviously, of enormous value.

But to see its limitations, let us be really utopian about humanitarian aid. Let us imagine that it is collected on a regular and automatic basis from rich countries according to some formula that more or less reflects ability to pay; for example, a shadow tax on GNP graduated by the level of GNP per capita. And suppose that the proceeds were pooled and dispersed through agencies of the United Nations, according to general criteria for entitlement to assistance.

Now, undoubtedly such a world would be an immense improvement over the present one, just as the modern welfare state has transformed, say, Henry Mayhew's London. But it would still have the division between the donor countries, free to spend "their" incomes as they pleased and the recipient countries, which would have to spend their incomes "responsibly." No doubt, this would be less objectionable if the criteria were drawn up in partnership between donor and recipient countries rather than, as now, being laid down by bodies such as the IMF and the World Bank in whose governing councils the rich countries have a preponderant voice. But funds earmarked and conditional upon approved use would still be basically different from income of the usual kind.

In contrast, transfers that were consequential upon considerations of justice would simply reduce the resources of one set of countries and augment those of another set. The distribution of control of resources would actually be shifted. It is therefore easy to see that the question of justice in the relations between rich and poor countries is by no means a purely "symbolic" one. Real issues are at stake, and it is no self-delusion that leads the poor countries to press for a recognition of the claims of justice and the rich countries to resist.

The conclusion we have reached, then, is that the crucial characteristic of justice is that the obligation to make the transfers required by it does not depend upon the use made of them by the recipient. At this point, I find that the following kinds of objection are usually made: What if the recipient country wastes the resources transferred to it? What if it is going to spend the money on armaments? What if it has a very unequal distribution of income and the additional income will be divided in the same unequal way? Such objections illustrate how difficult it is to get across the idea that if some share of resources is justly owed to a country, then it is (even before it has been actually transferred) as much that country's as it is now normally thought that what a country produces belongs to that country.

The answer that I give is that there are extreme circumstances in which the international community or some particular donor country would be justified in withholding resources owed as a matter of justice to some country. But these are exactly the same extreme conditions under which it would also be justifiable to refuse to pay debts to it or to freeze its assets overseas.

One could envisage a world in which there were indeed an international authority that allowed countries to keep only that income that would be justly distributed internally and used in approved, nonwasteful ways. Such a world would not be at all like ours, since it would accept no principle of national autonomy. It would be a world in which a presently nonexisting world society had inscribed on its banner: "From each according to his ability, to each according to his needs."

The alternative is a world in which the general presumption is of national autonomy, with countries being treated as units capable of determining the use of those resources to which they were justly entitled. This is the world that we now have, and the only modification in the status quo I am arguing for is a redefinition of what justly belongs to a country. It inevitably, as the price of autonomy, permits countries to use their resources in wasteful ways ("theirs," on my interpretation, being of course those in their own territories plus or minus transfers required by justice) and does not insist that a country that allows some to live in luxury while others have basic needs unfulfilled should lose income to which it is entitled as a matter of justice.

My point is that both of the models I have sketched are internally consistent. We could have a system in which there are no entitlements based on justice and in which, assuming that states are still the administrative intermediaries, funds are allocated for worthy purposes and cut off if they are misspent, just as in the United States the federal government cuts off funds to state and local governments that do not comply with various guidelines. Or we could have a world in which, once the demands of just distribution between countries are satisfied, we say that we have justice at the world level, and the question of domestic distribution and national priorities then becomes one for each country to decide for itself.

What is not consistent is to have a world in which those countries that are required by international justice to be donors live under the second system while those that are recipients live under the stern dispensation of the first. If the idea is going to be that countries should have their entitlements reduced if they are wasteful and fail in internal equity, then the obvious place to start is not with some poor country in sub-Saharan Africa or South Asia but with, say, a country that burns one ninth of the world's daily oil consumption on its roads alone and that, in spite of having a quarter of the world's GNP, is unable to provide for much of its population decent medical care, while a substantial proportion live in material conditions of abject squalor that (except for being more dirty and dangerous) recall the cities of Germany and Britain in the aftermath of World War II.

None of this, of course, denies the independent significance of humanity as a criterion in international morality. But we cannot sensibly talk about humanity unless we have a baseline set by justice. To talk about what I ought, as a matter of humanity, to do with what is mine makes no sense until we have established what is mine in the first place. If I have stolen what is rightfully somebody else's property, or if I have borrowed from him and refuse to repay the debt when it is due, and as a result he is destitute, it would be unbecoming on my part to dole out some part of the money that should belong to him, with various strings attached as to the way in which he should spend it, and then go around posing as a great humanitarian. That is, in my judgment, an exact description of the position in which the rich countries have currently placed themselves.

The need for humanitarian aid would be reduced in a world that had a basically just international distribution. It would be required still to meet special problems caused by crop failure owing to drought, destruction owing to floods and earthquakes, and similar losses resulting from other natural disasters. It would also, unhappily, continue to be required to cope with the massive refugee problems that periodically arise from political upheavals.

Beyond that, humanitarian aid in the form of food, technical assistance, or plain money is always a good thing, of course. How much the rich countries would be obliged to give depends first on the extent of redistribution we hold to be required by justice and, second, on the stringency that we assign to the obligation of humanity—how much sacrifice can be demanded to deal with what level of need.

As will be clear, this chapter is concerned only with a preliminary investigation of the principles relevant to an ethical appraisal of international distribution and redistribution. I must therefore leave any more precise statement of implications for future discussions—and not necessarily by me. Ultimately, if anything is to be done, it will require a widespread shift in ideas. Greater precision can be expected to develop *pari passu* with such a shift. I very much doubt the value of single-handed attempts to produce a blueprint in advance of that.

NOTES

1. *Oxford English Dictionary*, sub. Humanity, 3b. In the light of the central example to be discussed below, it is interesting to note that the title of a society founded in England for the rescuing of drowning persons in 1774 was the Humane Society (*OED*, sub. Humane, 1c).
2. 1 *Philosophy & Public Affairs*, 229–43 (1972). See, for a briefer and more recent statement of the same basic case, Peter Singer, *Practical Ethics* (Cambridge: Cambridge University Press, 1979), ch. 8, pp. 158–81.
3. *Ibid.*, p. 231.
4. *Ibid.*

5. *Ibid.*
6. *Ibid.*
7. *Ibid.*
8. C. D. Broad, "On the Function of False Hypotheses in Ethics," 26 *International Journal of Ethics* 377–97, at 389–90 (1916).
9. John Passmore, "Civil Justice and Its Rivals," in Eugene Kamenka and Alice Erh-Soon Tay, *Justice* (London: Edward Arnold, 1979) pp. 25–49, at 47 [italics in original].
10. For a sustained argument along these lines, see T. D. Campbell, "Humanity before Justice," 4 *British Journal of Political Science* 1–16 (1974).
11. Henry Sidgwick, *The Methods of Ethics* (London: Macmillan, 1907), p. 273.
12. Constantine V. Vaitsos, *Intercountry Income Distribution and Transnational Enterprises* (Oxford: Clarendon Press, 1974), esp. ch. 4.
13. See for an elaboration of these remarks "And Who Is My Neighbor?" 88 *Yale L. J.* 629–58 (1979).
14. Adam Smith expressed this view: "As a man doth, so it shall be done to him, and retaliation seems to be the great law which is dictated to us by nature. Beneficence and generosity we think due to the generous and beneficent. Those whose hearts never open to the feelings of humanity should, we think, be shut out in the same manner, from the affections of all their fellow-creatures, and be allowed to live in the midst of society, as in a great desert, where there is nobody to care for them, or to enquire after them." Adam Smith, *The Theory of Moral Sentiments* (Indianapolis: Liberty Classics, n.d.), p. 160.
15. Princeton, N.J.: Princeton University Press, 1979. The part of the book in question was first published in substantially the same form as "Justice and International Relations," 4 *Philosophy & Public Affairs* 360–89 (1975).
16. *The Liberal Theory of Justice* (Oxford: Clarendon Press, 1973), ch. 12.
17. H. L. A. Hart, "Are There Any Natural Rights?" 64 *Philosophical Review* 175–91 (1955).
18. See my extended review in 12 *Theory and Decision*, 95–106 (1980).
19. Hillel Steiner, "The Natural Right to the Means of Production," 27 *The Philosophical Quarterly* 41–49, at 44–45 (1977). The reference to Nozick is to *Anarchy, State, and Utopia* (New York: Basic Books, 1974), p. 154.
20. Bruce A. Ackerman, *Social Justice in the Liberal State* (New Haven: Yale University Press, 1980), p. 38.
21. Oscar Schachter, *Sharing the World's Resources* (New York: Columbia University Press, 1977), p. 124, references n, 52, p. 159.

22. David Hume, *An Enquiry Concerning the Principles of Morals*, 3d ed. (Oxford: Clarendon Press, 1975), pp. 193–94.
23. Eleanor B. Steinberg and Joseph Y. Yager, eds., *New Means of Financing International Needs* (Washington, D.C.: The Brookings Institution, 1978), ch. 3.
24. For a distinction stated in these terms see Ronald Dworkin, "The Original Position," 4 *Chi. L. Rev.*, 500–33 (1973), reprinted in Norman Daniels, ed., *Reading Rawls* (Oxford: Basil Blackwell, 1975) pp. 16–53. The relevant discussion is on pp. 38–40 of this reprint.
25. *Political Argument* (London: Routledge and Kegan Paul, 1965), pp. 43–44.

12

ON THE NEED TO POLITICIZE POLITICAL MORALITY: WORLD HUNGER AND MORAL OBLIGATION

KAI NIELSEN

I

Much of our talk about moral obligation and of what justice requires presupposes that we are talking about one society or at least a group of closely related societies. What is to be said when the whole world is our subject? Brian Barry's analysis of this tricky subject is sensible, and I am in substantial agreement with much of it; but all the same it fails, paradoxically enough, *both* through the lack of a sufficiently developed political sense and through a certain lack of moral idealism.[1] It is deficient both in its sense of *Realpolitik* and in its sense of the moral relevance of a vision of a possible future. Such a dark saying needs explaining; and in what follows, after I have set out something of Barry's case, I shall explain what I have in mind and attempt to justify it.

While not being at all shackled by positivist myths about *wertfrei* social science, Barry still wishes to be a tough-minded, no-nonsense analytical political theorist. But, for all his good intentions, his analysis suffers from an insufficient awareness of the reality of socioeconomic and political factors in the relations between human beings in very different material conditions and spread out in various parts of the world.

Starting from Peter Singer's influential "Famine, Affluence and Morality," Barry asks about the moral claims of poor

countries to economic assistance from rich ones.[2] What obligations, if any, do such countries have to make transfers to poor
ones? It is plain enough that in a rather straightforward way
they have an obligation not to harm them, parallel to the
obligation of individuals not to harm others. But the significant
question here is whether they have an obligation to help poor
countries where that comes to something more than simply not
harming them. Where rich countries do not make poor countries
worse off than they otherwise would be, do they have an
obligation to help them?

Singer takes an unyielding utilitarian line here, though for
him international redistribution, which he takes as something
that should be extensive, operates quite explicitly at the level of
individual obligation. Singer starts from a premise that has
rather general acceptance. Indeed, it will be widely taken as a
moral commonplace, though that of course is not an impediment
to its being true. I refer to Singer's claim "that suffering and
death from lack of food, shelter, and medical care are bad."[3]
His second key premise has a stronger and a weaker statement,
the stronger being that "if it is in our power to prevent
something bad from happening, without thereby sacrificing
anything of comparable moral importance, we ought, morally,
to do it," the weaker being that "if it is in our power to prevent
something very bad from happening, without sacrificing anything morally significant, we ought, morally, to do it."[4]

Barry has little difficulty in first showing that the stronger
form is too strong and then in showing that the weaker form
has a number of difficulties of detail in its specific formulation.
However, Barry recasts the weaker statement, plausibly captur-
ing what appears at least to be its intent, in what he takes to be
a vague but still a tolerably acceptable form. On Barry's formulation, and additional specification, it comes to be the claim
that, where it is possible to do so, "there really is an obligation
to relieve dire poverty out of superfluity and this [obligation]
is not limited by distance or lack of direct relations between the
parties." Just as I have an obligation to save a drowning child
from a wading pool when I am by it and no one else is, so I
have an obligation to give aid to starving children even though
I have never met and never will meet the child or children I
aid. The lack of face-to-face contact and not being from the

same culture or a similar culture is morally irrelevant, as is the fact that millions of others are in the same or in a similar position to help.

If we accept Singer's premises or his own modification, Barry argues, we have, if we are tolerably well off, a moral obligation to help such starving people even when they are from poor countries very distant from and dissimilar to our own. We have, that is, an obligation to help prevent starvation and the debilitating life that results from severe malnutrition. Daily thousands of people are starving in places like the sub-Sahara, while we (particularly the "we" who will be the readers of this chapter) live in moderate affluence or at least in reasonable security.

Living as we do in moderate affluence or at least in reasonable security, we have an obligation to relieve such suffering. Whether or not it is justice that requires it, at least we have an obligation to relieve suffering as a matter of humanity. This is not just something that it would be good or virtuous of us to do but something, Barry and Singer argue, we have an obligation to do. Morality requires this of us.

Barry takes up the neo-Malthusian argument that accepts the principle that suffering should be relieved but denies that aid to the impoverished countries is, in the long run, a way to relieve suffering. International aid at least appears to be an effective way to reduce, for the present at least, the amount of disease and suffering in the world, but, the neo-Malthusians argue, it also helps all over the world to bail out corrupt, exploitative, extremely class-stratified, antidemocratic regimes— regimes that continue to produce just these conditions that give rise to the suffering in the first place. Moreover, and perhaps more important, such famine relief will actually worsen an already desperate situation. With such aid the populations of these impoverished countries will increase even faster until we reach the state where even more people are starving, and we will not be able to do anything about it.

That such dire predictions will come true, that this will be the upshot of such aid, is of course a factual issue, and both Barry and Singer present telling reasons for doubting that that will be the upshot. However, what such considerations do, in effect, is to bring out the fact that the rich countries need to be very careful about what kind of aid they give. They need to help with the provision of various contraceptive devices; with aid that will build up the economic and agricultural base of the country; with aid that will increase the educational level of the country; and with military and other aid to revolutionary insurgents struggling, in places such as Latin America and Africa, to topple dictatorial, antisocialist regimes, regimes that are opposed to land reform and to an economic development of the country oriented to meeting the needs of the masses of the people.

The latter sort of aid is surely not going to be forthcoming from most capitalist countries. Capitalist giants, such as the United States and West Germany, the latter even with its Social Democratic government, are going to do just the opposite, but it is just such aid that is sorely needed. And if such aid is given, it is very unlikely that the horrendous consequences the neo-Malthusians predict will obtain. If these consequences are unlikely to occur, it seems plain that the rich nations of the world have a moral obligation to aid the poor nations and that we, as individuals in such countries, have an obligation to press for such aid. (I think, for roughly the reasons Barry gives, that it is governmental action, not individual action per se, that is required here. It is governments that should give such aid. Individuals should devote their energies to help bring about the reality that the rich nations come to have governments committed to such aid—aid that would take the form of a significant redistribution of wealth. It is such governmental aid that has the promise of really being effective.)

Barry concludes against Singer that the stronger and more rigorous utilitarian rationale for giving aid cannot be sustained; but, as we have seen, he argues that we can demythologize out of Singer's account the vaguer but still correct claim that "there really is an obligation to relieve dire poverty out of superfluity and [that] this is not limited by distance or lack of direct relations between the parties." Barry then remarks, correctly I believe, that the facts being what they are, a recognition of this obligation, along with an acceptance of Singer's first premise, that is, his uncontroversial premise "that suffering and death from lack of food, shelter, and medical care are bad," is sufficient to require an immense increase in the scale of aid from rich countries to poor ones.

Barry then proceeds to argue that both on the donor side and on the recipient side such obligations "are most effectively carried out if they are enforced by the state rather than left to individual charity."[5]

II

I agree, and for much the same reasons that he gives, that "individual charity" is not going to accomplish much in meeting the problems of world hunger. What is needed is state action on both the donor and the recipient side. But it is just here where the apolitical quality of Barry's account begins to bother me. (I should add that a similar criticism should be made of Singer's account.)

In considering an obvious criticism of Singer's account, to wit, that voters in a democratic society wouldn't buy such a scheme, that they would never vote for taxes that would make for a significant redistribution, Barry makes a number of responses that seem to me quite ineffective. He first points out that it is not the people but their elected representatives who vote for foreign aid and then claims that their elected representatives have a lot of latitude here in the amounts they can vote. But to this it should be responded that it is very unlikely, under the present system, that many of the representatives will be enlightened types with any considerable degree of moral sensitivity such that they will give much thought to starving and undernourished people in the poorer parts of the world. (Exceptions such as present-day [1979–80] Cambodia prove the point. Starvation of that magnitude goes on persistently in many places quite unnoticed. But in the Cambodian case the Americans can gain political advantage from publicizing it.) They will rather divide their attention between, on the one hand, having their ear to the ground to try to discover what they think their constituents want or could be readily sold, and, on the other, to serving faithfully the capitalist order and by so serving that order to enrich themselves. Neither of these activities is likely to lead to much increase in aid. What we need firmly to recognize is that it is hardly likely that from that lot any great move toward a redistribution of wealth will occur.

Barry also remarks that people may behave in a more public-spirited way when voting than in writing out a check for Oxfam. This may well be true, but it does nothing to show that with either they will tolerate the kind of redistribution necessary to help the poor countries significantly. And while it very well may be rational to prefer a collective decision to an individual decision, where you are seriously contemplating giving funds, this does nothing to show that it is rational to prefer a collective decision *sans phrase* where one of your options may be to give nothing at all or only a little "conscience money," which you then can conveniently deduct from your income tax. Indeed, as far as individual rationality is concerned, it is rational to opt to see everybody 10 percent worse off than be 10 percent worse off yourself while everybody else stays the same. But that is not the only option. You also have the option of giving nothing at all or only a fraction of a percent as "conscience money," which, where certain Nozickian ideological mystifications are at work, may do quite nicely. The question remains whether in capitalist societies, with their characteristic routines of ideological indoctrination, it is even remotely plausible to think that we would get anything even approximating the aid that is required from a moral point of view. With the mentality of proposition 13 around, do we have any reason at all to think that people, left to their own devices, will support anything like that? And is there any reason to expect that the consciousness industry will engage in the kind of sustained and rigorous campaign to turn around people's consciousness about such matters? I am inclined to think the prospects are nil, but at the very least they are extremely bleak.

The political and socioeconomic nature, as distinct from the ecological, scientific, or technological nature of the problem is in effect shown by some of Barry's own evidence. The crucial difference between malnutrition and a tolerably adequate diet is decided in many cases by the state's agricultural policy. If the poorer countries would avoid such an exclusive development of cash crops and the manipulation of the market for profit and would concentrate instead on agricultural production to meet the needs of their people, for some of the countries at least, there could be produced a reasonable diet for the people in their jurisdictions without an influx of aid from outside. The countries of middle wealth, such as the countries of the Middle East and the better-off ones in Latin America, could meet their famine problems adequately if they would engage in a redistribution of their existing wealth, including a parceling out of land—often very underused land—to the peasants. Even in the sub-Sahara the lack of food is in large measure a result of counterproductive agricultural policies of the states of that region. In these societies a minuscule elite, dependent on a capitalist order, based for the most part in the powerful capitalist countries, exploit, often in a very inefficient way, the poverty-stricken masses—many of whom, if employed at all, are only marginally employed. Even without pumping additional wealth into those countries, if the existing wealth were extensively redistributed and their agricultural policies reoriented, these societies could overcome their hunger problems.[6]

Singer speaks of people channeling their aid money into population control programs. An even better way for individuals to channel their money, if there were any general movement toward this at all, would be to channel it into those genuinely socialist insurgent movements that are trying to topple corrupt and dictatorial governments. If the U.S. government were serious about aiding such Latin American and African countries, it could threaten economic sanctions against their governments in the way the United States is presently harassing Iran. Indeed, if it cut off support of their elites and carried through economic sanctions, all sorts of corrupt and dictatorial regimes would quickly fall. At a minimum, it could do a lot of good by just leaving these countries alone to work out their own destinies. The World Bank, instead of being a policing device for capitalist interests, could be a genuinely liberating instrument, but it is simplistic to believe that it will play that role. The problem of world hunger is plainly political and socioeconomic. And the culprit is capitalism.

What I am arguing is, given the political consensus in the United States and in much of the bourgeois world, "way out" and "utterly utopian." Given the dominant ideologies in our societies, it will be generally perceived as the posturing of what Noam Chomsky ironically refers to as the irresponsible, critically oriented intellectual—the chap disputing about and using, so the story goes, ideology. (Chomsky, of course, both defends such critical intellectual "posturing" and brilliantly exemplifies, as did Bertrand Russell before him, what it is to be such a critical intellectual.[7]) And, of course, it is pure fantasy to expect that the United States, West Germany, Japan, Canada, France, or Great Britain—any of the major bourgeois countries—will do anything of the kind. Given the consciousness industry, the moral case for such alternatives will plainly never even get a hearing. The underlying causal agent generating the problem is not the development of science or medicine or overpopulation or pollution; it is capitalism.

Barry talks about the lack of political will in recipient and donor countries, but he never mentions the role of the capitalist economic order in all this, and he never discusses what difference it could make if we had a democratic, participatory socialism—I do not speak of an *Ersatz State* socialism—in place with its very different socioeconomic orientation, namely a socioeconomic order that treats production to meet human needs as central and capital accumulation as secondary and instrumental.[8]

Perhaps I am overly optimistic in thinking these changed priorities could make such a difference. Surely conventional wisdom in bourgeois societies would incline us to believe that I am being wildly overoptimistic. Indeed, for anything like what I hope for to become a reality, the relations between nation-states would have to be radically different than they are now, the tolerable inequalities far different and the rationale for production radically changed. It would seem at least, particularly given the truth of the factual claims Barry stresses, that this would be sufficient to overcome the problem of world hunger. But perhaps I am being overly sanguine? Perhaps, even with such radically changed socioeconomic priorities and concomitant changed conceptions of an adequate life that would go with a developed socialist consciousness, there would still be too great a drain on world resources? I am not claiming that the answers are obvious. But what I am claiming is that it is just such issues that need to be faced. We need to concern ourselves with such things rather than to worry about trivial issues such as whether present-day Indians starving in Calcutta are to be blamed or held responsible for the past mismanagement of Indian governments. But none of this gets aired in Barry's essentially apolitical account, an account that stays fastidiously clear of what he may well regard as ideological issues.

Perhaps Barry believes that the possibilities for socialist transformations of society are so remote that one should best opt, in such moral-cum-political arguments, for a normative position that would settle for the few crumbs we might get from a capitalist social order conjoined with liberal welfare states. (But with only that kind of aid in the offing, the neo-Malthusian arguments become more worrisome.)

There is, indeed, a tragic political morality, deeply rooted in cultural pessimism, that has honorably and sometimes intelligently opted for just that. But with the specter of Euro-Communism haunting Europe, social transformations in the offing in Scandinavia, liberation struggles in Southern Africa and Latin America seething under dictatorial boots, such historical possibilities are not so plainly fanciful. Cultural pessimism may itself be the romantic posture. We need, in thinking about these matters, to avoid being held captive by the rather myopic vision we can get from America. The world in fifty years, perhaps even in a decade, may very well look very different than it does now. And in a radically changed socioeconomic environment world food problems might look very different.

Indeed, it is fair enough to respond that that is a long time to wait, given the magnitude of the food problem (ten thousand people die of starvation every day) and its likely acceleration. But then what are the alternatives? Are we likely to get more than a few crumbs out of capitalist world order? Perhaps I am too pessimistic and too cynical? Capitalism, for whatever reasons—perhaps to achieve world stabilization—might come through with a little more, though its track record is not very good. It is just such issues that need airing in a discussion of world hunger. But that is radically to politicize the discussion and our conceptualization of the problem. But not a whisper of that comes into Barry's and Singer's through-and-through apolitical analyses. Yet it is just these issues that must be brought to the fore if we are to discuss problems of world hunger and moral obligation seriously.

III

I asserted at the outset that Barry's account was defective not only in its political sense—in its lack of *Realpolitik*—but also, and paradoxically in relation to my first claim, in its sense of the moral relevance of a vision of a possible future. In discussing the appropriate scope of political principles, Barry argues, sensibly and realistically, against the extension of such principles to the whole human race. Different countries have different laws and different customs, and this does not seem generally to be a source of injustice. Moreover, in different countries different conditions obtain so that, Barry claims, it is not an injustice to pay, say, steel construction workers of equal skill and doing the same kind of work with the same kind of tools, substantially lower wages in Lebanon than in the United States. Treating equals equally does not involve treating them the same in such different circumstances. As things stand, this is surely correct. There are in those circumstances justified inequalities and indeed inequalities that may even be just inequalities. However, such inequalities may not be just inequalities in what is not only a perfectly well ordered society but a perfectly well ordered world. And even if such a conception is but a heuristic device, a picture, used as a model of a perfectly just world, it still has that role. Ideals, even if they can only be approximated, still have their uses. And it is there, if we operate with Dworkinlike deep assumptions about the moral equality of all human beings, where it is not so evident that our extension of the scope of political principles, for such an ideal picture, must not be to the whole human race.

Barry rightly does not want to extend the notion of justice into an all-inclusive social ideal. That is an overextension of the concept, for justice is plainly not the only social end. A society might be rich or poor, cultivated or philistine, religious or secular, and still be just. A perfectly just society might still not be a perfect society, and it might very well still be a morally criticizable society. People, Barry argues, might still be treated justly and yet be treated differently because they are in different jurisdictions.

Consider, in trying to assess this, something as deeply affecting a person's vital interests as effective equality of educational opportunity. While Barry is sympathetic to Thurgood Marshall's claim that "the right of every American to an equal start in life" is so vital that the decision whether or not to provide genuine equality of educational opportunity cannot be left to the discretion of the various states in the United States, Barry will not extend this beyond the borders of the nation-state. Since "the world as a whole," he tells us, "does not form a single labor market," we are not justified in "extending the concept of equality of opportunity in education beyond national boundaries."[9]

Now, as things stand, and perhaps always will stand, what Barry says here makes perfectly good sense. For while it makes sense to argue about there being equality of educational opportunity between Americans and Canadians, it makes little sense to speak of equality of educational opportunity between an American and a Dinka living in his native condition in the Sudan. Their conditions of life are just too different to admit of meaningful comparison; moreover, since "ought" implies "can," it makes little sense, as things stand, to try to establish equality across such jurisdictions. But if our ability to think clearly about these matters is not so deeply ideologically deformed as to make such thinking impossible, it is important to try to distinguish between ideal and nonideal theory when we are trying to think what the design of a perfectly just world order would look like.

If, in setting out that structure, we start from a conception of the moral equality of persons—a conception shared in our societies, though with different readings, by egalitarians and inegalitarians, socialists and liberals, libertarians and state socialists—it is difficult to resist the claim that, for ideal theory, at least, where other equally crucial values are not being sacrificed, we should, in such a *perfectly* just world order, seek a situation in which not just every Canadian or every American but every human being, as far as that is possible, should have an equal start in life. If we start, as most of us do, with the deep underlying assumption—indeed an assumption that is one of our most deeply embedded considered judgments—of the moral equality of human beings, then it appears, at least, to be the case that the egalitarians have the edge on the others, at least as far as ideal theory is concerned.[10] People, if such a moral equality is accepted, must have equal life chances, as far as this is possible without undermining other things—such as moral autonomy—to which we are also deeply committed. In ideal theory, we cannot be as complacent about the moral relevance of different jurisdictions as is Barry. We think, when we reflect in a primitive gut way, about what is just and unjust, fair and unfair, that simply "being born into one country rather than another should not determine one's fate to the extent that it does now, so that a person born into a poor society is condemned to almost certain disease, malnutrition and poverty while another, who has the good fortune, to be born into a rich society, has an excellent chance of living a healthy and comfortable life."[11] It isn't that the criterion of fair exchange has been broken here but that justice as equality has not been achieved.

Barry sees justice as having three aspects: (1) the *formal* aspect, accepted even by Nietzsche, of treating equals equally; (2) justice as reciprocity, which itself has three aspects—justice as fidelity, justice as requital, and justice as fairness; and (3) the notion that everyone has an equal claim to the earth's natural resources. But he neglects another aspect of justice, an aspect that has been called *justice as equality*.[12] This conception, like justice as reciprocity, can take several different readings. (1) A perfectly just world order is a world order in which each person is treated in such a manner that we approach, as close as we can, to a condition where everyone will be equal in satisfaction and in such distress as is necessary for achieving their commonly accepted ends. (2) A perfectly just world order is one in which there is a complete equality of the overall level of benefits and burdens for all human beings. (3) A perfectly just world order is a world in which the institutions of all societies are structured in such a way that each person can, to the fullest extent compatible with all other people doing likewise, satisfy her or his needs. These articulations of justice as equality are both vague and distinct, though they all have a similar thrust. My preference is for the third formulation, for, with its stress on needs, it brings out, as Marx's second maxim of justice in the *Gotha Program* brings out, the importance of a respect for individuality and the differences among people within a fundamental commitment to an equality of treatment.[13] (In doing this it escapes Berlin's and Dahrendorf's basic criticism of egalitarianism.[14])

Though these conceptions are vague, they are no vaguer than other general conceptions of justice, and they do mark out an important domain of justice that is missed in Barry's account. It is such conceptions of justice as equality that give a partial moral vision of the future and provide a moral idealism lacking in Barry's account. If we really do believe in the moral equality of persons, we will naturally gravitate toward some such conception of justice as equality and seek, as I have, to find principles of justice to match it.[15] We will also, without making justice an all-purpose virtue, be inclined to argue not only that we have an obligation to relieve starvation, as a matter of humanity, but that we must also recognize that a world with starvation and malnutrition in it could not obtain in a perfectly just world order where conditions of a rather minimal moderate affluence could be worldwide.[16] A not inconsiderable number of us in certain countries live under conditions of moderate affluence, while other people, in less fortunate circumstances, suffer from malnutrition and, not infrequently, are threatened with starvation and indeed do regularly starve. Where this obtains it is correct to say that there is an injustice there that should be rectified if it can be done without reducing the more fortunate people to similar life conditions. (There is no justice in simply spreading the misery around.) But such a rectification can be made without such untoward effects. The struggle to achieve it is an obligation of justice, and not just of humanity.[17]

NOTES

1. Barry's ideas are further developed in his forthcoming volume, *Rich Countries and Poor Countries.* The quotations from Barry in this essay are taken from the version of his paper delivered at the Society's meetings. Although they do not appear in these words in his essay, *supra* pp. 219–52, he has not altered their substance.
2. Peter Singer, "Famine, Affluence, and Morality," *Philosophy and Public Affairs* 229–43 (1972).
3. *Ibid.*, p. 231.
4. *Ibid.*
5. Barry, "Humanity and Justice in Global Perspective," pp. 221ff.

6. *Ibid.*

7. Chomsky does this in a series of well-known books and articles, but in the last half of his book on Bertrand Russell he brilliantly shows (a) how Russell played this role of critical intellectual and (b) exemplifies it himself in his own discussions of social issues discussed by Russell and social stances taken by Russell. Noam Chomsky, *Problems of Knowledge and Freedom* (New York: Pantheon Books, 1971).

8. The case for this has, of course, been made repeatedly in the socialist tradition, but for one contemporary statement that is particularly powerful and that faces in an informed and tough-minded way a whole range of problems, see Richard C. Edwards et al., eds., *The Capitalist System*, 2d ed. (Englewood Cliffs, N.J.: Prentice-Hall, 1978).

9. Barry, "Humanity and Justice in Global Perspective." In the revised version of his essay published here, Barry does not discuss equality of education [The editors.]

10. Ronald Dworkin, "The Original Position," Norman Daniels, ed., *Reading Rawls* (New York: Basic Books, 1975), pp. 16–53.

11. Barry, *Rich Countries and Poor Countries* (unpublished manuscript).

12. Christopher Ake, "Justice as Equality," *Philosophy and Public Affairs* 69–89, (1975); Kai Nielsen "Class and Justice," in, John Arthur and William Shaw, eds., *Justice and Economic Distribution* Englewood Cliffs, N.J.: Prentice-Hall, 1978), pp. 225–45; Kai Nielsen, "Radical Egalitarian Justice: Justice as Equality," *Social Theory and Practice* 5, no. 2 (Spring 1979), pp. 209–26, and Ted Honderich, "The Question of Well-Being and the Principle of Equality," *Mind*, forthcoming.

13. Allen W. Wood, "The Marxian Critique of Justice," 1 *Philosophy and Public Affairs* 244–82 (1972); Ziyad I. Husami, "Marx on Distributive Justice," 8 *Philosophy and Public Affairs* 27–64 (1978), and Allen W. Wood, "Marx on Right and Justice: A Reply to Husami," 8 *Philosophy and Public Affairs* 267–95 (1979).

14. Isaiah Berlin, "Equality," in his *Concepts and Categories: Philosophical Essays* (New York: Viking Press, 1979); and Ralf Dahrendorf, "On the Origin of Inequality among Men" and "Liberty and Equality," both in his *Essays in the Theory of Society* (Stanford, Calif.: Stanford University Press, 1968).

15. See the reference in note 12, *supra*, to articles by me.

16. I certainly do not intend my reference to socialism to be treated as a magical formula to solve all problems. I see socialism as extensively flourishing only as a worldwide system and not as something extensively flourishing while it remains in deadly con-

flict with capitalism. But even with socialism in place in a worldwide system, redistribution between poor and wealthy areas will be required. Here something like the general schemes for International Taxation sketched by Barry in section 7 of his "Humanity and Justice in Global Perspective" (pp. 241–43 of this volume) seem to me entirely reasonable.

17. The editors have thought it necessary to remind me "that sometimes explicitly and sometimes by implication" I "make a great many debatable but completely unsupported assertions." They then suggest that I make "a brief statement . . . to the effect that this paper is an expression of a point of view, or set of beliefs, which in the space available it would be impossible to support by evidence or argument." This conservative liberal sensitiveness ("edginess" is perhaps the better term) is revealing. It is an expression of an ideology pervasive among liberal intelligentsia. It is surely not the case that my article is devoid of argument, but arguments require premises; and there are, of course, some premises that are not supported. In philosophical writing on social and political topics, it is routinely the case that a great many unsupported and debatable assumptions are made. This, as Peirce and Wittgenstein have taught us, is quite unavoidable in many contexts, if we are to say anything of substance. Where the debatable and unsupported assertions are part of the liberal consensus or (sometimes) even those of a right libertarian, they tend to pass unnoticed. Perhaps they are not even seen as being debatable and unsupported. But where they reflect the orientation of the Left, such disclaimers are often thought necessary. Noam Chomsky perceptively analyzes such liberal ideological reactions in the first chapter of his *American Power and the New Mandarins* (Harmondsworth, Middlesex, England: Penguin Books, 1969). See, as well, Noam Chomsky and Edward S. Herman, *The Political Economy of Human Rights* (Montreal, Canada: Black Rose Books, 1979). It should also be noted that in *The Political Economy of Human Rights* some of the factual support occurs on which some of my assertions rest.

13

POLITICAL FUNCTIONALISM AND PHILOSOPHICAL IMPERATIVES IN THE FIGHT FOR A NEW ECONOMIC ORDER

THOMAS M. FRANCK

Those of us who share with Brian Barry the political belief that the rich—including the *newly* rich—nations of the world ought to share their affluence with the poor in a new economic order may be tempted to "package" our belief in the wrappings of universal moral imperative. Why should the rich help to feed the poor? Because—we argue with passionate conviction—it is meet, right, and our bounden duty so to do. It is meet, right, and our bounden duty at all times and in all places. It is morally imperative for an advantaged society to share with disadvantaged societies: here and now, but also anywhere, at any time.

These assertions are significantly different from my stating: "I think the United States should transfer more of its assets to needy nations of the Third World," which is a mere declaration of a personal preference, which I shall call a "political preference."

A political preference may become a moral imperative in any of three ways, one anthropological, the second logically deductive, and the third rhetorical.

An anthropologically based moral imperative is one that can be verified by independent social data gleaned from many societies over a long time span. Take the proposition: "it is better to act to save life than to stand by and witness its destruction, provided this can be done without causing greater suffering than is to be prevented." Whether such a moral imperative is anthropologically rooted can be tested empirically by examining the moral/legal/religious attitude of various societies to the person who, in Professor Barry's example, stands by and lets the child drown when he could have prevented it at the cost only of muddying his trousers. Not that such empiricism can transform into black-and-white clarity the gray areas surrounding the normative proposition. What if the child drowning were afflicted with terminal cancer or a calamitous mental disease, or had recently committed a heinous murder? What if there were several available rescuers, of different ages and states of health?

The difficulties encountered at the fringe of the proposition should not, however, detract from the verifiable proposition that the existence of an omnipresent uniform response to a moral dilemma can be anthropologically proved or disproved. If, indeed, such a postulated moral imperative is shown to have been embraced by almost all cultures at almost all times, that would surely be something worth mentioning when recommending to one's fellow humans that they conduct themselves in accordance with the imperative in a specific new situation in which, in fact, it was being ignored because its implementation seemed inconvenient. If it were my political preference that the principle be implemented, and if I had empirical evidence of its universality, I would argue: "we must act in this fashion because to do so is a universally accepted imperative, as evidenced by the fact that it is how we have always acted, how we have expected others to act, how others have acted." As a political animal I would be grateful to the anthropologists for providing this datum and to the moral philosophers for investing it with higher significance. Privately, I think it prescriptively irrelevant; but publicly I might be tempted to play it in Topeka for all it was worth.

A logically deduced moral imperative is exemplified by the proposition: "without life (being) there is nothing; therefore life (being) is the first value and its preservation the highest principle of conduct." Unfortunately, few values and principles can be logically deduced as persuasively. To the extent that a foreign-aid program is designed to save life, I might be tempted to justify it by summoning up a moral imperative derived in this fashion. But most aid is not directed toward the saving of lives but to improving the quality of life. It may not be impossible to construct a logically deduced moral imperative that requires us to improve the quality of life of our deprived fellow beings, but—at least when made globally applicable—it may be less than overwhelmingly persuasive. If it proceeds along the line of egalitarian logic ("all persons are inherently equal and should therefore be treated equally"), it may be refuted by data suggesting that the assumed equality of human beings is biologically open to argument.

Perhaps the strongest evidence against the deductive-logic approach is that it has been relatively little employed by those seeking to advance social causes. Much more frequently, the advocate in search of an absolute turns to divine revelation or to other forms of pure assertion.

A rhetorically based moral imperative is like an anthropologically based one, except that the data are missing. Instead of data we have hortatory eloquence. Lack of evidence is compensated by moral fervor. Trial lawyers, prosecutors, ministers of church and of state, teachers of law and of liberty science—all slip into rhetorically based moral imperatives now and then.

Rhetorically based moral imperatives signify nothing and would be harmless enough, were they not also a factor in the growth of religious and political absolutism and, derivatively, pernicious contributors to fake certitudes that endow the human condition with brutishness. Moral imperatives that are not based on anthropological data or deductive logic are personal opinions masquerading as truth and demanding an undeserved deference.

Even anthropologically based moral imperatives may be intellectual scams. If I am empirically right in asserting that most societies at most times have acted in the belief that their prevailing opinions and prejudices should be invested with the status of the moral imperative, then it would follow that a moral imperative, supported by empirical anthropological data, may simply point to a universal bad habit, like nose-picking, devoid of valid claim to special deference: a mere social artifact.

While I believe—as a matter of personal political preference—that the United States ought to help poor countries, I cannot bring myself to elevate that passionately held but subjective preference to a moral imperative. If I had empirical evidence that rich societies everywhere have always acted on the belief, or at least truly believed, that they had an obligation to help the poor, then I might use this to commend my cause to others. But such evidence would not commend it to me. The anthropological fact that most people have usually attitudinized in a particular fashion is rather small change when it comes to figuring my bottom line.

My agnosticism, in this context, seems to be rather widely shared, which would seem to diminish the utility of dressing a political preference as a moral imperative in the first place. If one society does not care a fig about the moral imperatives of another, and if the moral imperatives of one generation are ignored by the next, then what use are they? Imperatives bereft of imperium fortunately cannot kindle the *auto-da-fé*, but neither can they be the engine of history. What could be more pitiful than the moral imperative with an empty dance card?

As T. S. Eliot might say, if I do not wish to travel the way of the mandatory principle, yet I wish to begin in the same place as Professor Barry and arrive approximately at the same place as he, then I must seek some other way to get where I am going. I believe a politics of expediency and self-interest—much maligned of late—can get me there.

To us Lockeans, the state exists primarily to advance the values of its constituents and to facilitate their own pursuit of those values. What are the currently predominant values of our society? Let me posit several:

1. That people should be free to express themselves.
2. That freedom of expression should include not only an open market in ideas, beliefs, and behavior, but also a free, competitive, economic market.
3. That the society must balance its freedom with compassion for the disadvantaged, protection of the consumer, and conservation of the environment.

These propositions are not, in my view, self-evident, sacred, or immutable moral principles. They are my estimate of what values empirical research might indicate are most widely shared at this moment in this society. Opinion pools cannot anoint these values with immutability. But would we really feel one

whit more committed to them if they had been carved in celestial
stone, informed the codes of Medes and the Persians, or were
irrefutably deduced from first principles?

So let us begin with social values and political preferences—
poor, fragile things, but our own. And let us begin with the
political belief that the state should advance them. It would then
follow that it is in our self-interest to assist those whose values
reinforce our own; and it would be appropriately the role of
the state to employ its assets to help achieve that policy.

Instead of arguing that we have a mandatory *moral* obligation
to assist all the world's poor, I would argue that it is in our
instrumental *political* self-interest to assist selectively those of the
world's poor who share our social goals and political values. I
would reason from our own history and that of other free,
compassionate societies, arguing that these values cannot survive
in an embattled Masada. Perhaps, too, our experience in selling
wheat to the Russians has demonstrated that when we deal with
a state-purchasing monopoly, we are at a tactical disadvantage
unless we create a defensive sellers' monopoly of our own. If
we wish to retain our values, we may have to support the effort
of others to emulate them.

In addition, I would argue, with fairly persuasive economic
data, that our most successful aid programs are developing
foreign economies that become some of our best trading
partners.

Does this political-functional approach bring me to exactly
the same conclusions as Professor Barry? Not quite. The principal difference in outcome, dictated by difference in method-
ology, is that his approach would seem to mandate an undif-
ferentiated moral obligation *ergo omnes*, whereas mine compels
me to prefer some states over the multitude. One of the
functional reasons I could not embrace Professor Barry's moral
imperative approach is that I do not believe many Americans
can be won over to a program of action that must respond
equally to 1 billion Chinese; 700 million Indians; to the poor of
North Yemen, South Korea, Uruguay, and Paraguay, as if they
were all part of an equally entitled underclass.

While a general system of welfare is sustainable in the United
States as long as the ratio of donors to recipients is sufficiently
high—and it tends to break down in those of our large cities

where it is not—it is simply not possible to nurture any such belief in our ability to transform the entire planet. A system of universal redistribution would impoverish us without significantly transforming the beneficiaries. This hard truth, alone, means that we must engage in a practice not defensible by Professor Barry's mandatory principles: picking and choosing the targets of any large-scale program of economic and social transfers. "Like should be treated alike" would reduce our good intentions to ashes not only by overextension but also by misdirection. For example, any deliberate improvement in the terms of trade in nonpetroleum minerals—a cause passionately pursued by the Third World—would benefit, first and foremost, Australia, Canada, South Africa, and the Soviet Union. Of course we must pick and choose.

Such a policy of picking and choosing may repel the philosophical purist, but it can be defended—up to a point—even on grounds of fairness. The Arab oil-producing states are already launched on a foreign-aid program that marshals some of OPEC's obscene surplus to aid like-minded states inclined in the direction of Islamic theocracy. The Soviet Union, East Germany, and Czechoslovakia expend billions to keep afloat their ideological kith and kin in Cuba, Angola, Mozambique, Ethiopia, Vietnam, Cambodia, and South Yemen. Oil-enriched Venezuela and Mexico have an increasing capacity to select like-minded beneficiaries in Latin America. There is bound to be some overlapping and responsibility sharing, particularly in Latin America where our own role should remain paramount, and in parts of Africa, where the Islamic and American roles should be mutually supportive. But since the practice of picking and choosing is already widely in effect to benefit those states that ally themselves to Islamic or Marxist values, it is fair as well as prudent that a preferential system should be devised for states that aspire to values similar to our own.

If we would rally the American taxpayer, the consumer and the worker, to endure more taxes, more expensive primary products, and more competition from labor-intensive imported secondary products, then there are essential functional, political steps that our government must take. *First*, it must develop priorities, targeting for preferential treatment states whose combined size can sustain a reasonable belief in adequacy of impact. *Second,* it must demonstrate to the American people that the targeted states share, or are likely to come to share, the basic American beliefs in an open politic, a free economy, and a compassionate society. *Third,* it must demonstrate that, by building up the fortunes of kindred states, we are serving American self-interest; directly adding to our national security; insuring the survival of our political, social, and economic systems; and building trading partnerships. Enlightened self-interest is the American ethic.

14

INTERNATIONAL DISTRIBUTIVE JUSTICE

DAVID A. J. RICHARDS

In this essay, I investigate the application of the concept of
justice to relations among states in contrast to the more familiar
issues of justice arising within states. My starting point is that
contractarian theory, in the form developed by John Rawls in
A Theory of Justice,[1] enormously clarifies critical discussion of
arguments about distributive justice in the forms in which they
arise within developed industrial states. In what way, if at all,
can or should this analytic framework be deployed in the
analysis and explication of issues of justice outside this context,
for example, claims of justice between or among states or claims
of intergenerational justice? This chapter addresses the problem
of international distributive justice, by way of an examination
of certain difficulties that contractarian theory allegedly experiences in this area. In general, I defend the coherent plausibility
of contractarian theory in providing foundations for strong
moral duties in the international area, both of mutual aid for
persons in life-endangering distress (in the form suggested by
Peter Singer,[2] and more precisely elaborated by Brian Barry[3]),
and of redistributive justice along the lines of Rawls's difference
principle[4] (in line with early suggestions of David Richards[5] and
Brian Barry,[6] and the more recent elaboration of Charles
Beitz.[7])

I. THE CIRCUMSTANCES OF JUSTICE AND MORAL RECIPROCITY

It is useful to begin a discussion of the application of con-tractarian theory to international justice by noting an alleged difference between the circumstances of justice classically as-sociated with discussion of claims of justice within states and the different circumstances associated with such discussions in other contexts (e.g., both intergenerational and international justice). These differences have been elegantly described by Brian Barry,[8] who notes that the Humean circumstances of justice,[9] which Rawls expressly assumes and elaborates,[10] may not apply in these latter contexts. Let us stipulate the form of these circumstances of justice as follows: (1) rough equality in the powers and capacities of persons; (2) "confin'd generosity" (Hume),[11] such that human nature is neither so vulpine as to make larger social cooperation impossible nor so benevolent as to take no reasonable steps to advance self-interest; (3) and moderate scarcity, such that goods are neither so scarce that social cooperation is pointless nor so abundant that it is unnec-essary. Such circumstances are alleged by Hume and Rawls to define the conditions within which the ethical virtue of justice and its associated principles find their natural home, namely, the principles of justice are those ethical principles that adju-dicate the conflicting claims on scarce goods of persons so described in circumstances so defined. If human nature were different than it is or moderate scarcity turned into superfluous abundance, the virtue of justice, like Marx's state, might wither away. Put roughly, these circumstances insure that the principles of justice, whatever they are, will secure a balance of reciprocal advantage to persons who regulate their conduct thereby. *Ex hypothesi*, everyone (being roughly equal) stands to gain from justice in the defined circumstances.

Contrast this form of reciprocal advantage (a net advantage to all if all conform their conduct to principles of justice) with the kind of radical nonreciprocity associated with international or intergenerational justice. With respect to international dis-tributive justice, nations are radically unequal, arguably not even capable of "confin'd generosity," and perhaps not in a condition of interdependent scarcity; put bluntly, a wealthy nation that conforms to international distributive justice in helping poor nations may thus secure no reciprocal advantage or secure it only with respect to certain other states (e.g., those wealthy in needed natural resources). Intergenerational justice appears even more radically nonreciprocal: the present generation appears to gain little reciprocal advantage from its conformity to justice. If justice is a jealous virtue that expects little and rests on a balance of fair reciprocity, how can international or intergenerational justice be cases of *justice* (as opposed to beneficence) at all?

It is doubtful, however, that these alleged differences reflect some different sense in the concept of justice applied to all these contexts. Rather, they bring out a certain ambiguity in the interpretation of the idea of equality fundamental to the deployment of the concept of justice in all of these contexts. Once we investigate this ambiguity, we see that the alleged differences cannot be sustained.

Arguments of justice are, I take it, forms of moral argument specially concerned with the distribution of goods and evils among the conflicting claims of persons. Qua moral, these arguments define forms of practical reasoning that persons would find reasonable whether they are on the giving or receiving end. Ethical argument or moral reasoning, thus, conceptually incorporates some significant constraint of reciprocity—what some philosophers would call universalizability or role reversibility.[12] This form of reciprocity or universalizability or role reversibility is not the same idea as actual reciprocal advantage, for we have the strongest forms of ethical obligation and duty, based on the moral idea of reciprocity, to persons from whom, in fact, we stand to gain nothing. We do not have to consider examples of international or intergenerational justice here, for we can find clear examples in the intrastate case. For example, when a philosopher like John Stuart Mill articulated new forms of moral argument criticizing injustices to women,[13] he conceded that men, as a class, would suffer some losses when they surrendered their unjust domination, just as slaveowners did when slavery was ended;[14] Mill's argument is quite clear that the gain is not one of actual reciprocal advantage to men (indeed, they lose), but the gain in justice when men regulate their conduct by principles they would reasonably

accept if they were women on the receiving end.[15] We call the
sensibility capable of such moral argument a form of growth in
moral imagination. Indeed, this example, which arises within a
state, brings out the inadequacy of the Humean idea of actual
reciprocity even on its own turf. Hume's idea of rough equality,
if accepted, would sanctify vicious intrastate injustices, which
rest on just such arguments (women are physically weaker).
That we do not accept them even within the state suggests that
the Humean interpretation of rough equality is not the morally
fundamental one in any context (intrastate, international,
intergenerational).

In my judgment, we should introduce at this point the Kantian
idea of treating persons as equals.[16] When we engage in moral
argument, of which arguments of justice are one subspecies, we
appeal to forms of practical reasoning whereby we inquire
whether certain conduct would be acceptable to persons whether
on the giving or receiving end. A growth in moral imagination,
of the kind signaled by Mill's argument, includes a group to
some degree unjustly excluded from the moral community of
persons. In Kantian terms, moral argument invokes our capacity
to think self-critically about our lives and to take personal
responsibility for them as beings capable of freedom and
reason;[17] we identify others as persons by their having the like
capacity; and in reasoning morally and acting accordingly, we
treat others in terms of principles we and they would reasonably
accept, thus expressing respect for their human dignity.

These remarks are obscure but are sufficient to suggest that
the idea of equality that is relevant to the deeper analysis of the
concept of justice is the same idea of treating persons as equals
as is relevant to moral argument generally. Accordingly, the
moral idea of reciprocity, which invokes this idea of equality, is
not that of reciprocal actual advantage, but the ethical idea of
treating persons in the way one would oneself reasonably like
to be treated.

II. CONTRACTARIAN THEORY AS AN
INTERPRETATION OF MORAL RECIPROCITY

Contractarian theory affords one useful way of organizing
these moral ideas in a way that, consistent with them, yields
determinate forms of practical reasoning.

The basic analytic model is this:[18] moral principles are those that perfectly rational persons, in a hypothetical "original position" of equal liberty, would agree to as the ultimate standards of conduct that are applicable at large.[19] Persons in the original position are thought of as ignorant of their specific situations, values, or identities, but as possessing knowledge of general empirical facts, capable of interpersonal validation, and as holding reasonable beliefs. Since Rawls's concern is to apply this conception of moral principles to develop a theory of justice, he introduces into the original position the circumstances of justice described above, namely, the existence of conflicting claims to a limited supply of goods, and considers a specific set of principles to regulate these claims.

The original position presents a problem of rational choice under uncertainty. Rational people in this position have no way of predicting the probability that they will end up in any particular situation. If a person agrees to principles of justice that permit deprivations of liberty and property and later winds up in a disadvantaged position, he will, by definition, have no just claim against deprivations that may render his life prospects meager and bitterly servile. To avoid such consequences, the rational strategy in choosing the basic pinciples of justice would be the prudential "maximin" strategy:[20] one would seek to maximize the minimum condition, so that if a person were born into the worst possible situation of life allowed by the adopted moral principles, he would still be better off than he would be in the worst situation allowed by other principles.

An important feature of the contractarian interpretation of moral personality is the assumption of ignorance as to specific identity and the consequent requirement that a decision be reached on the basis of empirical facts capable of interpersonal validation. This assumption assures that the principles decided on in the original position will be neutral as between divergent visions of the good life, for the ignorance of specific identity deprives people of any basis for illegitimately distorting their decisions in favor of their own vision. Such neutrality, a fundamental feature of the idea of political right, insures to people the right to choose their own lives autonomously as free and rational beings.[21]

In such ways, contractarian theory expresses the Kantian idea of equality and reciprocity in terms of those principles that would rationally be agreed to by persons from an original position of equal liberty, on the assumption that the principles can and would be generally accepted and acted on; and, the Kantian idea of autonomy is expressed by the thought that the contractors would make their choice behind a veil of ignorance whereby they do not know who they are, thus depriving them of any way of taking account of any fortuitous features of themselves other than their personhood.

In the context of an advanced industrial state, Rawls argues that the maximin strategy would require the contractors to give special weight to the liberties of free speech, religious tolerance, voting rights, and so on, over the general goods of wealth and status. Because such liberties are among the fundamental factors that shape a person's capacity to become a fully rational being and to enjoy the life of such a being, the rational contractors of this model of political morality could not, consistently with the maximin strategy of rational choice, agree to any configuration of principles except one providing equality in the distribution of such liberties. Use of the maximin strategy in choosing principles relating to these liberties, then, tends to eliminate the class disadvantaged with respect to these liberties; the highest lowest condition is equality for all persons.

By contrast, once a certain minimum level of property and wealth is guaranteed, the rational interest in property and wealth is not so fundamental as that in these liberties. Assuming the greatest amount of equal liberty for all and some measure of fair opportunity, inequalities in property and income above the minimum are tolerable if there are countervailing advantages. A relatively poor person, with full liberty and basic opportunity, may be better off in a system that allows inequalities in the distribution of wealth than in a system that requires equality: the consequences of inequality—for example, incentive effects on total production—may increase his absolute well-being although his relative share is less than it would be in a system with mandated equality of wealth.

The general consequence of such reasoning is a structure of principles that, very schematically,[22] we may summarize as follows:

1. *The principle of equal liberty.* Basic institutions are to be arranged so that every person in the institution is guar-

anteed the greatest equal liberty and opportunity compatible with a like liberty and opportunity for all.

2. *The difference principle.* Inequalities in the distribution by institutions of general goods like money, property, and status are to be allowed only if they are required to advance the interests of all persons more than equality would and they advance the interests of the least advantaged persons as much a possible.

Rawls puts these principles in lexical order: the difference principle applies only when the first principle is satisfied.[23] At least in the circumstances of an advanced industrial society, no inequality in the liberties of the first principle can be justified in order to advance the goods of the difference principle.

III. CONTRACTARIAN THEORY AND INTERNATIONAL DISTRIBUTIVE JUSTICE

Clearly, this form of analysis, and the underlying Kantian perspective it expresses, can be limited to the nation-state or to one generation only arbitrarily. Rawls himself acknowledges this when he suggests the applicability of some moral constraints governing the relations among states (nonaggression, diplomatic immunity, *pacta sunt servanda*, and so on[24]) and argues for a just savings principle as one specification of intergenerational justice.[25] Rawls does not, however, take either international or intergenerational justice as the main focus of his analysis; the central concern, rather, is to explicate principles of distributive justice applicable within a developed industrial nation-state. His account of international justice is, accordingly, schematic, and the conception of intergenerational justice is clearly inadequate to the whole problem.[26] For present purposes, the most striking limitation of Rawls's account of international justice is his focus on the conventional principles of international law described above and his express disavowal of the application of the difference principle internationally.[27]

In order to consider how the contractarian framework could be applied in the context of international justice, we should remind ourselves of the underlying ideas that the framework is intended to explicate, namely, treating persons in the way one would oneself reasonably like to be treated, that is, what I have called moral reciprocity. We apply this idea straightforwardly in our relations to persons currently existing insofar as our actions or failures to act relate to others in ways that we can reasonably assess in terms of moral reciprocity, namely, whether we, if our situations were reversed, would have wished to be treated, when we were ignorant of our capacities and values, in the way we now treat or fail to treat them. The factual relations among nation-states in the contemporary world would, when assessed from the perspective of the contractarian original position (each person not knowing, of course, specific identity, and thus which nation-state they are in), give rise to two *kinds* of moral obligations or duties: the natural duty of mutual aid, and complex institutionally based obligations of justice. Let us discuss each *seriatim*.

A. The Principle of Mutual Aid

While Rawls applies the contractarian model to a certain special case of institutional relations among persons (namely justice within a developed industrial nation-state), it is reasonably clear that the model, as one way of expressing moral reciprocity, may be suitably adapted to clarify other forms of moral principle.[28] Now, it is fundamental to distinguish two kinds of contexts that give rise to different kinds of moral principles: first, relations among persons, as such, whether or not the persons share common institutions (nation, community, clan, culture, or the like); and second, relations among persons in common institutions or in some institutional connection with one another.[29] Let us focus here on one subclass of the former principles, namely, requirements of duty that govern human relations, which we will call the principles of natural duty.

It is not difficult to see why, from the perspective of the contractarian interpretation of moral reciprocity, such principles of natural duty would be agreed to or universalized.[30] It is a familiar natural fact, which would be known by the contractors of the original position, that persons stand often in relation to one another, unregulated by any common institutional membership, whereby, at little cost to an agent's pursuit of her or his rational interests, the agent may forbear from actions or so act that other persons are either not harmed or are saved from prospective harms of grave and irreparable kinds. From the perspective of an original position in which persons behind a veil of ignorance would not know whether they would be on the giving or receiving end, it would be reasonable to agree to principles of natural duty, requiring forms of conduct and forbearance in these contexts, because they would, in any event, lose little of any significance to the pursuit, as agents, of their rational ends (if, as agents, they acted on such principles) and would gain protection from forms of irreparable harm (as beneficiaries of the observance of such principles). In this way, persons would secure, independent of any institutional nexus, basic forms of respect for personal integrity by which persons express to other persons the natural bonds of a common humanity.[31] Such principles would define duties because their observance costs little and secures such basic interests that coercion would, where appropriate, be regarded as justified in securing their observance.

One set of facts, relevant to the formulation of one such principle of natural duty, relates to forms of assistance and aid that, at only slight cost, one person may render in saving another from grave forms of harm. Consistent with the contractarian interpretation of moral reciprocity, persons would agree to or universalize this principle, enforceable by coercion if necessary, because, in this way, they would guard against the possibility that they might themselves end up in such a position of requiring assistance.[32]

It is important to see that agreement on the principle of mutual aid arises from the consideration of a certain circumscribed set of circumstances, not all possible circumstances of aid, that is, the principle is concerned only with aid, given at slight personal cost, that secures a great good to the person helped. Mutual aid, in contrast to beneficence, requires aid only where rendering the aid is of little cost to the person who does the helping: a person may save another from drowning by merely putting out her hand, or throwing out a lifebelt. This feature explains how the principle could be agreed to as one of duty, justifying coercion, and defining correlative rights: persons would agree to or universalize such a principle, as one of duty, only if they knew it did not require sacrifice of life or limb.[33] Of course, acts of heroism or saintliness, saving persons at such risks, are morally admirable on the ground of the moral principle of beneficence.[34] But we are here concerned, not with the moral ideals of saints and heroes, but with the basic minimum standards of human decency that cannot, consistent with human rights, be transgressed. The principle of mutual aid defines a natural duty that, properly understood and limited, imposes such enforceable rights.[35]

This distinction of mutual aid from different sorts of circumstances in which persons may do good to other persons must be contrasted with the traditional and contemporary failure of philosophers to draw this distinction, or, even where they draw it, to give weight to its full normative significance.[36] With respect to the failure to draw this distinction, utilitarian thought has most prominently and self-consciously insisted that no such distinction exists. Henry Sidgwick for example, describes both nonmaleficence (another natural duty) and mutual aid as a "somewhat indefinite limit of Duty" beyond which "extends the Virtue of Benevolence without limit"; but he sees these as only relative distinctions within the wider principle of beneficence in reference to which he grants that the "distinction between Excellence and Strict Duty does not seem properly admissible in Utilitarianism."[37] If we suppose, following utilitarians like Sidgwick, that the only ultimate normative principle is maximizing the aggregate net pleasure over pain of all sentient beings, there can be no fundamental moral distinction between mutual aid and beneficence, since both principles, to the extent they are justified at all, are based on maximizing the aggregate net of pleasure in the requisite utilitarian way. In short, both are principles of utilitarian duty and thus may be appropriately enforced by law in the way our duties may be. The perception of beneficence as supererogatory is simply a moral illusion.[38]

The consequence of this self-conscious utilitarian failure to distinguish mutual aid and beneficence is dramatically seen in the attempt of Peter Singer, a utilitarian, to apply mutual-aid arguments to international famine relief.[39] Singer poses his argument, in support of moral obligations of famine relief, in terms of mutual aid. His central example, to which famine relief is analogized, is an example of clear mutual aid:

> if I am walking past a shallow pond and see a child drowning in it, I ought to wade in and pull the child out. This will mean getting my clothes muddy, but this is insignificant while the death of the child would presumably be a very bad thing.[40]

If we acknowledge this as a clear moral duty, as Singer and the above contractarian account would agree, then we must, Singer argues, suppose famine relief to be a comparable moral duty insofar as it satisfies the same moral conditions: giving such famine relief is of little cost to people in developed nations and saves other persons from the irreparable harm of starvation. Again, the contractarian would concur. But Singer goes on to specify the extent of this moral duty of famine relief in a way that cannot be sustained, at least on grounds of mutual aid. Thus, Singer puts the requirement of little cost (instantiated in his example by the risklessness of saving the child and the muddy clothes) in terms of not "sacrificing anything of comparable moral importance."[41] In the context of famine relief, this requirement is interpreted, not in terms of little cost to the agent, but in terms of the marginal utility of the money forgone by the agent compared with the utility achieved by those who get it. This would require, as a matter of duty, that persons in developed countries should surrender substantial percentages of their income, at least to "the level at which, by giving more, I would cause as much suffering to myself or my dependents as I would relieve by my gift."[42]

Now, this is a remarkable non sequitur: it does not follow from the application of mutual aid to the small cost of saving Singer's drowning child or the small cost, fairly shared, of wealthy countries' relief of famine that any particular person in wealthy countries is under a *moral duty*, of a comparable kind, to surrender such significant percentages of their income. Singer here has played on the ambiguity of "at little cost," fundamental to the requirements of mutual aid as a natural duty, shifting the normative content of the idea from its proper locus in the agent and the insubstantial sacrifices of his or her rational interests, to the marginal utility comparison noted above. On this latter view, quite substantial sacrifices of an agent's rational interests are "morally" insignificant if the sacrifice and pain incurred is balanced with a surplus by the pleasure thus made possible in others. But the latter interpretation wholly fails to capture the moral basis of mutual aid as a natural *duty*. For example, it suggests that, in the drowning child example, quite severe risks of harm to the agent might be morally required (the water is deep; the agent a bad or incompetent swimmer; and the like) if the likely goods to the child or her family are greater than the likely harms to the agent and others. But it is precisely *such* sacrifices of the agent's interests that mutual aid, at least as a principle of enforceable natural *duty*, does not require. Singer betrays the force of his own example and the moral distinction on which it rests because, as a utilitarian, he must deem this a distinction without a moral difference.

The contractarian interpretation of mutual aid here proposed preserves, however, the important moral weight of this distinction in intuitive moral thought: the principle of mutual aid, like other enforceable moral duties, applies only where compliance does not require substantial sacrifice of the agent's responsible pursuit of his ends, whatever they are. Saving the drowning child, at the risk of muddy clothes, is governed by the principle; saving the child, at the risk of death (the water is deep; one cannot swim), is not. Correspondingly, the utilitarian failure to give weight to this kind of distinction (or, as in Singer, to elide it) is criticized on the ground that it dissolves moral personality, the fundamental datum of ethics, into utilitarian aggregates.[43] The consequence, I believe, is a sounder understanding of the moral force that mutual aid properly has or should have. Whereas Singer's utilitarian elision of mutual aid and beneficence tends, mistakenly, either to attribute to beneficence a moral obligation it does not have or to characterize mutual aid as a form of supererogatory charity that it is not, the present account marks off the moral stringency of mutual aid as a natural duty from the supererogatory grace of self-sacrificing beneficence.[44]

So understood, we can preserve Singer's central point but see its institutional implications more clearly. Famine relief, in the circumstances Singer describes, is a requirement of the natural duty of mutual aid, since wealthy countries can, when fairly shared, at little cost per person save other persons from irreparable harms. Individual persons are under a natural duty of mutual aid to make the small contributions that, if made by many or a substantial number, would suffice to give famine relief. Obviously, it would be institutionally fairer if such natural duties were met by the state with the burden equitably assessed through the tax system. Citizens may be under moral obligations to use their political power to realize such an end. Absent their success, however, the duty of mutual aid would fall on them individually to make contributions in the required way.

Finally, this account of mutual aid enables us to perceive its moral basis in ideas of human rights. Brian Barry, whose general account of mutual aid preserves the distinctions here insisted upon, nonetheless disassociates mutual aid from rights, supposing it to be goal-based.[45] On the view here proposed, this residue of utilitarian reasoning, for the same reasons that the utilitarian account of mutual aid is unacceptable, should be dissolved in the clearer understanding of the moral basis of mutual aid that the contractarian interpretation of moral reciprocity here affords. On this view, the requirements of mutual aid are specified by a moral principle of natural duty, whose requirements correlatively define moral or human rights. Some philosophers of stature have, I know, questioned the linguistic naturalness of asserting rights to mutual aid.[46] But the linguistic intuitions here adduced are, I believe, widely controverted, and I do not believe that the controversial moral views, which these intuitions may reflect, can be regarded as decisive against a critical moral argument that may show these intuitions to be undefended and indefensible. The gravamen of the present argument is that these intuitions are wrong, resting as they do on the mistaken assimilation, supported by unexamined assumptions of Anglo-American law,[47] of mutual aid (a natural duty, which defines correlative rights) to beneficence (a principle of supererogation, which is a matter of grace, not of enforceable rights).

B. International Distributive Justice

If we interpret justice in terms of the actual reciprocities of benefits among persons in schemes of mutual cooperation, as Hume's notion of the circumstances of justice appears to require,

justice among nations will play a role only where such reciprocities exist; for example, where ongoing trade relations bring
into play appropriate obligations of fair dealing, fair play,
fidelity, and the like. Moral requirements of such kinds place,
as Brian Barry has shown,[48] critical moral constraints on international economic relations, especially in cases, which often
exist, where developed countries have, in the past, unfairly
dominated undeveloped countries, using resources and markets
on unfair terms, and continue to do so. Barry mentions, in this
connection, the current unfair transfer pricing of transnational
corporations.[49]

I should like, however, here to focus on the different moral
question whether, in addition to such requirements of fair
dealing now, there are general obligations of international
distributive justice. In particular, I shall discuss whether Rawls's
difference principle has any international implications, which
Rawls, as we earlier saw, sharply limits.

Brian Barry supports Rawls's limitation on three grounds.[50]
First, the idea of justice as reciprocity is importantly governed
by the cooperative relations of a society. If the cooperative
scheme does not extend to certain institutions (e.g., having a
pension scheme), then there are no associated obligations of
justice, for there is no fair reciprocity of actual benefits and
burdens. Perhaps the society is collectively irrational in not
instituting such a scheme, but—until it does so—no obligation
of justice obtains. In the international sphere, pertinent schemes
of mutual support are notably undeveloped; and, accordingly,
obligations of justice are undeveloped. Second, the world is not
a cooperative partnership in the same sense the nation-state is.
And third, international redistribution cannot plausibly be
regarded as advantageous to rich as well as poor countries.
Barry queries Charles Beitz's argument,[51] for the global extension of the difference principle on the ground that the network
of international trade, appealed to by Beitz,[52] does not sufficiently constitute the kind of reciprocal interdependency of the
nation-state, and thus cannot be the natural subject of the
principles of justice appropriate to the nation-state.

Clearly, Barry's critical argument against a global difference
principle deploys the conception of actual reciprocity in the
circumstances of justice discussed earlier. But, as we saw there,

uses of the concept of justice that appeal to actual reciprocity implement one form of moral reciprocity; but other claims of justice, in which actual reciprocity is not implemented (indeed, one party loses, the other gains), are justified by moral reciprocity. We adduced an intrastate example—Mill's argument against the subjection of women,[53] a clear argument of justice in this latter sense: men lose, women gain, but the change is nonetheless just because it secures the elimination of a distribution of power and goods that violates moral reciprocity. The existing inequalities between men and women (some of which may be natural—men are physically stronger) are critically assessed in the light of deeper values of moral equality and reciprocity; the weight given to these inequalities is unjust because it reinforces morally irrelevant natural inequality by creating socially induced forms of inequality that, as self-fulfilling prophecies, deny capacities for human dignity.[54] We concluded that actual reciprocity is necessary neither in the intrastate nor in any other context; issues of justice turn on a deeper ideal of moral reciprocity. Indeed, we appeal to this ideal in criticism of perceptions of "natural" equality that, on examination, exclude illegitimately from the scope of moral criticism questionable forms of equal treatment.

I submit that, from the perspective of moral reciprocity, the exclusion of poor nations from the scope of justice on the ground that they are not in the requisite relation of equality and actual reciprocity to wealthy nations, is a mistake on a par with the failure of moral imagination that Mill revealed in the moral arguments supporting the subjection of women. We start, as we should, not with the world as it is in which, as Rousseau saw,[55] we see everywhere the effects of continuing injustice and morally arbitrary forms of thought and treatment, but with the idea of moral reciprocity. We assess current forms of thought and treatment in terms of moral argument that invokes our capacity to think self-critically about our lives and to take personal responsibility for them as beings capable of freedom and reason; we identify others as persons by their having the like capacity; and in reasoning morally and acting accordingly, we treat others in terms of principles we and they would reasonably accept, thus expressing respect for our common human dignity. The contractarian interpretation of these ideas uses the veil of ignorance to strip away fortuitous characteristics (e.g., one's race, gender, religious affiliation, and the like) as morally irrelevant, and focuses only on personhood and those aspects of human circumstances that are relevant to the task assigned to the original position—agreeing on critical standards that constitute a publicly understood, accepted, and acted on conception of what shall be moral conduct. Now, from this perspective, one's membership in one nation as opposed to another and the natural inequality among nations may be as morally fortuitous as any other natural fact. Certainly, consistent with the veil of ignorance, persons cannot be aware of which nation they are born into, and thus of the degree of wealth or poverty of that nation. Rather, without such knowledge, they must agree on appropriate critical standards regulating relations among nations, which persons would reasonably accept whether on the giving or receiving end.

From the perspective of the original position and the concern of the contractors for the worst off, there would be a natural tendency to agree to some critical standards fairly allocating the basic scarce natural and cultural resources that enable persons, no matter what nation they should live in, to have a decent opportunity and capacity to pursue a life of personal dignity on whatever terms they define their rational good. Thus, the contractors would know that certain natural resources are necessary to realize many human goods; that these resources are unequally distributed over the earth; and that, accordingly, one fundamental problem of distributive justice, which they must address, is how such scarce resources should be allocated.[56] In addition, the contractors would know that forms of knowledge and technology would exist unequally in different cultures and that certain of these cultural resources would afford new opportunities, not previously available, by which persons may better achieve their rational ends (e.g., better child care, improved diet and health care, longer life, and the like). From the point of view of the original position, neither the actual location of natural resources in certain territories occupied by certain nations nor the good fortune of other nations in fostering the cultural resources can confer on them any moral title to the exclusive use and disposition of the resources. Certainly, the mere location of natural resources is quite obviously fortuitous, and a principle of justice would be agreed to requiring that, to the extent feasible, all persons be granted equal access to them, consistent with obligations to future generations as well.[57] Cultural resources appear no less fortuitously present in certain nations; fortunate material and historical circumstances explain how new forms of knowledge and technology appear in certain cultures. Certainly, whatever personal responsibility may be part of the explanation can be attributed only to certain persons (who should be appropriately rewarded consistent with the difference principle[58]), not to everyone who happens to be born into those cultures;[59] correspondingly, the failures of responsible and capable persons in other cultures to foster such resources cannot justly be imputed to everyone in the culture. From the point of view of the original position, such cultural resources should be distributed so that all persons, no matter what the accident of their birth, have fair access to them. Even if the contractors of the original position would give greater weight to equality within the political community in which they find themselves over global distribution, they could not, consistent with hedging against the possibility of ending up in a disadvantaged nation, fail to give some weight to claims of such nations for fair access to basic material and cultural goods.

The principles governing such claims are, of course, principles of justice: the contractors of the original position focus here on critical standards that are to regulate conflicting claims over scarce goods, which is the problem of social justice. But *these* principles of justice operate at a more fundamental evaluative level than those principles, associated with the classic definitions of the circumstances of justice, that govern distribution within the unit of the nation-state; nor do they depend on any assumption of actual reciprocity among those subject to their requirements, whether those relations are those of national interdependence or of international trade and common markets. Nations could, hypothetically, be completely autarkic and yet be subject to these requirements of justice, which insure, from the perspective of treating persons as equals, that each person has been guaranteed the equal respect of being in a nation with fair access to these basic natural and cultural resources. Human life chances and prospects are basically shaped by the kind of nation into which one is born and in which one lives, and access to natural and cultural resources shape in fundamental ways the opportunity that life in a nation affords to realize one's rational vision of one's good. Accordingly, persons, situated in the moral impartiality of the original position, could no more leave the distribution of these resources to an amoral fortune than they could the distribution of goods within the nation-state.

On examination, then, the natural inequality of nations no more justifies a blanket exemption of international relations from requirements of distributive justice than the comparable claims regarding the natural inequality of women, debunked by Mill, justify the subjection of women. In both cases, current forms of powerlessness appear, on examination, to be subject to deeper moral criticism. We need not, in this connection, abandon entirely ideas of reciprocity, as Barry suggests,[60] in order to explain this moral criticism; rather, we must focus, as we have here, on the deeper idea of moral reciprocity and show how it gives rise to claims of justice of some force that do not rest on actual reciprocity, indeed fundamentally criticize the limitation of international moral evaluation within such confines.

The consequence of this analysis is, I believe, support for Beitz's recent elaboration of a global difference principle[61] that does not rest, as his account does,[62] on facts of international trade and common markets. On the view here suggested, any inequalities in wealth and real income among nations that are atttributable to unfair inequalities in resources are justified only if, over time, they make the worse off in poorer nations better off than they would be with equality. This is a global form of the difference principle.[63]

Nothing in this account denies the right of persons to define the meaning of their own lives, including their cultural lives; nor does it deny the right of persons, on fair terms, to establish communities or nations in which they can express their own conceptions of the good life; nor does it imply that the liberties defined by Rawls's first principle of justice must enjoy priority over the difference principle in undeveloped nations.[64] Certainly, a person may choose reasonably to live a life free of the empty distractions of the consumerist wealth of advanced countries; and, nations may, consistent with justice, define their cultural life in ways that eschew wealth as an end in itself. The global difference principle, here supported, requires only that persons and, derivatively, nations be given fair access to certain basic natural and cultural resources; whether, how, and to what degree persons accept or use such resources may, assuming fair processes of decision making, be left to them.

IV. THE PLACE OF INTERNATIONAL DISTRIBUTIVE JUSTICE AS A MORAL DUTY; AND WHY BE MORAL?

In this essay, I have suggested that duties of aid in the international sphere take two forms: the natural duty of mutual aid, which is triggered by extreme deprivation, like imminent starvation; and a principle of fair distribution of natural and cultural resources. These principles have different scopes of application (e.g., the fair distribution principle applies wherever resources are distributed unequally, whether or not the inequality results in starvation, or the like), but sometimes also converge.[65] Both, however, are forms of moral duty or obligation,[66] which appear to apply in circumstances where actual reciprocity is lacking. Arguments on behalf of mutual aid or international redistribution to poor countries are, I have argued, ethical arguments, which do not require the kind of actual reciprocity familiar in some contexts of intratemporal justice within the nation-state; it suffices, rather, that personal relations in certain circumstances may be assessed in terms of what I have called moral reciprocity. Now, even granting that these arguments do define ethical obligations and correlative rights, one may ask, following Plato, Why be moral?[67] This question, as traditionally discussed in philosophy, often rests on various conceptual confusions: most obviously, the conceptual confusion that moral reasons for action must, as such, be in the agent's interests.[68] Nonetheless, undoubtedly, at some point in moral reasoning certain moral reasons for action require such severe personal sacrifice that the question arises whether such reasons can be given controlling weight:[69] Does the moral life require us to endure privation or misery, something we admire in saints or heroes but do not usually demand of ordinary and decent people of good will? Skepticism about moral arguments for mutual aid or international distributive justice may express doubt of such forms, namely, that the moral arguments demand too much personal sacrifice to be properly credited.

So stated, such skepticism deserves no weight whatsoever. The fact that we do not stand immediately to benefit from acting on mutual aid or international redistributive justice does not suggest or imply that such action requires us to lead lives of misery and privation, any more than the elimination of the subjection of women compelled masculine impoverishment. Rather, such actions requires no more than is reasonable in the circumstances. Mutual aid might require the small costs in an increased tax burden per citizen that, fairly distributed, would be incurred to maintain a fund for famine relief and the like. Distributive justice would call for the moderate scaling down of national consumerist avarice and cupidity that, equitably administered, might lead to a more just sharing of natural and cultural resources (e.g., a reduction in luxury spending fairly imposed). It is, in my judgment, a disturbing feature of the ways in which American philosophers deploy Kantian arguments that the little personal costs that arguments of humanity or justice require are assimilated to the rape of one's personhood.[70] Moral philosophy, in my opinion, becomes an expression of unjust American ideologies, which legitimate crass failures of humanity and elementary justice in the interest of class and national selfishness when it fails to draw moral distinctions of such kinds. The point applies to the whole range of contexts of justice: distributive justice within the nation-state, intergenerational justice,[71] and international justice.

I have little hope that a change in the underlying social attitudes, which these ideologies reflect, can be worked easily or soon. Brian Barry[72] is, however, correct to compare the slowness of the shift in conceptions of international redistributive justice with the gradual and invisible transformation of ideas that undergirded the emergence of the welfare state; and certainly, just as political action by the poor and powerless accelerated such changes in developed nation-states,[73] comparable action by poor nations, with whatever leverage they possess and may fairly exercise,[74] will play a part now in the dawning recognition of international distributive justice. For philosophy, the task must be to preserve the integrity of language and thought, to acknowledge the force of moral arguments consistently pursued, to insist on the authentic articulation of the voice of the invisible world whose moral demands are ever more audible and urgent.

NOTES

* This essay profited from conversations with Donald Levy, Brooklyn College (Philosophy).

1. John Rawls, *A Theory of Justice* (Cambridge, Mass.: Harvard University Press, 1971).
2. See Peter Singer, "Famine, Affluence and Morality," in Peter Laslett and James Fishkin, *Philosophy, Politics and Society* (Fifth Series) (Oxford: Basil Blackwell, 1979), pp. 20–35; reprinted from *Philosophy and Public Affairs* 1 (1972), 229–43. See, for a similar statement, Peter Singer, *Practical Ethics* (Cambridge: Cambridge University Press, 1979), ch. 8, pp. 158–91.
3. See Brian Barry, "Humanity and Justice in Global Perspective," pp. 219–52 in this volume.
4. See John Rawls, *supra* note 1, 65–83.
5. See David A. J. Richards, *A Theory of Reasons for Action* (Oxford: Oxford at the Clarendon Press, 1971), pp. 138–41.
6. See Brian Barry, *The Liberal Theory of Justice* (Oxford: Clarendon Press, 1973), ch. 12. See also T. M. Scanlon, "Rawls' Theory of Justice," 121 *U. Penn. Law Review* 1020–69, at 1066–67 (1973).
7. See Charles R. Beitz, *Political Theory and International Relations* (Princeton, N.J.: Princeton University Press, 1979), pp. 127–76.
8. See Brian Barry, "Circumstances of Justice and Future Generations," in R. I. Sikora and Brian Barry, *Obligations to Future Generations* (Philadelphia: Temple University Press, 1978), pp. 204–48.
9. See David Hume, *A Treatise of Human Nature*, ed. L. A. Selby-Bigge (Oxford: Clarendon Press, 1964), pp. 485–95; David Hume, *An Enquiry Concerning the Principles of Morals*, in *Enquiries*, ed. L. A. Selby-Bigge (Oxford: Clarendon Press, 1902), p. 190.
10. See John Rawls, *supra* note 1, 126–30.
11. See Hume, *Treatise*, *supra* note 9, at 495.
12. See, for different forms of statements of these ideas by recent philosophers, Kurt Baier, *The Moral Point of View* (Ithaca, N.Y.: Cornell University Press, 1958), pp. 187–213; Alan Donagan, *The Theory of Morality* (Chicago: University of Chicago Press, 1977), pp.

210–43; Charles Fried, *Right and Wrong* (Cambridge, Mass.: Harvard University Press, 1978), pp. 7–29; David Gauthier, *Practical Reasoning* (Oxford: Clarendon Press, 1963); Alan Gewirth, *Reason and Morality* (Chicago: University of Chicago Press, 1978), pp. 129–98; G. R. Grice, *The Grounds of Moral Judgment* (Cambridge: Cambridge University Press, 1967), pp. 1–35; R. M. Hare, *Freedom and Reason* (Oxford: Clarendon Press, 1963), pp. 86–183; R. M. Hare, *The Language of Morals* (Oxford: Clarendon Press, 1952); John Mackie, *Ethics* (Harmondsworth, Middlesex, England: Penguin Books, 1977), pp. 83–102; John Rawls, *supra* note 1; David A. J. Richards, *supra* note 1.

13. See, in general, John Stuart Mill, *The Subjection of Women*, in J. S. Mill and H. T. Mill, *Essays on Sex Equality*, ed. A. S. Rossi (Chicago: University of Chicago Press, 1970).

14. See *id.* at 157–80.

15. *Id.*

16. The classic Kantian text is *Foundations of the Metaphysics of Morals*, trans. L. W. Beck (New York: Liberal Arts Press, 1959).

17. Cf. R. M. Hare, *Freedom and Reason, supra* note 12.

18. See John Rawls, *supra* note 1; see also David A. J. Richards, *supra* note 5, at 75–91.

19. See John Rawls, *supra* note 1, at 11–22.

20. *Id.* at 150–61.

21. Cf. Ronald Dworkin, "Liberalism," in Stuart Hampshire, *Public and Private Morality* (Cambridge: Cambridge University Press, 1978), pp. 113–43.

22. I adapt this formulation from Richards, *supra* note 5, at 121, focusing on the priority of the liberties to wealth for purposes of simplicity of exposition. The treatment of opportunity issues, thus, is not here focused on; and questions of capacity distribution are put aside. For Rawls's more complex formulation, see John Rawls, *supra* note 1, at 302–3.

23. See *id.*, 243–51.

24. John Rawls, *supra* note 1, 377–82.

25. *Id.*, 284–93.

26. See Brian Barry, "Justice Between Generations," in P. M. S. Hacker and Joseph Raz, *Law, Morality and Society* (Oxford: Clarendon Press, 1977), pp. 268–84; see also David A. J. Richards, "Contractarian Theory, Intergenerational Justice, and Energy Policy," in volume of essays on energy policy to be published by Center for Philosophy and Public Policy, University of Maryland; see also in the same volume, Brian Barry, "Intergenerational Justice in Energy Policy."

27. Cf. the discussion of this point in Charles R. Beitz, *supra* note 7, at 129–36.

28. See, in general, David A. J. Richards, *supra* note 5.
29. See *id.*, 92–95.
30. See, for a general discussion of the derivation and content of the principles of natural duty, *id.*, ch. 10.
31. Brian Barry, thus, correctly refers to mutual aid as a principle of humanity. See Brian Barry, *supra* note 3, p. 221.
32. See, for a fuller discussion, David A. J. Richards, *supra* note 5, 185–89.
33. *Id.*, 187.
34. See *id.*, 205–8.
35. For the relation of moral principles of obligation and duty and ideas of moral rights, see *id.*, 95–106.
36. For a fuller discussion of the traditional and contemporary literature, see *id.*, 185–86.
37. See Henry Sidgwick, *Methods of Ethics*, 7th ed. (London: Macmillan, 1963), pp. 253, 492.
38. For a recent utilitarian defense of this view, see Jonathan Glover, *Causing Death and Saving Lives* (Harmondsworth, Middlesex, England: Penguin Books, 1977), pp. 92–112, 292–93.
39. See Peter Singer, "Famine, Affluence and Morality," *supra* notes 1–2.
40. *Id.*, 23–24.
41. *Id.*, 23.
42. *Id.*, 33.
43. Cf. Bernard Williams, "A Critique of Utilitarianism," in J. J. C. Smart and Bernard Williams, *Utilitarianism For and Against* (Cambridge: Cambridge University Press, 1973), pp. 77–150.
44. See David A. J. Richards, *supra* note 5, 185–89, 205–11.
45. See Brian Barry, *supra* note 3, at pp. 244–46.
46. The point has been put in terms of denials that mutual aid and even nonmaleficence can be regarded as duties. Against the existence of a duty of nonmaleficence, see H. L. A. Hart, "Legal and Moral Obligation," in A. I. Melden, *Essays in Moral Philosophy* (Seattle: University of Washington Press, 1958), pp. 82–83; against the existence of a duty of mutual aid, see Kurt Baier, *supra* note 12, at 226–27; against the existence of a duty of nonmaleficence, *id.*, at 221; similarly, David Gauthier maintains that no duty of nonmaleficence exists (*Practical Reasoning, supra* note 12, at 194), yet upholds a duty of mutual aid (*id.* at 203). This view has, however, been criticized by other philosophers who maintain, for example, that "duty" has no more natural use, in moral contexts, than to express requirements of mutual aid. See Eric D'Arcy, *Human Acts: an Essay in Their Moral Evaluation* (Oxford: Clarendon Press, 1963), pp. 50–57; J. N. Findlay, *Values and Intentions* (Lon-

don: Allen & Unwin, 1961), pp. 310, 343, 363; G. R. Grice, *Grounds of Moral Judgement* (Cambridge: Cambridge University Press, 1967), pp. 124, 155, 159 ff., 173.

47. See David A. J. Richards, *The Moral Criticism of Law* (Encino, Calif.: Dickenson-Wadsworth, 1977), pp. 221–24; also see David A. J. Richards, "Human Rights and the Moral Foundations of the Substantive Criminal Law," 13 *Georgia L. Rev.* 1395–1446, at 1429–30 (1979).

48. See Brian Barry, *supra* note 3, pp. 227–29.

49. See *id.* at 227–28.

50. See Brian Barry, *supra* note 3, pp. 232–33.

51. See, in general, Charles R. Beitz, *supra* note 7, at 127–76.

52. *Id.* at 143–53.

53. See note 13, *supra*.

54. See *id.* at 125–55.

55. See Jean Jacques Rousseau, *The Social Contract*, in *The Social Contract and Discourses*, trans. G. D. H. Cole (New York: E. P. Dutton, 1950), at pp. 3–4.

56. Cf. Charles R. Beitz, *supra* note 7, at 136–43, where Beitz develops such an argument in terms of entitlements to natural resources. He does not, however, extend it to cultural resources.

57. On the form of these intergenerational obligations, see the essays of Brian Barry and David Richards cited at note 26, *supra*.

58. Charles Beitz suggests a principle of the form here discussed applied to natural resources, but not to cultural resources. See Charles R. Beitz, *supra* note 7, at 136–43. Beitz makes the distinction between natural and cultural resources on the ground that the former, unlike the latter, is not tied to persons and involved with personal identity, so that the distribution of the former does not involve costs of the kind that appropriation of the latter would involve. But, the issue is not forcing people to work, but whether the results of their work, as much the result of good fortune and context as natural talent, should—after appropriate reward to elicit such performance—be subject to principles of fair distribution. At most, the distinction between natural and cultural resources is that the latter, unlike the former, calls for special forms of recognition and reward consistent with the difference principle, which is, paradigmatically, concerned with encouraging precisely such contributions to the general good. But, once such just rewards are met, the considerations requiring fair distribution are the same in both cases.

59. Perhaps, since a cultural environment of education may be part of the background leading to such discoveries, the difference principle would require some broader dispersion of rewards to those

aspects of the environment which facilitated such discoveries. But, again, this would not apply to everyone in the culture and would, in any event, only apply to the extent required to encourage such invention, which would hardly justify a claim in perpetuity to such resources.

60. See Brian Barry, *supra* note 3, at pp. 234–39. Barry appeals, instead, to intuitive ideas of equal rights to natural resources which, while appealing, express more a conclusion than the kind of moral argument that, in fact, is available to support such a conclusion.

61. See Charles R. Beitz, *supra* note 7 at 127–76.

62. *Id.* at 143–53.

63. Cf. Brian Barry, *supra* note 3, at p. 232.

64. For some of the complexities of fairly assessing these issues and the implications for conventional doctrines of international law, see Charles R. Beitz, *supra* note 3, 69–123.

65. See Brian Barry, *supra* note 3, at pp. 243–50, for further elaboration.

66. The principle of just distribution of natural and cultural resources would, like the principle of mutual aid, be regarded as a principle justifiably enforced, if necessary, by coercion (and thus, define obligations or duties), because it secures, without requiring privation or misery, goods fundamental to leading lives with a fair chance of achieving one's rational ends with dignity.

67. See, in general, David A. J. Richards, *supra* note 5, at 279–91.

68. *Id.* at 279–83.

69. See *id.* at 277.

70. I have in mind, especially, Robert Nozick. See R. Nozick, *Anarchy, State, and Utopia* (New York: Basic Books, 1974). Cf. Brian Barry, "And Who Is My Neighbor?" 88 *Yale L. J.* 629 (1979).

71. See David A. J. Richards, *supra* note 26.

72. See Brian Barry, *supra* note 3, at pp. 239–41.

73. See, for example, E. P. Thompson, *The Making of the English Working Class* (New York: Vintage Books, 1966). Cf. Barrington Moore, Jr., *Injustice: The Social Bases of Obedience and Revolt* (White Plains, N.Y.: M. E. Sharpe, 1978).

74. I assume certain moral constraints of proportionality and not harming the innocent. Cf. Michael Walzer, *Just and Unjust Wars* (New York: Basic Books, 1977).

PART IV

A HISTORICAL STUDY
OF LEGAL DYNAMICS

15

LAW AND THE IMPERATIVES OF PROGRESS: PRIVATE RIGHTS AND PUBLIC VALUES IN AMERICAN LEGAL HISTORY

HARRY N. SCHEIBER*

Recent studies in American legal history have devoted much attention to problems of law and economic development, especially in the nineteenth century. From these scholarly efforts has come a new appreciation of the extent to which law was mobilized to shape and channel economic change.[1] Innovations in statute law provided new forms for enterprise—both "purely" private and "mixed" enterprise—while most of the antebellum eastern states created public bureaucracies and developed creative sources of state funding to provide the emergent industrial economy with essential transport infrastructure. Apart from the well-known tariff, land-disposal, free immigration, and fiscal efforts (including the erratic banking policy) of the national government, states developed greatly varied programs, designed to foster development—or, as in the most conservative southern states, at least to enhance productivity even if systemic change that might threaten the slave plantation economy was eschewed.[2] What recent scholarship has illuminated, in particular, is the extensive reach of the law in shaping nineteenth-century economic institutions and the dynamics of economic change, both during the antebellum years and (to the surprise of many, given the Supreme Courts's notorious conservatism) even in the late nineteenth century.[3] Especially notable is the

role played by the state courts. This role was twofold. First, the
state judges engaged in doctrinal innovation across a broad
front to establish the parameters of the great trinity of governmental powers, namely taxation, eminent domain, and the
police power.[4] Second, they regularly advanced the common
law in ways that either impelled or constrained rights of contract,
in both respects greatly enlarging the overall formative influence
of public authority on the workings of the private marketplace.[5]

In Willard Hurst's studies, the purview of the legal historian
came to embrace all manifestations of law-in-action; Hurst
sought to discover "working principles," expressed and defined
not only in the great cases, nor even only in judicial decisions
at all levels, but also in the full range of activity of the legal
system. In his inquiries into the history of Wisconsin resource
law and in his more general research, Hurst has tended to
emphasize that nineteenth-century Americans were dedicated
to "promoting growth"; they gave high priority to material
values; they produced a consensus, despite evidences of serious
conflict, on the proposition that "it was common sense, and it
was good, to use law to multiply the productive power of the
economy."[6]

Of special interest to any investigation of ethics in the relationship of law and economy, historically considered, is Hurst's
contention that in nineteenth-century American law,

> Productivity was the central test and validating canon. By
> this criterion the legislature and the judges confidently
> wielded authority over the waterways [of Wisconsin's lum-
> ber region].[7]

Although the statement quoted is directed specifically to one
state's waterways policy and law, much the same contention is
applicable, in Hurst's view, to the nation's law generally.
Throughout the first half of the nineteenth century a kind of
"bastard pragmatism" marked the posture of legislators and
jurists striving to advance the economy and to accommodate
new technologies, new investment, new enterprise.[8]

Hurst's work made clear that productivity as a validating
canon of law was regularly (and tellingly) invoked by American
courts to abridge severely, at times rather brutally, what are

commonly termed "vested rights." The bias in favor of expediting growth meant that when courts defined the rules of property, contract, torts, eminent domain, or taxation, they tended to give preference to "dynamic" over "static" institutions. Law was an instrument of change; it tended to be heedless of long-term consequences when it came to bear on exhaustible resources; it worked as much through "drift and default" as through purposive decision making.[9]

Friedman's studies of contract law, my own work on eminent domain and property law, and, above all, Leonard Levy's close study of the Massachusetts Supreme Court under Chief Justice Lemuel Shaw, have provided evidence across a broad front generally supportive of Hurst's depiction of nineteenth-century law.[10] A controversial new study by Horwitz, addressed to the "transformation of [all] American law," 1780–1860, but in fact based on cases from only a few (admittedly important) eastern states, similarly describes the common law as supportive of new enterprise.[11] But Horwitz's work stridently contends that the law was exploitative of the society's poorer elements; that it worked uniformly to the advantage of industrial interests, at the expense (regularly) of older agrarian interests; that "consensus" is a fiction; and that pragmatism—what he rechristens "instrumentalism," a word that also had been used occasionally by Hurst—became the dominant judicial style in the pre-1860 period, giving way to a competing style, "formalism," in the Civil War era.[12] These arguments have received critical treatment elsewhere and need not concern us in any detail here.[13]

What is of concern here is the question of how judges and other participants in legal process in nineteenth-century America squared the application of pragmatic, growth-oriented norms—the validating canon of productivity—with other competing claims for government's protection and positive support.

The first, and of course best known, of such competing claims was that of "vested rights." Edward S. Corwin once termed the protection of vested rights "the basic doctrine of American constitutional law," historically considered.[14] Based upon natural law foundations, the doctrine of vested rights established that it was a violation of "the great first principles of the social compact" for government to seize private property arbitrarily or capriciously deprive private owners of the harmless use of their property.[15] As G. Edward White has shown, this powerful doctrine, rooted in Lockean precepts and the legacy of natural law writers, early became embedded in the fabric of "the American judicial tradition":

> The role of the judiciary in demonstrating the inviolability of property rights and in preserving their sanctity had been an important concern of Marshall; maintaining this aspect of the judicial function was a central, self-designated task of Kent and Story.[16]

But even the most conservative formulations of jurists such as Kent retained the power of the state (1) to take property, if done for public use and on payment of compensation; and (2) to abridge property rights in the course of proper exercise of the police power, namely for protection and advancement of the health, welfare, and safety of the community.[17] How the U.S. Supreme Court, especially in the area of contract clause adjudication, and the state courts dealt with private vested rights on the one hand, and with the competing claims of the state on the other, constitutes one of the enduring themes of American constitutional and legal history.

The second competing claim, posed against the pragmatism, or instrumentalism, of the antebellum courts, is by comparison with vested rights little known and little appreciated. It is the claim of "rights of the public," a claim advanced in argument and decision in hundreds of American cases—a claim that was advanced on the premise that when the interests of the community were vitally at stake, private rights (whether "vested" or "dynamic") must yield and societal values be given priority. What follows here will concentrate attention upon the history and functions of this neglected doctrine, supportive of societal interests that were alleged to transcend individual rights and so warranted their abridgment.

Two conclusions seem warranted, from the evidence we are about to examine. First, American law exhibited a continual tension between the classic doctrines of private rights and the competing doctrine of "rights of the public." Second, the doctrine of public rights provided an ethical foundation and justification for a variety of rules laid down by the state courts—

rules that in some instances were supportive of an "instrumental" judicial style but that in other instances served to impose the most stringent regulations upon the very same "dynamic," entrepreneurial interests that Horwitz contends were uniformly the beneficiaries of judge-made law. That is to say, the doctrine of public rights cut sharply across some of the established doctrinal categories of common law; if it was sometimes invoked to expedite economic progress, it was at other times used to place burdens and constraints on capitalistic interests, whether agrarian, commercial, or industrial. Withal, even though American society may have had its full share of expectant capitalists (whether or not there was "consensus"), the positive doctrine of public rights was not submerged or altogether overwhelmed by the clash of struggling selfish interests.[18] Although the notion of public rights could be used (as will be seen below) to force economic change into specific channels, it could also be used, and was used, to interpose the power of government where business interests proved heedless of community needs and rights.

What is perhaps most interesting is the fact that the tension we have described continued throughout the heyday of laissez-faire and conservative jurisprudence, in the age of freedom of contract. Similarly, instrumentalism itself continued to appear, sometimes as the partner of public rights, sometimes as antagonist, in the decisions of American courts long after the Civil War decade, when "formalism" allegedly had crowded out the older growth-oriented pragmatic judicial style and established itself as the dominant judicial style.[19]

I. DOCTRINAL VARIANTS OF "RIGHTS OF THE PUBLIC"

Public rights were asserted in formalist terms, on the basis of the natural law concept of "sovereignty," in many important American decisions. References to inalienable power, inherent in sovereign governments, abound in decisions relating especially to eminent domain, taxation, and the police power. Even in one of the earliest federal decisions asserting the inviolability

of private vested rights, Justice Paterson thus acknowledged
that "the despotic power . . . of taking private property when
state necessity requires, exists in every government."[20] The first
American treatise on eminent domain, by J. B. Thayer in 1856,
drew extensively from Grotius, Vattel, Pufendorf, and Bynk-
ershoek in defining the taking power as "that attribute of
sovereignty by which the State may take, appropriate, or devest
[sic] private property whenever the public exigencies demand
it . . . for public purposes."[21] The Supreme Court endorsed this
view of eminent domain as rooted in sovereignty when, in the
West River Bridge Case, in 1848, it held that every state of the
Union inherently enjoyed "the right and the duty of guarding
its own existence, and of protecting and promoting the interests
and welfare of the community at large" through exercise of the
eminent domain power.[22] Moreover, the Court even endorsed
the position of New York's Chancellor Walworth, set down in
1831, that the state might legitimately take any sort of private
property when "the interest, or even the expediency, of the
State" is the end.[23] Of course, the obligation to provide compensation followed as a necessary concomitant of the taking
power; as I have shown elsewhere, this obligation was often
honored only nominally, and eminent domain could become a
heavy-handed instrument of the state.[24]

The same type of formalistic basis for the police power found
expression in both state decisions and Supreme Court doctrines.
Indeed, the whole concept of "concurrent powers" rested on
the notion that the states could legitimately exercise the police
power, because it was rooted in sovereignty, within the context
of commerce clause limitations.[25] Employment of the police
power, of course, required no compensation when property was
damaged or taken.

Closely linked to the attribute-of-sovereignty basis of the
police power was a somewhat independent source of legitimacy
for police regulations: the common law doctrine of *sic utere*,[26]
requiring that one's property be used so as not to damage the
rights of others. It was only a step from that doctrine, the basis
of private nuisance law, to the doctrine that property might not
be used in ways that damaged the rights *of the community*.[27] The
step was formalized by Chief Justice Shaw, who in the leading
case of *Commonwealth* v. *Alger* (1851) declared that "the rights of

the community," no less than private rights, were a consideration validating public regulations. "Rights of property," Shaw wrote,

> like all other social and conventional rights, are subject to
> such reasonable limitations in their enjoyment, as shall
> prevent them from being injurious, and to such reasonable
> restraints and regulations established by law, as the legis-
> lature, under . . . the Constitution, may think necessary and
> expedient.[28]

To assure protection of "the acknowledged public right," the courts bore the responsibility of formulating clear rules "which all can understand and obey."[29] Just as "public use" or "public purpose," in tandem with at least nominal compensation, validated the pursuit of rights of the public through the eminent domain power, so, then, did "reasonableness" become the judicial standard for validating police-power regulations.[30]

Still another doctrinal foundation for assertions of "rights of the public" was the common law concept of property that is private in ownership but public in its uses. This concept was found particularly in the law of water rights, codified by Lord Matthew Hale (ca. 1670) in a treatise given wide attention after 1787.[31] Hale's *De Jure Maris* distinguished waters entirely private, waters private in ownership yet *publici juris* (subject to public rights of use, as for navigation, fisheries, and wharves), and waters entirely public. The distinction, stressing rights of servitude to the public, or "public purpose," came into American property law extensively in the nineteenth century.[32] The concept of public use was applied regularly in development of eminent domain doctrines, and later it found application as well in taxation decisions; but ultimately its great importance in constitutional law was its reformulation regarding property "affected with a public interest" in the Granger Cases, to validate state regulation of privately owned business facilities that served the public, namely, warehouses and railroads.[33]

Even further over on the spectrum of property rights, beyond the *publici juris* concept drawn from the common law, was the related category of property held by government itself as a "public trust." Here, in stark and dramatic form, was a concept of rights of the public that could serve as counterweight to the claims of private or "vested" rights. In American jurisprudence, the public trust doctrine represented a fusion of common law concepts drawn from Lord Hale with natural law ideas concerning obligations of the sovereign; the latter tradition found concrete expression, moreover, in the heritage of civil law that operated in property disputes in California and other formerly Spanish, French, or Mexican jurisdictions.[34] In the first seven decades of the century, the state courts of California, Louisiana, and Texas advanced the public trust doctrine to protect rights of the public in *pueblo* lands, alluvial property, and other special assets of government which had been designated as "trusts" under predecessor regimes.[35] The federal courts meanwhile formulated the powerful doctrine of navigable waters, to assure public rights on inland streams and lakes; and they validated the doctrine that public rights to fish and conduct commerce transcended private rights in riparian property.[36] After 1870, moreover, both the state courts and the Supreme Court advanced public trust doctrines across a broad front. Not only did California and the New England states assure growing cities of water supply by application of the doctrine, and numerous states expedite urban transport improvement, but in a startling application of public trust notions the Supreme Court in 1892 invalidated long-standing private title to waterfront lands in Illinois; it did so on grounds that the state had alienated the waterfront property, "in disregard of a public trust, under which [the state] was bound to hold and manage it."[37]

Confounding any neat dichotomization of "instrumental" versus "formalistic" judicial reasoning (or modes of decision making) is the pervasive tendency of American judges, throughout the nineteenth century, to employ the language and forms of inherited law—but they so used the common law in ways that produced new concrete rules, adaptable to the peculiarities of their own resource-use and regulatory problems. (Further discussion these peculiarities and their adaptation is given below). As Chief Justice Shaw asserted, he sought to govern new cases by applying from common law "the general principle . . . , modified and adapted to new circumstances by considerations of fitness and propriety, of reason and justice."[38] Well-known distinctions in modern jurisprudence, such as the principle/rule distinction that Lon Fuller, Ronald Dworkin, and others have explored, found a prominent place in nineteenth-century American courts' struggles to legitimize their applications of common law precepts in dealing with property questions. "We are not bound to follow the letter of the common law, forgetful of its spirit, its *rule* instead of its *principle*," the New York appellate court early asserted.[39] Similarly, the Connecticut judges adverted to the "well-settled rule that the law varies with the varying reasons on which it is founded," so that a law manifestly inappropriate or unjust simply "abrogates itself."[40]

Lawmakers did not delude themselves when they confronted the dilemmas inherent in such rule making and rule adaptation: that private rights, often highly valuable, were being abridged was fully recognized. The several variants of "rights of the public" offered a doctrinal foundation, however, for the inevitable ordering of economic priorities—the placing of certain types of property and activity above other types—that accompanied such judicial action. Although "vested rights" and their protection were at the very center of American jurisprudence in the nineteenth century, so too were doctrinal variants of "rights of the public." Neither the doctrine of public rights nor that of vested rights was monolithic or static; both underwent successive redefinitions throughout the century, and the tension between them manifested the continuous role of American courts in balancing the widely accepted policy goal of economic growth with the obligation to extend judicial protection to acknowledged rights.[41]

II. PRAGMATIC FOUNDATIONS OF DOCTRINAL CHANGE

In effect, the nineteenth-century American courts attached an imperative to adaptability to common law: they made it a rule of law, a principle, that adaptation should be a legitimate option, if not mandatory, under certain circumstances. But what circumstances?

The tension between the claims of the public and the claims of private (vested) property—and also the tension between the twin goals of possessive individualism, the stability of ownership rights and the need to clear the channels for new enterprise— were manifest in the rhetoric of property law decisions. Space is lacking here to provide detailed analysis of even the major cases,[42] but a few examples will indicate how pragmatic considerations typically triggered judicial reexamination of inherited rules.

Judicial rule making in property law was perhaps nowhere so difficult as in California, where during some seventy years or more of hectic, diversified development there was remarkably little statute law in many areas of economic policy and even less in the way of explicit constitutional guidance. This was true even in the vital area of water law.[43] Left on their own, the courts gradually produced a full-blown rationale for rule adaptation, as was expressed in a decision of 1903 on riparian law:

> Whenever it is found that, owing to the physical features and character of the state, and the peculiarities of its climate, soil, and productions, the application of a given common-law rule by our courts tends constantly to cause injustice and wrong, . . . then the fundamental principles of right and justice on which that law is founded . . . require that a different rule should be adopted, one which is calculated to secure persons in their property and possessions, and to preserve for them the fruits of their labors and expenditures.[44]

The court admitted that "an ordinary difference in the [geographic] conditions would scarcely justify the refusal to adopt the rule of the common law, . . . but where the differences are so radical," as between England or the East and California, as in this case (relating to rights to percolating water), "a different rule is imperative."[45] In support of that proposition, the California judges were able to reach far back into the early part of the nineteenth century for New York and other eastern precedents that had adapted English riparian rules to American geographic peculiarities. They cited a decision of seventy years' standing, that portions of the common law "inconsistent with the spirit of our institutions" and also those "framed with specific reference to the physical condition of a country differing widely from our own" must be modified or rejected.[46] Ever since the establishment of American rule in California, in fact, the courts had adhered to the maxim handed down in 1855 that they were "bound to take notice of the physical and social conditions of the country which they judicially rule."[47]

What is germane to our present concerns above all is the degree to which considerations of geography and other special local conditions led to expansion of the "public rights" concept, not only in California but in American states more generally and ultimately in the nation's constitutional law.

It was not unique to California for courts to assert that jurisprudence in the property rights area "must be controlled and modified by the peculiar nature of the subject and by surrounding circumstances."[48] Indeed, the pragmatic basis for creation of public rights doctrine and abridging of private rights had found strong expression in the 1830s, when eastern courts were shoring up the foundations of eminent domain law. Thus, in validating takings of property for industrial purposes, the New Jersey court declared in 1832 that "the ever varying condition of society is constantly presenting new objects of public importance and utility; and what shall be considered a public use or benefit, may depend somewhat on the situation and wants of the community for the time being."[49] Law must be "a practical system, adapted to the condition and business of its society," as a Kentucky court averred in 1836.[50]

Both in general terms and in terms specific to local geographic peculiarities, American courts deployed the concept of public rights (and also "public use") in order to respond to what was deemed a necessity—either the necessity for exercise of eminent domain powers or the necessity to permit actions that were damaging to property owners yet were not compensable. Exemplary of such decisions were those of the arid-land states upholding the devolution of extraordinary powers on irrigation agencies and corporations.[51] Similarly, in the Rocky Mountain region the remoteness of mineral resources, and to some extent timber resources as well, induced courts to rule it was "imperative necessity"[52] that common law riparian rules be abrogated in favor of mining and lumbering interests. Only so could peculiar western "advantages and resources . . . receive the fullest development for the general welfare."[53] In the same manner, drainage projects in midwestern wetlands districts were given eminent domain powers; the courts also validated the formation of drainage district governments that taxed all property owners, whether or not directly benefited by the projects.[54] In several landmark decisions from the late 1870s to 1911, the U.S. Supreme Court approved state-by-state variations in water law, designed to adapt to arid climates and the special needs of mining properties "to the value of many millions";[55] upheld application of the "public use" concept to irrigation districts;[56] validated an extreme rule, adopted by the Utah court, that authorized even a private individual irrigator to appropriate a neighbor's land;[57] and approved devolution of eminent domain and taxation powers to drainage districts, on grounds that the states could properly enhance the productive capacity of arable land through such innovations.[58] As the Court indicated in the Utah case, it believed that property rules and definition of public use ought to be left so far as possible to the state courts, as they "appreciate the results upon the growth and prosperity of the State."[59]

As this last quotation indicates, the narrow ground of geographic necessity, as a foundation of public rights doctrine building, verged over into a much broader criterion. This was the criterion of the general welfare and advantage of the state economy, most vividly given expression in the 1860 Massachusetts decision of *Talbot* v. *Gray*. The interests of the public, validating a taking by a private corporation, were defined as:

> everything which tends to enlarge the resources, increase the industrial energies, and promote the productive power of any considerable number of the inhabitants of a section of the state, or which leads to the growth of towns and the creation of new sources for the employment of private capital and labor, [and so] indirectly contributes to the general welfare and to the prosperity of the whole community.[60]

In some states, especially in the Far West, the concept of public use was given concrete expression in key provisions of their constitutions; many authorized the devolution of eminent domain powers on transportation enterprises and some combination of mining, drainage, irrigation, log-boom, and wharf companies.[61]

To be sure, the Supreme Court placed some constraints upon this development in its 1874 decision of *Loan Association* v. *Topeka*, striking down a Kansas law authorizing public aid to a bridge-building company.[62] But given the range of comparable legislation the Court did sustain, it must be admitted that American law had come a very long way from Blackstone's assertion that the right of private property consisted of "that sole and despotic dominion which one man claims and exercises over the external things of the world, in total exclusion of the right of any other individual in the universe"![63]

CONCLUSION

It can hardly be denied that a pragmatic ethic, with policy-oriented decision making aimed at promotion of economic growth, animated American lawmakers in the nineteenth century. As the evidence offered here suggests, however, there was also a principled ethic, based on the concept that rights of the public must be defined and given play by the courts; and this ethic, taking specific form in various doctrinal declarations of public rights and public use, was invoked both to release entrepreneurial energies and to regulate them in certain vital respects. Such issues and institutions in the law as eminent domain, special-district government, and regulation under the police power proved no less prominent a feature of American courts' work than their better-known activities in the protection of "vested rights" and the rank-ordering of "static" and "dynamic" propertied interests. In the history of the tension between the tenets of "possessive individualism" and the tenets of public rights is to be found the genesis of modern formulations of "the public interest." And like these modern formulations, "rights of the public" as used historically by American courts was a concept rife with perplexities about objective standards.[64]

NOTES

* The author is indebted to the Rockefeller Foundation for a Humanities Fellowship, under which research for this paper was conducted.

1. Jamil S. Zainaldin, "The New Legal History: A Review Essay" 73 *Northwestern U. L. Rev.* 205–25, (1978); Harry N. Scheiber, "Legal History," 26 *Amer. Jnl. of Compar. Law,* 350–64 (1978); Lawrence M. Friedman, *A History of American Law* (New York, 1973), passim.
2. Scheiber, "Government and the Economy: Studies of the 'Commonwealth' Policy in 19th-Century America," 3 *Journal of Interdisciplinary History* 135–51 (1972).
3. Robert W. Gordon, "J. Willard Hurst and the Common Law Tradition in American Legal Historiography," 10 *Law & Society Rev.* 9–56 (1976). See also Wythe Holt, "Now and Then: The Uncertain State of 19th-Century American Legal History," 7 *Indiana L. Rev.* 615–43 (1974).
4. James Willard Hurst, *Law and the Conditions of Freedom in the Nineteenth Century United States* (Madison, Wis., 1956); Scheiber, "The Road to *Munn*: Eminent Domain and the Concept of Public Purpose in the State Courts," in Donald Fleming and Bernard Bailyn, ed., *Law in American History,* (Boston, 1972), pp. 329–402; Charles W. McCurdy, "Justice Field and the Jurisprudence of Government-Business Relations: Some Parameters of Laissez Faire Constitutionalism," 61 *Journal of American History* 970–1005 (1975), reprinted in Lawrence M. Friedman and Harry N. Scheiber, *American Law and the Constitutional Order: Historical Perspectives* (Cambridge, Mass., 1978) pp. 246–65.
5. Morton Horwitz, *The Transformation of American Law, 1780–1860* (Cambridge, Mass., 1977); Tony Allan Freyer, *Forums of Order: The Federal Courts and Business in American History* (Greenwich, Conn., 1979).
6. Hurst, *Law and Economic Growth: The Legal History of the Lumber Industry in Wisconsin, 1836–1915* (Cambridge, Mass., 1964), pp. 203, 171–72. Cf. Scheiber, "At the Borderland of Law and Economic History: The Contributions of Willard Hurst," 75 *American Historical Review,* 744–56 (1970).
7. Hurst, *Law and Economic Growth,* note 6 *supra,* at 172.
8. Hurst, *Law and Social Process in United States History* (Ann Arbor, Mich., 1966), pp. 238–39 et passim.
9. *Law and Economic Growth,* note 6 *supra,* at 262–63; see also Hurst, *Law and the Social Order in the United States* (Ithaca, N.Y., 1977), pp. 48 ff., 213, et passim.
10. Friedman, *supra* note 1; *id., Contract Law in America* (Madison, Wis.,

1965); Scheiber, "Road to Munn," *supra* note 4; *id.*, "Property Law, Expropriation, and Resource Allocation by Government: the U.S., 1789–1910," 33 *Journal of Economic History* 232–51 (1973); Leonard W. Levy, *The Law of the Commonwealth and Chief Justice Shaw* (Cambridge, Mass., 1954).

11. Horwitz, *supra* note 5. For a critique, see Scheiber, "Back to 'The Legal Mind'? Doctrinal Analysis and the History of Law," 5 *Reviews in American History* 458–66 (1977).

12. Horwitz, *supra* note 5.

13. Cf. Scheiber, "Instrumentalism and Property Rights: A Reconsideration of American 'Styles of Judicial Reasoning' in the 19th Century," *Wisc. L. Rev.* 1–18 (1975). William Nelson pursued further the theme of "formalism" and its alleged hegemony in post-1860 judicial reasoning in American courts; cf. Nelson, "The Impact of the Antislavery Movement upon Styles of Judicial Reasoning in Nineteenth Century America," 87 *Harv. L. Rev.* 513 (1974). A. W. B. Simpson, "The Horwitz Thesis and the History of Contracts," 46 *U. Chi. L. Rev.* 533–601 (1979) subjects Horwitz's book to devastating criticism; little remains of his section on contract. Lynda Sharp Paine, "Instrumentalism vs. Formalism: Dissolving the Dichotomy," *Wisc. L. Rev.* 997 ff. (1978), very tellingly attacks, on logical and evidentiary grounds, the distinction on which much recent work rests. Hurst has responded at some length to critics of his work who subscribe to a "ruling-class explanation" of legal innovations, in "Old and New Dimensions of Research in United States Legal History," 23 *Amer. Jnl. of Legal Hist.* 1, 9–18 (1979).

14. Corwin, "The Basic Doctrine of American Constitutional Law," 12 *Mich. L. Rev.* 247–76 (1914). The relationship between vested rights doctrines and dual federalism is explored by Stuart Bruchey, "The Impact of Concern for the Security of Property Rights on the Legal System of the Early American Republic," *Wisc. L. Rev.* 1135–58 (1980).

15. *Calder* v. *Bull*, 3 U.S. 386, 387–89 (1798) (Chase, J.). Cf. Joseph M. Snee, "Leviathan at the Bar of Justice," in *Government under Law* (Cambridge, Mass., 1955), pp. 69–70. The standard account, still valuable both for its analytic overview of natural law concepts and for its examination of individual decisions, is Charles Grove Haines, *The Revival of Natural Law Concepts: A Study of the Establishment and of the Interpretation of Limits on Legislatures with special reference to . . . American Constitutional Law* (1958; reissued, 1965); on *Calder* v. *Bull*, cf. *ibid.*, pp. 86–89.

16. White, *The American Judicial Tradition: Profiles of Leading American Judges* (New York, 1976), p. 47.

17. *Ibid.*, p. 49. Cf. Levy, *Law of the Commonwealth, supra* note 10, passim.

18. See the sensible comments on "consensus" or lack thereof, vis-à-vis nineteenth-century legal development, in Stephen Diamond, "Legal Realism and Historical Method: J. Willard Hurst and American Legal History," 77 *Mich. L. Rev.* 784–94 (1979).

19. See note 13, *supra,* and accompanying text.

20. *Vanhorne* v. *Dorrance,* 28 F. Cas. 1012 (No. 16, 857) (D. Pa. 1795). An excellent discussion of the English and colonial background, and of the context of this case as well, is in William B. Stoebuck, "A General Theory of Eminent Domain," 47 *Wash. L. Rev.* 553–603 (1972), esp. at 573.

21. Thayer, "The Right of Eminent Domain," *Monthly Law Reporter,* new ser., 9 (1856); cf. Stoebuck, *supra* note 20, at 583–85; and Arthur Lenhoff, "Development of the Concept of Eminent Domain," 42 *Colum. L. Rev.* 596–605 (1942).

22. *West River Bridge* v. *Dix,* 6 How. 507 (U.S. 1848) at 531–32.

23. *Beekman* v. *Saratoga, &c. R.R.,* 3 Paige ch. 45 (N.Y., 1831) at 73.

24. Scheiber, "Road to *Munn,*" *supra* note 4.

25. W. G. Hastings, "The Development of Law as Illustrated by the Decisions relating to the Police Power of the State," 39 *Proceedings of the American Philosophical Society* 359–406 (1900); Scheiber, "Federalism and the American Economic Order, 1789–1910," 10 *Law & Society Rev.* 57–118, esp. at 72–84 (1975); Edward S. Corwin, "The Extension of Judicial Review in New York, 1783–1905," 15 *Mich. L. Rev.* 281, 299–306 (1917).

26. *Sic utere tuo ut alienum non laedas:* "Use your own property in such manner as not to injure that of another."

27. This critical development is explored in depth in Scott M. Reznick, "Empiricism and the Principle of Conditions in the Evolution of the Police Power," *Wash. U. L. Q.* 1–92, at 6–19 (1978).

28. 7 Cush. 53 at 84–85 (Mass., 1851).

29. *Ibid.*

30. Cf. Levy, *Law of the Commonwealth, supra* note 4, at 253–54 and 254n., contending that Shaw left definition of reasonableness principally to the legislature; *contra,* White, *American Judicial Tradition,* p. 90.

31. Actually three tracts written c. 1670 constituted the treatise, viz., Francis Hargrave, ed., *Collection of Tracts Relative to the Law of England* (1787). For full bibliographic information, cf. Scheiber, "Road to *Munn,*" *supra* note 4, at 334–35 and 334 n. 18; Charles Fairman, "The So-called Granger Cases, Lord Hale, and Justice Bradley," 5 *Stan. Law Rev.* 587–679 (1953).

32. Scheiber, "Road to *Munn,*" *supra* note 4, at 329–55.

33. *Ibid.*, passim.
34. *Ibid.*, 348–49; Molly Selvin, "The Public Trust Doctrine in American Law and Economic Policy, 1789–1920," *Wisc. L. Rev.* 1403–42 (1980).
35. E.g., *Hart v. Burnett,* 15 Cal. 530 (1860); *Mayor v. Hopkins,* 13 La. Rep. 326 (1839).
36. *Martin v. Waddell,* 16 Pet. 345 (1842); *Pollard's Lessee v. Hagen,* 3 How. 212 (1845). See also *Barney v. Keokuk,* 94 U.S. 324 (1877), discussed in Scheiber, "Road to *Munn*," *supra* note 4, at 351–53.
37. *Illinois Central R.R. v. Illinois,* 146 U.S. 387 (1892), remarkable for the fact that Justice Stephen Field, alleged defender par excellence of private rights, wrote the opinion. See discussion in McCurdy, "Justice Field," *supra* note 4. The context and latter-day impact, in modern environmental regulation litigation, are considered in Selvin, *supra* note 34, at 1437–40.
38. Quoted in White, *American Judicial Tradition, supra* note 16, at 60.
39. *Morgan v. King,* 30 Barb. 16 (New York, 1858).
40. *Beardsley v. Hartford,* 47 Am. Rep. 677, 682 (Conn., 1883).
41. Levy, *Law of the Commonwealth, supra* note 10, portrays brilliantly the way in which the Shaw Court worked through these problems creatively and with sweeping impact on American law and the economy. On a smaller canvas, but equally well, Charles McCurdy portrays the California State Supreme Court's "balancing" of property-protection and growth-expediting doctrines and goals, in "Stephen J. Field and Public Land Law Development in California, 1850–1866," 10 *Law & Society Rev.* 235–66 (1976).
42. I have attempted a preliminary overview and analysis in a paper, "Property Rights and Public Purpose in American Law," *Proceedings of the International Economic History Association, 7th Congress* (Edinburgh University Press, 1978), 1: 233–40.
43. H. N. Scheiber and Charles McCurdy, "Eminent-Domain Law and Western Agriculture, 1849–1900," 49 *Agricultural History* 112–30 (1975); Gordon R. Miller, "Shaping California Water Law, 1781 to 1928," 55 *Southern California Quarterly* 9–42 (1973).
44. *Katz v. Walkinshaw,* 141 Cal. 123, 124 (1903).
45. *Ibid.* at 133–34.
46. *People v. Appraisers,* 33 N.Y. 461 (1865), citing Bronson, J. (diss.) in *Starr v. Child,* 20 Wend. 149, 159 (N.Y., 1840).
47. *Irwin v. Phillips,* 5 Cal. 140 (1855) at 147. Similarly, the California court abrogated its own rules, from precedent, when "destruction to public and private rights" were the consequence; in *People v. Gold Run Co.,* 66 Cal. 138 (1884) at 151.
48. *English v. Johnson,* 17 Cal. 108 (1860) at 117.
49. *Scudder v. Trenton & Del. Falls Co.,* 1 N.J.Eq. 694 (1832).

50. *Steele* v. *Curle*, 34 Ky. (4 Dana), 381, 390 (1836).
51. E.g., *In re Madera Irrigation Dist.*, 92 Cal. 296 (1891); cf. Samuel Wiel, "Fifty Years of Water Law," 50 *Harv. Law Rev.* 252 ff. (1936).
52. *Coffin* v. *Left Hand Ditch Co.*, 6 Colo. 443, 447 (1882).
53. *Oury* v. *Goodwin*, 3 Ariz. 255, 274 (1891); cf. *Irrigation District* v. *Williams*, 76 Cal. 380 (1888); *contra, In re Drainage*, 39 N.J. L. 433 (1877).
54. E.g., *Hager* v. *Supervisors of Yolo County*, 47 Cal. 222 (1874).
55. *Jennison* v. *Kirk*, 98 U.S. 453 (1878) (Field, J., that without water mining could not be carried on in the West); cf. Scheiber, "Instrumentalism," *supra* note 13, at 15–16.
56. *Fallbrook Irr. Dist.* v. *Bradley*, 164 U.S. 112 (1896). Cf. Kay Russell, "The Fallbrook Irrigation District Case," 21 *Journal of San Diego History* 23–40 (1975).
57. *Nash* v. *Clark*, 27 Utah 158 (1904), *affd. Clark* v. *Nash*, 198 U.S. 361 (1905).
58. *Wurts* v. *Hoaglund*, 114 U.S. (1885). I am indebted on this point to an article by Charles W. McCurdy, "The Concept of Confiscation in the Industrial Age: General Theory and Judicial Strategy, 1860–1910" (in manuscript).
59. *Clark* v. *Nash, supra* note 57, at 368.
60. 82 Mass. 417 (1860). See discussion in Scheiber, "Law and American Agricultural Development," 52 *Agricultural History* 439, 456–57 (1978).
61. Gordon Bakken, "The Impact of the Colorado State Constitution on Rocky Mountain Constitution Making," *Colorado Magazine* (1970), pp. 152–75.
62. 20 Wall. 655 (1874).
63. *Commentaries*, 2:1–2, quoted in John E. Cribbet, "Changing Concepts in the Law of Land Use," 50 *Iowa L. Rev.* 245, 247 (1965).
64. The two-faceted quest for objective standards in defining the public interest is dramatically exemplified by development of the doctrine of public necessity and convenience; on the one hand, a substantive standard of determination was sought, and on the other, an impartial agency for its determination had to be given power to act. See William K. Jones, "Origins of the Certificate of Public Convenience and Necessity: Developments in the States, 1870–1920," 79 *Colum. L. Rev.* 426–516 (1979).

INDEX

Adèle

Adèle

Mary Flanagan

W. W. NORTON & COMPANY
New York   London

Copyright © 1997 by Mary Flanagan
All Rights Reserved
Printed in the United States of America

First American edition 1997

For information about permission to reproduce selections from this book,
write to Permissions, W. W. Norton & Company, Inc., 500 Fifth Avenue,
New York, NY 10110.

Manufacturing by The Courier Companies, Inc.

Library of Congress Cataloging-in-Publication Data

Flanagan, Mary.
Adèle / Mary Flanagan. — 1st American ed.
p. cm.
ISBN 0-393-04547-1
I.   Title.
PS3556.L32A65   1997   97–6775
813'.54—dc21   CIP

W. W. Norton & Company, Inc., 500 Fifth Avenue, New York, N.Y. 10110
http://www.wwnorton.com

W. W. Norton & Company Ltd., 10 Coptic Street, London WC1A 1PU

1 2 3 4 5 6 7 8 9 0

With thanks to Liz Calder,
Mary Tomlinson, and Nigel
Greenhill. And to the Authors'
Foundation for their generous grant.

'*Clitoris*. 1615. Phys. A homologue of the male penis, present in the females of many of the higher vertebrata.'

The Oxford English Dictionary

'The marvellous is always beautiful, anything marvellous is beautiful, in fact only the marvellous is beautiful.'

André Breton
The First Manifesto of Surrealism